CROWN
INSIDERS'
GUIDE™
TO CALIFORNIA

Also in the series:

CROWN INSIDERS' GUIDE™ TO CALIFORNIA

Jane E. Lasky
and David Reed

Crown Publishers, Inc.
New York

Copyright © 1988 by Crown Publishers, Inc.

Published by Crown Publishers, Inc., 225 Park Avenue
South, New York, New York 10003 and represented in
Canada by the Canadian MANDA Group.

CROWN and CROWN INSIDERS' GUIDE are trademarks of
Crown Publishers, Inc.

Manufactured in the United States of America

Library of Congress Cataloging-in-Publication Data

Lasky, Jane E.
    Crown insiders' guide to California.

    Includes index.
    1. California—Description and travel—1981–
—Guide-books. I. Reed, David, 1950. II. Title. III. Title:
Insiders' guide to California.
F859.3.L37 1988   917.94'0453   87-22264
ISBN 0-517-56824-1 (pbk.)

10 9 8 7 6 5 4 3 2 1

First Edition

CONTENTS

CALIFORNIA INSIDE OUT

EDITOR'S NOTE

California has always been a land of dreams, even a few nightmares, maybe. Enough of the former have come true, in gold mines and on the silver screen, to keep the dream alive. Few places on earth are so dedicated to the joy of living or, as Californians see it, "livin' the good life."

For all the smog, fog, earthquake warnings, and highway shootouts, this western edge of the contiguous forty-eight United States is a land of wonder—of joy, beauty, sun, and fun.

If this all sounds like a sales pitch, well, it is, sort of. California is one of those states you can't ignore in America, like Texas, Florida, or Alaska. Most Americans envy California, or at least want to go there to share in its warmth and excitement. A few hate it, I suppose, but maybe they'd change their minds if they experienced the place. California, it seems, is on the minds of a lot of people.

The problem is, *which* California? Two of its exciting cities come first to mind: Los Angeles and San Francisco. But then there are the great national parks, like Yosemite, Redwood, and King Canyon. For the nostalgic, perhaps the smaller towns, such as Pasadena with its Rose Parade, or Santa Barbara of bed-and-breakfast fame, mean California. The great golf courses and artists' retreats on the Monterey Peninsula also form an image. Or is it the wonders, natural and man-made, that beckon, such as Death Valley and Disneyland? Could it just be the beach—but again, which one? The sandy stretches of the south or the dramatically rocky shores in the north?

The Golden State (its official nickname) offers untapped riches for the millions who visit each year and the thousands who decide to stay. The phrase that is usually a gross exaggeration in travel writing is true of California—it has "something for everyone"—and more than can be discovered in just one vacation.

Hollywood has done much to hype and stereotype the California life-style, laid back with Rayban sunglasses, Ferraris, and more kidney-shaped swimming pools than citizens. Well, this may be the case in Palm Springs, but let's be real, as Californians would say. The whole state is by no means that rarified. Although the phrase "casual elegance" may have been coined here, stuffy pomposity does exist in some business circles and in a few private clubs. But friendly smiles and a priority on fun outnumber arched eyebrows and studied arrogance in this land of nice and easy. Monday's gray-suited banker is Saturday's Hawaiian-shirted surfer. Margaritas, not martinis, are what the doctor ordered.

You'll learn to appreciate the Spanish legacy, still apparent in the red tile roofs on stucco mission-style homes throughout the state. Even the names are Spanish, from San Diego to San Francisco, not forgetting that wonderful mouthful everyone loves to cite—El Pueblo Nuestra Senora la Reina de Los Angeles, City of Our Lady, Queen of the Angels. Even more apparent is California's legacy of new peoples, from Hispanics, who have been here since before the Anglos arrived, to new communities of Japanese, Chinese, Filipinos, Vietnamese, and others from other parts of Asia and the South Pacific. The new Americans, like you, will be busy learning how to live like a Californian, or, in other words, how to enjoy life every minute of every day.

THE CROWN INSIDERS' GUIDE™ SERIES

Knowing California inside out isn't enough, by itself, to make a good travel guide. A good writer has to get inside his subject, yet keep the perspective right. The best authors learn to think like the people they portray. At the same time, they can't be chameleons, all things to all readers. In this series the authors try to show the reader what each place looks like from the viewpoint of a trained observer, someone who knows the ground thoroughly but isn't blinded by tradition, connections, or misplaced loyalties. Our Insiders, in short, have to be Outsiders for the very reason that natives of the place have too many obligations, too much cultural baggage of their own, too little knowledge of what readers want.

You'll learn from a Crown Insiders' guide the perils and pitfalls of travel, items that most travel books ignore. We'll make it a point to highlight the good things too, calling attention to special finds, such as movie star hangouts in Los Angeles.

THE AUTHORS

The Crown Insiders' authors have all lived in the places they write about. The co-authors of this book on California, Jane E. Lasky and David Reed, live in Los Angeles now (Lasky for eight years, Reed for four). The two met in New York as fellow editors at *The Travel Agent*, one of the nation's top industry travel publications. Since then, together and apart, they have written countless travel stories for *Bon Appétit, Connoisseur, Signature, Travel & Leisure, UltraSport, Los Angeles, Financial Planning*, and numerous airline in-flight magazines. Since 1983, they have shared bylines in *Esquire* each April and October covering "Business Travel News and Advice." In 1987, they launched a weekly business travel tips column for the *San Francisco Chronicle Features Syndicate*.

Oddly enough, given their close collaboration, Lasky and Reed have never traveled together. ("She's a shopper and I'm a sightseer," says David.) Jane loves big city glitter, David delves into historic sites. She does the theater scene, he goes to the movies. They both live in the hills of Hollywood, she with her TV director husband, he with shelves of books about bygone cinema stars. Indeed, Jane produced feature segments about Los Angeles for the popular local CBS television show "Fridays at Sunset."

In 1986, Lasky published, with co-author Brenda

Fine, *The Women's Travel Guide: 25 American Cities.*

Other contributors to this Crown Insiders' guide include Carol Canter, Amy Gordon, Melisa Sanders, Rebecca Singleton, Stacey Singleton Henry, Shawn Hartley Hancock, Helena Zukowski, Anne Framroze, Karen Hunter, Richard L. Schmidt, Steven C. Smith, Ellen Alperstein, Peter Segal, Mary Jane Horton, Sean Kelly, and Carole Saville.

In addition, we'd like to thank Julie Zirbel, Darlene Papalini, Beverly Chang, Gerry Cohen, Bill Brown, the California State Office of Tourism, and Pacific Southwest Airlines for their valuable assistance.

THE INSIDERS' RATING SYSTEM

The authors and the editor jointly award 1, 2, 3, 4, or 5 crowns to hotels, restaurants, and such places as museums, monuments, churches, landmark buildings, and other sights or sites that seem important to them. Here is our interpretation of the awards:

Hotels and Restaurants

♔ ♔ ♔ ♔ ♔	Best in the state
♔ ♔ ♔ ♔	Outstanding
♔ ♔ ♔	Excellent
♔ ♔	Very Good
♔	Recommended

Sights and Sites

♔ ♔ ♔ ♔ ♔	Once-in-a-lifetime
♔ ♔ ♔ ♔	A "must see"
♔ ♔ ♔	Worth a considerable detour
♔ ♔	Important
♔	Interesting

BECOME AN INSIDER

Nobody's perfect, and though our Insiders have tried to include everything worthwhile, omit the tourist traps, and maintain up-to-date prices and other information, the ever-changing aspects of travel ensure that something in this book will change between the time we wrote about it and the time you read or visit. Let us know, by writing to the authors and/or the editor at Crown Insiders' Guides, Crown Publishers, Inc., 225 Park Avenue South, New York, New York 10003. We'll be grateful for corrections, suggestions for new listings, or any comments you care to make.

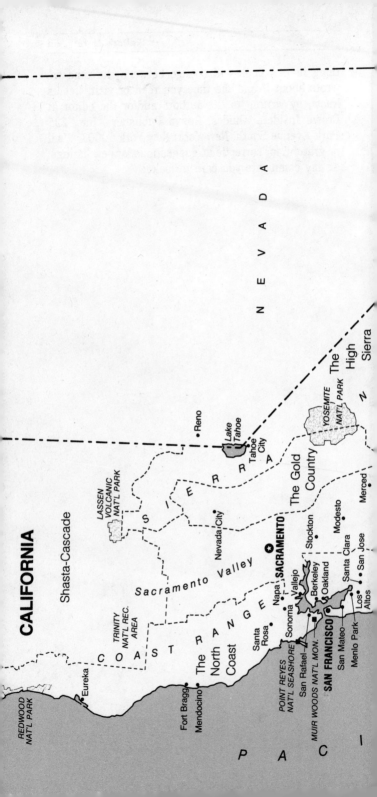

BEFORE YOU GO
WHY YOU SHOULD VISIT CALIFORNIA NOW

One hundred million visitors a year can't be wrong. No place has it all, but no place comes as close as California. From the Mediterranean-style languor and athletic leisure of the south to the dark, majestic forests and intellectual stimulation of the north, this state and state of mind offers something for everyone year-round. After all, if both Jerry Brown and Ronald Reagan could become governors of the Golden State, as they did, there has to be room for diversity—lots of it.

California has always been a land of individualists, some rugged, like the forty-niner gold prospectors, and some refined, like the artists, chefs, and designers now creating a distinctive California style. The state's sunlight inspires colorful art; its rich agriculture has spawned fine wines and a healthy new cuisine; and its stars have lit up the world—its Hollywood stars, that is.

Indeed there is more than one California. "The Californias," as the state tourism office calls the dozen geocultural areas comprising the state, include:

- The Greater Los Angeles Area—Hollywood, the J. Paul Getty Museum, Rodeo Drive, and ribbons of freeway linking mountains and beach
- Orange County—Worlds of amusement, Disneyland and others, plus fashionable seaside resorts like Newport Beach and Laguna Niguel
- San Diego County—Sparkling sands and boats, Horton Plaza's multicolored shopping playground, and the world's greatest zoo
- The Deserts and Inland Empire—Starkly contrasting scenery, rich resorts in and around Palm Springs with golf courses and cacti galore

- The Central Coast—Bed-and-breakfast inns of Santa Barbara, the cliff-top Hearst Castle, dramatic Big Sur coastline, and cozy Carmel
- The Central Valley—One of the country's richest farmlands, capped by the historic capital of Sacramento
- Gold Country—Old West towns of wooden sidewalks and calico, not much changed from the saloon and mining days, just quieter
- The High Sierra—Yosemite, Mammoth, Tahoe for winter skiing or summer hiking, nature with plenty of creature comforts
- The Shasta-Cascade—snow, glaciers, high mountains, and down-to-earth people—rodeo cowboys and salmon-fishing Indians
- The North Coast—Redwoods and the wine country, giant sequoias and rugged splendor
- San Francisco Bay—Fun and sophistication in Chinatown, Nob Hill, Fisherman's Wharf—or even Alcatraz

Did you say you were planning a week's vacation? Two? Well, you might cover two or three of the Californias in that time. If you're quick. More likely you will succumb to the laid-back pace by which Californians live. It may even tempt you to move here.

HISTORY IN A HURRY

The 16th-century Spaniards looking for the legendary city of gold, El Dorado, failed to see what California hid in its northerly hills. When Mexico won independence in 1821, it kept California as a colony—and tried to keep American settlers out. The gold was still nature's secret, but Americans seeking their "manifest destiny" kept coming in. Finally in 1846–48 (and there is no polite way to say it) the United States stole California from Mexico—by military force. When gold was found two years later, the rush to riches and statehood was on. Since then, oil, aviation and space technology, microelectronics, movies, and tourism have created a state so rich it could be a country: California, the Golden State, El Dorado at last.

1542	Portuguese mariner João Rodrigues Cabrilho, sailing north from Mexico, lands at San Diego Bay, claims it for Spain.
1579	Sir Francis Drake claims San Francisco Bay for England.
1769	Padre Junípero Serra builds first of Spain's 21 Franciscan missions, San Diego de Alcalá; era lasts until 1832. Gaspar de Portola's expedition reaches San Francisco Bay.
1776	As Great Britain is forced out of its American colonies, Spain establishes a mission and presidio at San Francisco.
1781	First pueblo at Los Angeles is founded.
1812	Russian fur traders set up a colony on the Sonoma coast.
1821	Mexico wins independence from Spain, keeps "Alta" (upper) and "Baja" (lower) California as its own colonies.
1845	Increase of American settlers prompts Mexico to attempt a ban on such immigration.
1846	Big Bear Revolt by American settlers overthrows Mexican colonial government at Sonoma; U.S. government declares war on Mexico, seizes California, and assumes control in 1848.
1848	James Marshall discovers gold in the American River.
1849	Gold rush forty-niners pour in to mine the Mother Lode.
1850	California becomes the 31st state in the union.
1854	Permanent state capital established at Sacramento.
1861	California a distant observer with divided sympathies in the Civil War years.
1869	First campus of University of California opens at Berkeley. Golden spike links transcontinental railway in Utah; pony express mail era ends as does need for Cape Horn clippers.
1872	Last major Indian war in California concludes.
1887	Hollywood founded as sleepy village of fruit farmers.

1902	First Rose Bowl game
1905	Silent movie era commences.
1906	The Great Earthquake and Fire level San Francisco, but its residents immediately build anew.
1913	Cecil B. De Mille, Jesse Lasky, and Sam Goldwyn make the first feature-length motion picture in Hollywood.
1921	Oil discoveries at Long Beach set the Los Angeles area on a boom tide of growth and development.
1929	First Academy Awards presentations.
1932	Los Angeles hosts the Xth Summer Olympics.
1935	The Central Valley project begins to dam waters and enrich the soil of California's coming farm region to the south; the DC-3 of Donald Douglas inaugurates California's aerospace industry.
1941	The Pacific military buildup makes California first in the nation for armed forces installations and personnel.
1942	110,000 Japanese-Americans are evacuated to inland "relocation" camps for the duration of World War II.
1945	Founding meeting of the United Nations held in San Francisco.
1950	The first of 30 freeways to entwine Los Angeles links the city through three tunnels to Pasadena.
1955	Disneyland opens in Anaheim, Orange County, defining a new style of amusement American-style.
1958	Breakthroughs in transistor technology in the Santa Clara Valley south of San Francisco presage microelectronics boom and the new nickname Silicon Valley.
1964	California replaces New York as the most populous state.
1968	Peace and Freedom Party at UC-Berkeley leads to hippie era, flower power in San Francisco's Haight-Ashbury district.
1975	"Manson Murders" terrify Los Angeles.
1980	Two-term Governor Ronald Reagan elected U.S. President.
1983	Assassination of Harvey Milk in San Francisco.
1984	Los Angeles hosts the twenty-third Summer Olympics.
1987	Major earthquake in Los Angeles with fatalities.

HOW MUCH WILL IT COST?

"As little or as much as you want to spend" is our answer. The state that created the budget Motel 6 chain and a circuit of campgrounds unequaled in the country can also welcome you to the posh pool cabanas of the Beverly Hills Hotel (Howard Hughes lived in one once), or the European-style elegance of San Francisco's Nob Hill (known as Snob Hill to some jealous cynics).

Getting to California is perhaps the easiest part. Airlines arrive from all over the country and the world, and promotional fares can make for happy landings indeed—especially the under-$100 tickets out of New York (from where so many seek a bicoastal escape). Deals depend on the time of year: spring and fall offer the best off-season breaks—and some of the best weather.

If you don't come by car, you are likely to want and need one to cover California, even if you stay in one part of it. This is the state that keeps Detroit in business, because public transportation cannot accommodate the freewheeling mentality here. A car is freedom (note "freeway"), and rentals range from humble sub-compacts for $15 a day to proud, sporty Porsche 911S for $200 and more. But don't miss San Francisco's cable cars—a $1 memory forever. Of course, recreational vehicles (RVs) rate high, and there are more than 1,000 parks to hook up at for $10–$30 a night.

Cruise ships sail in and out of California, and you could come on a transcanal voyage from the East Coast or up from the Mexican Riviera (Acapulco, Puerto Vallarta, etc.) to either Los Angeles or San Francisco—or occasionally San Diego. Fares vary with the various cruise lines, most notably Sitmar, Cunard, Princess, Royal, Royal Viking, Western, and World Explorer.

Amtrak trains roll along some of their most scenic routes, coastal and mountain, in California. Train trips are popular, especially between Los Angeles and San Francisco on the Coast Starlight (and on to Seattle), and between San Francisco, Denver, and Chicago on the California Zephyr. Individuals and couples may find train travel more affordable than renting a car, which can cost 35¢ a mile. Families and groups more likely will save by driving, if you think per person.

Lodging varies from modest motels to full-service resorts, from quaint bed-and-breakfast inns (usually gracious old homes) to opulent hotels. Park visitors will find comfortable campgrounds and elegant lodges. The bed-and-breakfasts and some of the new all-suite hotels include a breakfast in their rates, which can save $7–$12 per person. Hotels in resort towns like Palm Springs and Santa Barbara compare in cost to hotels in Los Angeles and San Diego.

	Deluxe	*Moderate*	*Inexpensive*
Hotel (double room)			
L.A.–San Diego	$150–$200	$90–$125	$45–$65
San Francisco	$125–$200	$70–$100	$35–$60
Elsewhere	$70–$ 90	$55–$ 70	$20–$40
Restaurant (per person, w/o drinks)			
Breakfast	$20	$10	$ 5
Lunch	$20	$12	$ 7
Dinner	$50	$25	$15
Daily Totals (approx.)			
Cities and resorts	$215–$290	$115–$200	$60–$95
Elsewhere	$160–$180	$100–$120	$45–$70

INSIDERS' TIPS

Look for surprisingly alluring weekend packages at city hotels you might think are out of your league; when midweek travelers on expense accounts check out, these hotels get more eager for business.

While lodging costs vary by location, meal costs are fairly consistent throughout California. Naturally, metropolitan and resort areas have a greater share of fine dining experiences and sometimes slightly higher prices even in more modest eateries.

Discounts for children and senior citizens are widespread, especially in amusement park areas, at museums, and at other cultural attractions. Many state and national parks and museums are free. So are libraries, beaches, and churches (some with lunchtime organ concerts). And then there's all the scenery you can see.

THE BEST TIME TO GO

Weather, like so many things in California, is a subject of north and south. In summer, when Angelenos beat the heat with cardboard sunshades in their car windshields, San Franciscans are using fog lights to find their way around the chilly Bay Area. As Mark Twain said, "The coldest winter I ever spent was a summer in San Francisco." But then, nearly year-round sun has been the magnet for millions of immigrants to southern California, from the fruit farmers of the late 1800s to the moviemakers of today.

Don't believe the pop song that proclaims, "It never rains in southern California," because in the early months of the year it often does. That is when the desert south turns green, drying to a parched brown by summer, and turning kindle-wood-dry by fall. The north always looks lush, and the far north from the wine country just above San Francisco to the Oregon border offers all the seasonal changes any Easterner might miss.

Newcomers often complain that they miss the change of seasons in L.A., but isn't that why they came here to live? To escape the bitter winter cold and humid summer heat of wherever they were? California may be the one place where a gray day is considered a refreshing change of pace—except in San Francisco, where even the chauvinistic locals admit their need for sun by the end of a foggy summer. Fall is the warmest season there.

In the coastal south, temperatures average 80 degrees in the summer, 69 degrees in the winter. The inland desert is yet hotter by day and cooler by night, and its infamous Santa Ana winds can blast the otherwise comfortable coastline like a furnace. The agricultural Central Valley up to Sacramento can exceed 100 degrees in summer and plunge to freezing in winter. San Francisco, with its natural air-conditioning blowing off the Pacific Ocean through the Golden Gate, declares a heat wave if the mercury tops 75 degrees. A typical summer day in the Bay City may hit 65; winter days hover around 50.

Thus, when considering clothes, pack your cottons, linens, and silks (and a sweater or light jacket for cool evenings) for the south; knits, light wools, worsteds (and furs if you're fancy) for the north. Down jackets are *de rigueur* in wilderness areas as are sturdy hiking shoes. Polyester is common at Disneyland but hot in midsummer's long lines. The most fun is to shop when you arrive. California sets quite a fashion pace now, especially in sportswear, so take home a souvenir wardrobe—including Mickey Mouse ears, of course.

Unlike more traditional places where families gather at home for the holidays, California families get in the car and go. You will find crowds at Christmas wherever kids like to play. Even adult playgrounds like ski-mecca Lake Tahoe and spa-heaven La Costa are booked solid well in advance. Do plan ahead.

HOW TO GO

Most Californians speak English, though a smattering of menu Spanish will serve you well when trying the Mexican cuisine so popular here. Practice at your local Taco Bell. Chinese, Japanese, and Thai communities offer enticing taste treats, too, but the only words you need are "No MSG, please."

PERILS & PITFALLS

This is a pleasant state in which to get lost because people are generally friendly and helpful. It often seems as though everyone is on vacation. Just allow yourself time to get where you want to go: Distances are great, and traffic in the cities is often frustrating if not infuriating. Rent a car with music.

We all love feeling independent, finding our own way, and setting our own pace. This guidebook should help you do that. But package tours or a guided tour here and there can enhance your experience of places, too. In cities bus tours can orient you to sights you want to spend more time at on your own. A tour of movie stars' homes is a Beverly Hills must; the maps you can buy on street corners are hopelessly outdated since many of the stars listed are deceased and the rest have moved.

PERILS & PITFALLS

Unfortunately, we cannot ignore the reality of crime. This is a prosperous place, and visitors in particular can be prey to robbery. By avoiding known danger zones, one's risks diminish—and that is not too hard to do. Ask your hotel or motel manager about any cautions you should take, any areas to avoid. Do not take valuables to the beach!

Study the package tours available (see If You're Taking a Package Tour, page 14), and consult your travel agent if you think an organized itinerary would enhance your trip here. For additional information, contact the local convention and visitor's bureaus in the areas that interest you, or the California Office of Tourism, 1121 L Street, Suite 103, Sacramento, CA 95814; tel. 916-322-1396. Airlines, car rental companies, and, of course, American Express have tours and travel help, too.

In this book, we will provide you with as many phone numbers and notes about specific restaurants, accommodations, and attractions as we can fit between the covers. These will include where to rent a surfboard, find a fantasy honeymoon hotel, dine on *dim sum*, and much more you might not have known awaited you in sunny, sexy, delicious, and delightful California. So c'mon, surf's up!

WHAT TO PACK

Our weather report (see page 7) gave you some idea of the variable conditions you can encounter in "sunny" California. For the most part, springlike weather does prevail, and casual clothing is a tradition as old as Levi Strauss, the San Franciscan who invented (not "designed") the first blue jeans for gold rush pioneers (now *there* was a leisurely lot!).

San Francisco puts on a more Eastern establishment formality, whereas southern California leans to sporty pastels that reveal plenty of tan. Half the golfers in Palm Springs look as though they dressed in a Baskin-Robbins ice-cream kitchen—sunny climes bring out the colorful side in all of us.

Unless you are going straight to a ski resort or campground, men should bring one dress-up outfit—a dark suit or navy blazer and tie for the north (San Francisco, Carmel, Sacramento), and/or a lightweight sports coat and tie for the south (Los Angeles, San Diego, Palm Springs). You may not need the tie except at 4- and 5-crown restaurants and hotels (the posh Ritz-Carlton, Laguna Niguel requires it just to roam the corridors after sunset). Casual clothes for sightseeing, golf, etc. And white, white, white for tennis.

Women will find comfortable blouses, skirts, pants, or sundresses appropriate for most daytime activity; a handy sweater is always advised for air-conditioned museums, shopping malls, and theme park pavilions (such as the Penguin Encounter at San Diego's Sea World). You could bring a special dress or two for romantic meals at more elegant restaurants, but you will probably see "something Californian" you would prefer once you're here.

Any upscale hotel worth its crowns will provide you with an iron. Many now affix hair dryers, European-style, to their bathroom walls and supply terry-cloth robes for him and her (ask when you book a reservation). Baskets of toiletries and minibars of snacks are common, too. Any essentials you are missing can be bought nearby; this may be a foreign land, but you are still in America.

The fitness fervor in California means you can find any sports equipment you may desire if bringing your own is too awkward to contemplate. But airlines that fly here are used to transporting water skis, skin-diving equipment, surfboards, bicycles, golf clubs, windsurfing sails, downhill skis, and every variety of camping gear. We still say renting is much less troublesome.

Most important are comfortable and supportive walking shoes, even hiking boots if you plan any serious exploration beyond the major cities. Pack warmly for the wilderness, and plan to dress in layers (a good rule for San Francisco, too) to adjust to cool shade and hot sun. Raincoats are rarely used other than in winter.

HINTS ON YOUR HEALTH

Fitness and health are near obsessions for Californians, so never fear that you are far from comfort and care in case of emergency. Medical services and alternative (holistic) therapies abound here where Western and Eastern healing philosophies meet. Remember not long ago when Chinese acupuncture was considered close to voodoo? Many Californians have found it an invaluable import.

For emergency medical service in any California city, call 911 for police/ambulance and 0 (Operator) for connection to a hospital closest to you. Hospitals and specialty clinics are plentiful. In an emergency, dial 911.

INSIDERS' TIPS

Always carry an insurance identity card when traveling. You will not be refused service without one, but it can take longer to get it, and it may not be as thorough if the hospital is not assured of payment. Also, if time permits, ask the hospitals you call if they honor your insurance; most are "preferred providers" for particular policies but not for all. If they do not recognize your particular policy, you could end up paying 20–80 percent of the bill out of your own pocket.

If you plan on traveling into Mexico, even just Tijuana, take precautions. Tourist-oriented restaurants serve bottled water, but avoid ice, salads, fruit without hand-peelable skin (bananas are safe, apples are not) and carry Pepto-Bismol just in case. Before going, call the Tijuana Visitor and Convention Bureau for current information on travel conditions, 619-298-4105

(San Diego), or 800-522-1516 (California). Upset stomachs respond well to tea with lemon, yogurt, rice, and banana, which can all feel quite soothing when you're sick.

PERILS & PITFALLS

California law requires children under 4 years old or weighing less than 40 pounds to be strapped into a car seat when on the road in a private auto. A $50 fine is the penalty for ignoring this safety rule. Most car rental agencies offer these seats; most hospitals will loan them. Call any Children's Council; there are dozens around the state.

TRAVEL FOR THE HANDICAPPED

Much has changed in recent years, the very term handicapped being replaced by such positive phrases as "physically challenged." California has made the going easier with special considerations passed into law in 1978.

Special license plates now designate vehicles carrying handicapped and blind people and those with serious heart problems. With these plates—or other proof—such vehicles can park in blue-marked parking spaces prohibited to anyone else. Virtually every large parking lot has them, always near the building's entry and often adjacent to wheelchair ramps. Handicapped parking is free at meters and unlimited in limited-time zones.

Many popular hotels and most of the newly built ones have made their properties handicapped-accessible and have included some specially fitted handicapped guest rooms (wide doors, larger bathrooms, bath rails). For referrals to such hotels, contact the California Travel Industry Association, 2500 Wilshire Boulevard, Suite 603, Los Angeles, CA 90057; tel. 213-384-3178.

Most helpful may be the Society for the Advancement of Travel for the Handicapped, 26 Court Street, Brooklyn, NY 11242. This activist organization has praised Ramada and Holiday Inns for their handicapped guest programs.

INSIDERS' TIPS

Be sure to clearly identify a wheelchair checked with luggage, so it will not be confused with airline property. Allow plenty of time if meeting plane, train, or bus schedules, and make frequent rest stops if driving. Plan sightseeing carefully in San Francisco to avoid difficult and dangerous hill sites.

National park and worldwide airport accessibility for handicapped visitors is spelled out in two government guides, *Access to the National Parks* ($3.50) and *Access Travel* (free). Write the U.S. Government Printing Office, Washington, DC 20402, for copies.

Wheelchair travelers can send a self-addressed, stamped envelope for a free copy of *Round the Town with Ease,* a guide to Los Angeles' wheelchair-accessible historic sites from the Junior League of Los Angeles, 3rd and Fairfax streets, Los Angeles, CA 90036.

GETTING TO CALIFORNIA
IF YOU'RE TAKING A PACKAGE TOUR

Package tours can be fun for making friends, practical if you don't drive, and informative if you are not put off by canned tour lectures and wisecracking commentary. Their structure and scheduling eliminate much of the spontaneous exploration for which California is so perfect, but if your time is limited and your scope is grand, a tour can be an efficient choice.

We will discuss city tours in each city section. Here we have compiled examples of quality tours covering large areas or special themes. Most follow fairly beaten tracks—the coast, the redwoods, wine country, gold country, various parks (wilderness and amusement), and Palm Springs. But on those familiar routes lie the wonders of California that never cease to delight. (We have one friend who has been to Disneyland over 50 times!)

Two of the best tour operators, Tauck Tours and Maupintour, offer similar bus itineraries from San Francisco. Tauck's new California Tour takes 9 days to reach Long Beach via the redwood forests and assorted wineries of the north, the scenic 17-Mile Drive at Carmel on the central coast, Hearst Castle at San Simeon, and Catalina Island offshore from Los Angeles.

Maupintour's more elaborate Grand California tour spends 2 weeks with stops at top hotels, restaurants, and attractions in San Francisco, Sacramento, South Lake Tahoe, Yosemite, Monterey, Carmel, the San Joaquin Valley, Solvang, Hearst Castle, Santa Barbara, Hollywood/Los Angeles, and San Diego. The company also combines California and the Oregon coast in one itinerary and spends Christmas week in San Francisco for another.

Frontier Tours, a well-regarded Western travel company, has added a Skunk Train Tour to its product line. Beginning in the San Francisco Bay Area, the tour heads north for a half-day rail trip through the redwood forests and up to Willits, a picturesque logging and mining town that once relied on the stinky, gas-engine Skunk Train to get its goods to and from the markets. Diesels have replaced the 19th-century engines, but the name endures.

American Express Vacations focus on folks who like to go their own way but with accommodations prearranged. Their menu of city tours—minimum 2-night/ 3-day car-and-lodging packages—now include Carmel/ Monterey and the Napa/Sonoma Wine Country in addition to their standard tours. Stays can be extended on request.

More involved Independent Drive Vacations from American Express include an 8-day rental-car-and-hotel combination for Coastal California (San Francisco, an inland detour to Yosemite, Carmel, Solvang, and concluding in Los Angeles) and a 12-day West Coast Package providing car and accommodations on a grand circle (Los Angeles, San Diego, Scottsdale, AZ, Grand Canyon, Las Vegas, Yosemite, Carmel, and San Francisco—a *lot* of driving).

Mayflower Tours, in addition to the traditional coast motorcoach itinerary from San Francisco to San Diego, has added side trips (optional and geared to repeat visitors seeking something new)—one from San Francisco to wine country and gold country, the other from Los Angeles to Palm Springs and Las Vegas.

Gadabout Tours designs the most innovative trips of all. Their "settle in and sightsee" philosophy focuses on covering less territory but enjoying it more: Chinese New Year in San Francisco (February); gourmet Christmas celebrations in San Francisco or the Danish township of Solvang; a Civil War battle reenactment at Roaring Camp; or Death Valley Stays.

For more on these possibilities, call your travel agent or:

Tauck Tours, 203-226-6911 (CT), 212-689-9110 (NY), or 800-468-2825 (U.S.)

Maupintour, 913-843-1211 (KS), or 800-255-4266 (U.S.)
American Express Vacations, check local Yellow Pages.
Frontier Tours, 800-648-0912 (U.S.)
Mayflower Tours, 312-960-3430 (IL), or 800-323-7604 (U.S.)
Gadabout Tours, 619-325-5556 (San Diego), 800-521-7309
(California), or 800-952-5068 (U.S.)

AIRLINES

California is served by 37 domestic airlines and 37
foreign carriers. A flurry of mergers and acquisitions is
changing the names of some intrastate airlines: Pacific
Southwest Airlines (PSA) has become part of USAir;
AirCal has been bought by American; and Western was
absorbed into Delta. But the market for service, especially between the three major cities, indicates there
will always be convenient flights available. Fares between Los Angeles and San Francisco, the most competitive route, rarely exceed $60 and in fare wars go as
low as $29.

INSIDERS' TIPS

Less frequently than the carriers that fly numerous California intracity flights each day, some of the major
airlines, such as Pan Am, TWA, and United, have L.A.–
San Francisco hops as part of longer routes. To fill these
spot flights, they often offer low fares to win passengers
away from the better-known, hourly services.

SHIPS AND CRUISES

With so much coastline, California had to become a
cruise center. From San Diego, San Pedro (Los Angeles), and San Francisco, cruise lines set sail year-
round—in winter months to Mexico and the South
Pacific, in summer as far as Alaska or as close as
Catalina Island. Transcanal cruises are popular West
Coast–East Coast links via the Panama Canal and a
number of Caribbean island ports. Less frequent sailings head for the Far East or even around the world.

You cannot cruise to Hawaii, but if you fly there (as Californians do even for long weekends), you can take an American Hawaii interisland cruise to find your favorite.

Visitors with little time or a limited budget may enjoy an Azure Seas Friday or Monday sailing from Los Angeles to Ensenada, Mexico, and back. It's a quick hit of casino gambling, partying, and shopping south of the border, especially good for first-time cruisers—not fancy. Call Admiral Cruise Lines, 213-548-8411, 800-262-1128 (California), or 800-421-5866 (U.S.).

Count on a typical 8- or 10-day cruise to cost upwards of $1,500, and more deluxe choices over $4,000. Last-minute bargain space is always available if you are willing to weigh anchor on a moment's notice. Alaska trips generally cost more than Mexico due to the longer time and distance involved.

Among the top cruise lines to check for what you want are Royal Viking Line, Princess Cruises (well known here for their role in "The Love Boat" television series), Sitmar Cruises, and Royal Cruise Line. Royal Viking gets our nod as most upscale, with the most exotic itineraries and elegant service.

The Channel Islands, a string of uninhabited wildlife preserves, now a protected parkland, make for a memorable trip. Island Packers Company makes day trips from Ventura Harbor north of Los Angeles to Anacapa and Santa Cruz for under $40. The Santa Cruz cruise can include an overnight at the refurbished 1800s Ranch House for $100 (which includes the boat fare). The Ranch House has complete kitchens; you bring food and bedding.

BY TRAIN

The famed Twentieth Century Limited used to be the way movie stars shuttled from coast to coast in the heyday of Hollywood. Its art-deco luxury is long gone, but some of Amtrak's best rolling stock, including Superliner and Vistadome cars for fabulous views, come west to California each day.

The Coast Starlight travels the north-south route between San Diego and Seattle, its 11-hour leg from Los Angeles to San Francisco being most popular with visitors. The tracks run right along the coastline at many points for spectacular panoramas.

The California Zephyr departs Chicago daily for San Francisco crossing the High Sierras via Reno, NV, and chugging through the historic Donner Pass, where parties of covered-wagon settlers perished in mountain blizzards. Call 800-USA-RAIL for details.

BY CAR

The most automobiling state in the nation with over 9 million registered vehicles can certainly be reached by car. Interstate highways aim at the 3 major cities—I-80 via Salt Lake City and northern Nevada to Sacramento and San Francisco (or turn south at Salt Lake onto I-15 for Las Vegas and Los Angeles); I-40 across northern Arizona (closest to Grand Canyon) to Los Angeles: or I-10, the southernmost route, via Tucson and Phoenix for Los Angeles (turn left onto I-8 halfway between those two cities for San Diego). I-5, the main north-south highway, runs between San Diego and Seattle, but the more scenic drive is the Pacific Coast Highway, Route 1—slower and longer but vastly more beautiful.

Membership in an automobile club such as AAA is invaluable in California—for trip planning, road service, and phone-call assistance in strange territory. Insurance and fastened seat belts are required by California law.

PERILS & PITFALLS

There is no way to get to the coast without crossing miles of desert. While roadside services are plentiful enough to assure regular gas fill-ups, be sure your car is mechanically sound before leaving home, especially the cooling system. If the ride feels rough, lower tire pressure a bit as the desert heat causes expansion beyond normal conditions.

ARRIVING IN CALIFORNIA
A LITTLE GEOGRAPHY

We always hear how you can swim in the ocean and ski in the mountains on the same day in California. It's true, just one of the wonders of the Golden State where such geographic diversity abounds.

From the highest point in the contiguous United States (Mt. Whitney, 14,495 feet) to the lowest (Death Valley, 282 feet below sea level) is but an 85-mile hang glider's flight. In addition to 1,340 miles of coastline (that's counting all the curves and coves), California has 30,000 miles of rivers and streams and 5,000 lakes. Nearly half the land is under government ownership, and thus, in the public domain.

No wonder one in three California households has a recreational vehicle. Many of them are off-road conveyances such as dirt bikes, 4-wheel drives, and dune buggies. Balancing these hordes of wilderness explorers is one of the nation's strongest conservation movements—after all, the Sierra Club started here.

PERILS & PITFALLS

Quake, rattle, and roll. Yes, we have earthquakes—about 5,000 a year, few of which even rattle a windowpane. A notable lurch in the San Andreas Fault occurs about every 4 years, and the Big One is commonly forecast for the 1990s. If it hits during your visit, stay calm. Indoors, the U.S. government advises, get in a corner or a doorframe or under a solid desk or table; outdoors, get out in the open away from anything that can fall; in a car, stay in it with the radio on.

Basically California consists of an agriculturally rich central valley surrounded by mountain ranges and, below that, a vast desert. Coastal ranges form a backdrop to the beaches from Oregon south to Los Angeles. There, smaller mountain ridges create canyons and valleys stretching east toward the desert.

More than 20 million acres—one fifth of California—belong to 17 national forests. National parks and monuments cover another 4.5 million acres; and national wildlife refuges, 250,000 acres. Ocean beaches, though cold, rough, and dangerous for swimming in most parts, have been vehemently protected and kept public despite constant development pressures. The Channel Islands, scattered from San Diego to Santa Barbara and once rife with Indians, are now barren wildlife preserves—except for Santa Catalina Island where the wildlife is in the form of tourists.

Objective eyes would award San Francisco Bay the prize for prettiest cityscape—one of the world's most dazzling harbors. But it is southern California that draws the millions with little more than its climate. The Mediterranean-style flowering gardens of the south owe more to the air, sun, and sea than to the arid land. The only drawback of the climate is its monotony—or as one bumper sticker says, "Damn, another sunny day in paradise."

GETTING TO AND FROM THE AIRPORTS

Los Angeles

Los Angeles International Airport (LAX) lies about 22 miles or $25 by taxi from downtown, slightly less from Beverly Hills, a bit more from Hollywood. Airport-area hotels have their own courtesy shuttle vans. So do some more distant hotels.

Most affordable, if you're paying, is Super Shuttle, royal blue vans with bright yellow lettering that fan out to all corners of the metropolitan area for $11 per person from many of the city's hotels (more expensive if the distance is farther). You share the van with 4 or 5 others going your way, but the service is speedy in any case. Call from a courtesy phone after you have claimed your baggage; a van will come by for you within 10 minutes. For going back to the airport, call at least 5 hours in advance and plan on pickup 2 hours before your flight time; tel. 213-417-8988, or 800-554-6458 nationwide.

San Francisco

Three airports serve the Bay Area—San Francisco International (SFO), Oakland, and San Jose, each interconnected by shuttle services. Most likely, you will land at SFO, a 30-minute drive from downtown in good traffic, 15–30 minutes more at rush hour. Taxis cost $20–$30 plus tip. Associate Limousines is one upscale company that offers shared rides in its fine cars at taxi rates; single passengers pay $40–$100; call 415-563-1000.

Super Shuttle operates its door-to-door service here as in Los Angeles (call 415-871-7800, or outside California 800-554-6458). But the best deal in compact San Francisco (if you are staying in the center of the city) is the Airporter, a bus to a central terminal (Taylor and Ellis streets) for less than $2 that leaves you within a less-than-$5 taxi ride of most major hotels (call 415-673-2433).

San Diego

Easiest of all, San Diego International Airport, also called Lindbergh Field, is at the northern edge of downtown—just a 5-mile drive and a mere $3 by taxi to any hotel in the city center. Count on $7 or more to the beach areas, and $10 or so to Mission Valley and Hotel Circle. But ask your hotel if it offers a shuttle service; many do at low cost or for free. When confirming your outbound airline reservations, ask whether your flight departs from the east or west terminal in order to give your driver precise directions.

TIPPING

We admit that service is not what you'd expect in other parts of the world. But nothing ruins a good time more than quibbling over a tip. We say that unless the service is extraordinarily lousy, leave the going rate—and a bit more if it is especially nice. In many travel and hospitality jobs, the worker depends on tips for the better part of his or her income, unlike most of us enjoying a guaranteed wage whether we have a bad day or not. Standard minimums are:

Baggage porters. Airport or bus station: 50¢–$1 per bag; extra for loads of cameras, coats, golf clubs, etc. Railroad station: 40¢–50¢ per bag is a fee the porter must pay the station for each ticket stub; add 50¢–75¢ per bag as a tip.

On trains. Steward who seats you, nothing; sleeping car porter, $1.50 per night; dining car waiter, 10–15 percent per meal.

Drivers. Taxi drivers, 15–20 percent of the fare, plus 50¢ per bag they heave in and out; bus drivers, normally nothing, but if it is a sight-seeing tour, $1 per person or $25–$30/day per charter or package-tour busload (check to see if this is included in the price).

Hotels and resorts. Doorman, $1 for taxi hailing, baggage help; bellhop, 50¢ per bag in modest places, $1 each in the glamorous ones—plus a bit extra for excess paraphernalia; parking attendant, $1.50 for valet service; chambermaid, $1 a day for visits longer than one day, $5 per person per week for double occupancy; laundry or valet service, 15 percent; pool attendant, $1 per day that you use it; locker attendant, 50¢ per day; golf caddy, 15 percent of the greens fee for 18 holes, $3 a day on free courses, $1–$5 per bag otherwise; hairdressers, $3; barbers, $1; shoeshiners, 50¢–75¢; manicurist/pedicurist, $1.50; masseur or masseuse, $2.

PERILS & PITFALLS

Some tony restaurants automatically add a service charge to their bill; read the fine print on the menu, and don't tip twice. Only tip on the pretax amount of the meal. If paying by credit card, break down the waiter and wine steward's tips in writing on the restaurant bill (not the credit card receipt). For long stays, tip generously early on; it can help assure consistently good service.

Restaurants. Maitre d', no requirement for standard seating, but $5–$20 if it's special-to-very-special treatment in a glamorous place; bartender, 15 percent; waiter/waitress, 15–20 percent; at counters, 25¢ on anything up to $1 and 10 percent thereafter; wine steward, 15 percent of the wine bill.

THE INSIDERS' CALIFORNIA

WHERE TO STAY

Grand hotelier César Ritz proclaimed the three keys to success for a hotel were location, location, location. They are the keys to a California visitor's success, too. Decide where most of your activity will be, and then choose a hotel, or motel, campsite, or bed-and-breakfast nearby. Otherwise, you'll be driving for days!

Californians themselves tend to travel their state a lot, so lodgings from inexpensive to elegant, traditional to eccentric have grown up to accommodate explorers. The epitome of California kitsch, the Madonna Inn at San Luis Obispo, is a pink monument to bad taste and good times (that means we love it). But if every room is a different storybook fantasy scene there, the pink Beverly Hills Hotel's homey rooms come stocked with movie-land legends. San Diego's historic Hotel del Coronado beckons with white-clapboard, Victorian-seaside panache, while San Francisco's Westin St. Francis welcomes presidents, emperors, and kings to its stately, high-ceilinged suites.

Variety is the spice of overnight life in California where you may regret you don't have more time to spend in your room. If you plan to be out and about, stroll through a few of the exotic hotels, but stay somewhere simpler. Major chains abound—from budget Motel 6 (rarely more than $21 a night, often less) to Travelodge, Holiday Inn, and Best Western properties ($45–$75).

More and more popular are destination resorts where guests have no intention of wandering beyond the farthest fairway of the golf course—where varied dining and recreational facilities make for a one-stop vacation, usually in pampered luxury. These can be found on beaches, in the southern desert, or the mountains.

"Dude" is now a term heard mostly among sunbleached-blond teenagers acting cool rather than from cowboys who open their bunkhouses to tourists. But guest ranches, as they are called, remain a fun time for those seeking an Old West slice of life. On the luxurious side, some serve up more tennis than cattle branding these days, such as Santa Barbara's San Ysidro Ranch where John and Jacqueline Kennedy honeymooned.

Spa resorts are the ultimate California contribution to hedonism, often set near hot springs and staffed by masseurs, nutritionists, and other types for whom you become willing to suffer in order to look and feel good. You can pay through the nose job for the most luxurious shape-up at lavish La Costa near San Diego in the south, or you can steam in economic, volcanic-clay baths at modest Calistoga motels in the Napa Valley of the north.

California's other burgeoning bargain is the bed-and-breakfast inn, now spreading to big cities and quaint towns, wherever an amiable host has a spacious house with extra bedrooms. Just be sure they have extra bathrooms, too. This European concept lets visitors stay in romantic, often historic homes, some furnished like Grandma's house, others like modern designer showrooms. Breakfast can be Continental with croissants and coffee or Californian, complete with fruits, eggs, and home-baked muffins.

Just remember, the word for hot tub out here is "spa"—and you will be surprised how many hostelries have one. They have become a California mainstay and a wonderful way to relax after a busy day. Late at night they can be sinful.

WHERE TO EAT

The prototypical California girl is so slim and trim we have all come to believe she eats nothing but bean sprouts and the occasional celery stick. But these blonde beauties must just be blessed with amazing metabolisms for how could they resist all of the exciting gastronomic treats their home state has to offer?

From California cuisine and a rich variety of ethnic food to fresh fish and the exuberant bounty of fresh fruit and vegetables grown here, eating is a worthwhile pastime. Traveling the length of the Golden State, you'll be bound to come across just about everything it takes to make the perfect meal: fresh lobster from oceanside lobster shacks that dot the coast near San Diego; acres of fresh herbs from Taylor's Herb Gardens in Vista near Orange County; juicy apples from See Canyon near Morro Bay; strawberries growing in Oxnard fields; chèvre and olallie berries produced in Atascadero; fresh abalone and various other maricultural offerings such as California bay mussels, purple-hinged rock scallops, ridgeback shrimp, angel shark, sea urchins, belon oysters, rock crab, and for the adventuresome, sea vegetables or edible seaweed, all raised in offshore beds in Santa Barbara.

The perfect meals we are speaking of are expertly prepared in restaurants of all kinds, from one end of the state to the other. Dress codes at these places vary according to the area you are visiting. With the exception of San Francisco, the operative word is *casual;* and in the better restaurants, it's best to be elegantly casual. San Francisco is a dressy city with a fashion sophistication that's often compared to New York, whereas restaurant attire in Los Angeles ranges from the ridiculous to the ultra chic. A tie for a gentleman is the exception to the rule in Los Angeles, except for a few grand French restaurants, and you can count on one hand the number of restaurants that won't admit women in slacks. Still, bare feet and bare chests remain no-nos, even in casual beach restaurants. If you are dining out in San Diego or Orange County, lean toward more conservative attire; it's best to find that happy medium between couture and informality.

A word on California cuisine. Is it still an institution? What is it? Did it ever exist? There are still two sides to the argument which was first discussed in 1981. You will find many restaurants described as serving California cuisine, which usually means an eclectic or ethnic mix of food from something as ludicrous as goat-cheese sorbet to something as sublime as brie-and-grape quesadilla with sweet pea guacamole, as prepared by Chef Michael Robert at Trumps restaurant in West Hollywood.

INSIDERS' TIPS

Because of the eating-out syndrome in L.A., the clamor for dining reservations can be a difficult game. If you can, make reservations at least two weeks in advance (or even a month if the place is a celebrity haunt). San Francisco has been an eating town far longer than Los Angeles, and the restaurant frenzy is not as great, yet early reservations are suggested here as well, especially in the touted food citadels. Another tip, if you haven't planned ahead, is to seek out your friendly concierge and see what he or she can do for you. Recently, concierge extraordinaire Cynthia Reid of San Francisco's Huntington Hotel got us into the popular Stars restaurant with only a few hours notice.

If you come across the words *spa cuisine* on California menus, it does not mean food as prepared at expensive health resorts—although it *is* healthy food, cooked with a serious nod to dining without butter, flour, and other fattening ingredients. Also known as cuisine naturelle, this fare is the epitome of light and delicious, savory food, prepared with stock reductions and the use of herbs and spices in place of salt. If you would like to check into a spa to literally taste spa cuisine, try the Golden Door in Encinitas, California where both body and palate will be pampered.

Chicago and New York *used* to be the kingpins of pizza, but L.A. knocked down the pins for a strike in 1981. A talented Austrian transplanted to California got the country thinking about pizza in terms other than mozzarella, pepperoni, and tomato sauce. As Wolfgang Puck envisions pizza, it is better served with artichokes, leeks, radicchio, zucchini, garlic, fresh oregano, and garnished with edible flowers. Several other inventive pizza restaurants followed suit. The day of the everyday pizza is over—at least in L.A.

PERILS & PITFALLS

In Los Angeles, in spite of a beautiful coastline with public access beaches, there are only a handful of restaurants overlooking the beach that are worth the price of the food. With few exceptions, there are either nautical-theme restaurants or hot-dog stands in close proximity to the blue Pacific. In Los Angeles, the places to dine with the most beautiful views of the water are the private clubs. On the other hand, San Diego and environs have lovely waterfront restaurants with beautiful vistas of either boat marinas or the California coastline, and San Francisco tops them all with extraordinary views of the water and the Golden Gate Bridge.

Speaking of Los Angeles, let's look at Mexican cuisine. L.A. has a very large Mexican population, yet short of venturing into unknown territory in the barrios, where excellent, family-style cooking can be found, the Mexican fare all seems to look and taste the same. Excellent, regional Mexican cuisine is hard to find with only a few exceptions (noted in the restaurant listings), like San Francisco's Mission District, which has some fine Mexican restaurants. For families traveling on a budget, however, Mexican restaurants are a bonanza— and filling too.

Leaders of the California wine industry send their disciples to restaurateurs all over the state to encourage them to taste their vineyard's premium wines for placement on the wine list. It is the diner who benefits from this surfeit of California wines, many of which you won't find on wine lists in the rest of the country.

HOW TO GET AROUND

In the Cities

When the Beach Boys sang "I Get Around," they did not mean via surfboard. Renting a car—even a little deuce coupe—is the best way to get around California's 3 main cities and beyond. San Francisco has the state's only viable urban mass transport, and even there you will want wheels to cross the Golden Gate Bridge and to explore outlying areas.

Fly-drive packages from major airlines can do the trick. No need to worry that there will be a car shortage at a busy airport if you have booked in advance. Drop off the car as you depart. Major rental agencies charge the same rates all over town. Smaller companies can offer better deals, but you may sacrifice convenience, comfort, and mechanical reliability.

Taxis work well in San Francisco because it is compact. They cost $2.50 for the first mile and $1.20 for each additional mile. Rates are similar in Los Angeles, but distances between popular sites are greater. This can make for meter readings that boggle the budget. Cabs do not cruise as much in L.A., so count on making a phone call for pickup. San Diego is fairly compact and convenient for taxi trips.

As for mass transit, let's take the cities one by one:

Los Angeles has just started digging itself a subway to be called MetroRail. We will update this guidebook 10 times before it is finished to a degree useful for visitors. That leaves the bus.

The city's RTD service (Southern California Rapid Transit District), while cheap, is anything but fast— mostly because of the huge distances and the congestion of surface streets as opposed to freeways. If you will be bussing it, find a hotel on or near Wilshire Boulevard, anywhere between downtown and Santa Monica (the beach). Lots of buses, lots of sights along there.

For RTD routes, schedules, and self-guided tours, call 213-626–4455. Fares are normally 85¢ plus 10¢ for transfers, a true bargain. There is no all-you-can-ride day ticket as in San Diego and San Francisco.

Frankly, we recommend renting a car in Los Angeles. Check local listings for Alamo, Avis, Budget, Dollar, Hertz, National, Thrifty, and General, or for a jazzy sports car that will make you feel like a movie mogul, Showcase (800-345-2277) or 7-11 (*not* the convenience store chain, 714-650-1180).

Whether navigating by car or bus, get a good map (*The Thomas Guide* is the best). When given an address to find, always ask, "What's the cross street?" After all, Sunset Boulevard, from downtown to beach, is 30 miles

long! By asking which street intersects, you'll sound
like a native.

San Diego also depends on bus service for mass
transit, but with a few colorful twists. The Bus That
Goes in Circles will take you to the airport, major
tourist attractions, and hotels on its circuitous route.
Day Tripper all-you-can-ride tickets are on sale for one
day, $3; two days, $5; or three days, $7 (they must be
consecutive days). The Light Rail Transit, better known
as the Tijuana Trolley, is the best way to reach the
Mexican border 18 miles from downtown, and at $1, it
is also the cheapest. For general San Diego Transit
information, call 619-233-3004.

As in Los Angeles, we recommend renting a car in
San Diego. Though the hotels are fairly concentrated,
the city sprawls. Call Avis, Budget, Hertz, National, or
Sears for best quality.

San Francisco has excellent bus service, various
forms of speedy subway and, of course, its cable cars.
You will not need (or want) a car in town; the meter
maids are merciless, and hillside parking can be per-
ilous to the novice. Rent one for out-of-town excursions,
such as to the wine country or Carmel. Call AVCAR,
Avis, Budget, Dollar, Hertz, or Thrifty; ask about lower
weekend rates.

The cable cars, shut down from 1984 to 1986 for a
complete overhaul, are once again climbing halfway to
the stars. You just might have to wish on one to get
aboard; lines can be unbelievably l-o-n-g, especially in
the summer tourist season. Still, it's the best dollar
you'll ever spend.

Bus fare is 75¢ per ride, allowing for two transfers
within 90 minutes. An all-day pass, available in ticket
machines along the routes, costs $5. Route information

is in the Yellow Pages. *Tours of Discovery*, a pamphlet, points out 100 interesting sights one can find via public transportation ($1.25).

All this comes under the purview of the San Francisco Municipal Railway or MUNI. (Call 415-673-MUNI for information.) The other initials to remember are BART for Bay Area Rapid Transit, a light-rail system that can whisk you under the bay to Berkeley or Oakland. Call 415-788-2278 for where and when to catch it.

PERILS & PITFALLS

Be careful about nightcaps. Bars and clubs close in San Diego at 1:30 A.M., in Los Angeles and San Francisco at 2 A.M. with some open later on weekends. Late at night buses run less frequently, and light-rail transit (subways, trolleys, cable cars) stop altogether (in San Diego at 1:30 A.M., in San Francisco at midnight). Have cab fare.

Walking in California's major cities should be called hiking. In hilly San Francisco, it is climbing. Everywhere but there city blocks can be deceptively gigantic. "Nobody walks in L.A." is as true as it is trite; in Beverly Hills you are likely to be picked up by the police for questioning (your motives, not your sanity). San Diego welcomes walkers to its Gaslamp Quarter, its waterfront pedestrian paths, and its peaceful, sprawling Balboa Park. Ask at your hotel or motel about where walking is scenic and safe. Everyone likes sunny California, even street crooks.

PERILS & PITFALLS

We can tell you the legal speed limits, by the way—55 or 65 mph on the freeways and most highways; 30—35 mph on major city thoroughfares; and 25 mph on any normal street. We will not encourage you to exceed those — not that many Californians do. Be warned and beware—of drivers *and* police.

Bicycles may outnumber cars at California's beaches. Special bikeways are built for them, and the only trouble comes when skateboarders and roller skaters vie to use the asphalt strips. You can rent any or all of these conveyances at the more popular beaches. In-city cycling is risky given the way cars crowd in and turn right on red (legal unless posted otherwise).

Outside the Cities

By air. There are frequent shuttle services between the 3 major cities and competitive commuter hops to the popular resort areas such as Palm Springs and nearby Las Vegas. Look in the Yellow Pages for local numbers to learn fares and schedules.

INSIDERS' TIPS

Little-known and under-used airports can be more convenient than the majors, and all have national connections: John Wayne Airport in Orange County (if Disneyland is your main destination); Hollywood/Burbank Airport in Burbank (much closer to touristy L.A. than LAX); and Oakland Airport just outside of San Francisco (and just a bit farther from the city center than SFO).

By motorcoach. Motorcoach travel can be tiresome and time-consuming for all but short excursions. Tour company coaches pace their itineraries for passenger comfort and sightseeing (see If You're Taking a Package Tour, page 14). Greyhound Lines and Trailways (being acquired by Greyhound) serve the intercity market. Check local listings.

By water. Short trips traveling by water include Catalina Island jaunts from Los Angeles, Ensenada (Mexico) excursions from San Diego and Los Angeles, Channel Island explorations from Ventura, and, in San Francisco Bay, boats to Alcatraz, bay cruises, and ferries to Sausalito.

SHOPPING

Crossroads of the World, a quaint complex of stucco cottages in Hollywood, marked by a neon-lit globe on a soaring tower, claims to have been America's first shopping center. Gold miners' money made San Francisco a center for fancy goods from the beginning. And San Diego's proximity to Mexico as well as its famous port have made it an international marketplace to this day. In this state, when the jogging—or golfing, boating, skiing, or tennis—gets tough, the tough go shopping.

For visitors, the most popular and truly California take-homes include wine from the Napa and Sonoma valleys (homes of the state's finest vintages); chocolates from See's in the south and Ghirardelli's in the north; sourdough bread (on sale in every airport); and fashions and home furnishings designed in bright, distinctive California styles.

Whether you prefer the comfort and convenience of an enclosed shopping mall (often called gallerias here), or window-shopping and movie-star-gazing on high-fashion streets—or perhaps browsing among antique shops and country stores in the gold country or wine country, or discovering arts and crafts at friendly street fairs—California has it all: From T-shirts to high tea, this land was made for shopping.

Most famous of all the meccas is Rodeo Drive, the Fifth Avenue of Beverly Hills, but on a scale of much more concentrated luxury—just two and a half blocks of one famous designer name after another and the wealthy of the world with their elegant, lacquered shopping bags and valet-parked Rollses and Mercedes.

PERILS & PITFALLS

The word *sale* has become a cliché on Rodeo Drive and, except at the end of a fashion season, means little. For designer bargains, head downtown in Los Angeles to the California Mart (110 E. Ninth Street) and the Cooper Building (860 S. Los Angeles Street).

The most fun place to shop, we feel, is San Diego's new Horton Plaza, a multicolored, postmodern jumble of toylike building blocks stacked around a lively open-air atrium and filled with shops both funky and fashionable. A real hit. So is the city's Seaport Village, a waterfront cluster of art, craft, and ice-cream shops, looking like an early fishing town. We also like Old Town for its quality Mexican marketplace.

San Francisco has given California some of its finest family-owned department stores, namely I. Magnin, Gump's, and Wilkes Bashford. It also has an Eastern city-feel with Saks, Macy's, and Neiman-Marcus. The waterfront offers Pier 39—touristy but fun. And there are Chinatown and Japantown for oriental exotica and Union Street for fashionable boutiques.

NIGHTLIFE

Inside the Cities

Let's be honest: California is a day-tripper's dream. This land of natural beauty has geared itself to sunshine more than to moonlight, and Californians, for the most part, are early to bed and early to rise. You will have trouble finding late-night restaurants. Theater is a year or two behind Broadway, except for occasional previews of Broadway-bound productions. Nightclubs dwindled in number when Las Vegas stole the show. And since disco died, dancing has become pretty much the province of upscale-hotel hot spots.

> ### INSIDERS' TIPS
> Broadway-bound shows are much cheaper here than they are later in New York City.

Then again there are gems that sparkle after dark—some of the nation's best comedy clubs in Los Angeles (The Comedy Store, The Improvisation, and The Groundling Theater); jam-packed dance floors in San Diego (Club Diego's, Halcyon, and Spirit); and cultural treasures in California's more major cities (opera, symphony orchestra, and dance—ballet and modern—are all superb and popular here).

Some of the best nighttime pleasure can be found in scenic overviews of the cities—looking down on San Diego's downtown, its navy berths of big ships and its marinas of sailboats from Hillcrest, a revitalized neighborhood of shops and cafés; seeing San Francisco Bay from any of many hilltop vantages on either side of the Golden Gate; and parking in awe atop Mulholland Drive to enjoy the glitter of Los Angeles that seems to stretch forever.

Beyond the main cities, the Lake Tahoe resort area carries on late with legalized gambling at such dazzling casino hotels as Caesar's, Harrah's, and The Sahara. Palm Springs in the southern desert draws celebrities, corporate executives, and gays to its variety of luxury resorts and lively night spots where leisure is the area's only business.

If you miss the Los Angeles Philharmonic in winter at the Dorothy Chandler Pavilion of the downtown Music Center (where the Oscars are handed out), you might enjoy the orchestra even more at the Hollywood Bowl in summer—after the Playboy Jazz Festival in June. Picnics are a tradition for this season of nightly concerts under the stars. Only the performances with fireworks are a difficult ticket. Buy tickets in advance.

INSIDERS' TIPS

Many film and television actors and actresses yearn for the energy of a live-audience, stage-acting experience. At any given time, you are likely to find a famous face behind the footlights of Los Angeles' many smaller theaters and playhouses, those in Westwood and Pasadena being most famous. Check *Los Angeles Magazine* for the month's celebrity star turns.

But for the most authentic California entertainment, why not take in a movie? No place built cinema palaces like Los Angeles, and a $6 visit to Mann's (formerly Grauman's) Chinese Theater on Hollywood Boulevard is worth it for the theater alone. That means the *inside*, not just the famed footprint forecourt.

Some of the most exciting live theater in California can be found at San Diego's Old Globe Theater, a 50-year-old stage newly rebuilt after it had burned down (just as Shakespeare's did) in Balboa Park. Its outdoor Old Globe Festival Stage and the nearby Starlight Bowl amphitheater offer summer Shakespeare and musicals respectively.

INSIDERS' TIPS

Ticketron, Ticketmaster, Bass, and other ticket agencies sell tickets to the major pop, cultural, and sports events throughout the state. San Diego has an arts hot line (234-ARTS). San Francisco has a half-price service (STBS) for day-of-performance deals, cash only; call 433-STBS, or go to STBS on Stockton Street in Union Square.

Hotels hold some grand nighttime possibilities for both star entertainment and stellar views. The Venetian Room of San Francisco's Fairmont Hotel (the one featured in TV's "Hotel" series) presents top-name performers while the Top of the Mark atop the Inter-Continental Mark Hopkins towers over the entire Bay Area. Humphrey's, the fern-and-ceiling-fan restaurant at San Diego's Half Moon Inn, offers dinner with a breathtaking view of the marina and Point Loma. And a bubble elevator to the top of Los Angeles' Westin Bonaventure leads to sky-high fine dining.

Outside the Cities

Winter brings plenty of warmth to ski lodges at the major mountain resorts and plenty of programs open to the public on the state's numerous college campuses. Spring, summer, and fall are festival seasons—except for Pasadena's Tournament of Roses on New Year's Day and San Francisco's Chinese New Year in February. Many outlying cities and smaller towns stage colorful cultural and agricultural festivals and fairs lasting weeks on end. Most prominent are:

Cherry Blossom Festival, Japantown, San Francisco, April

The Ramona Pageant and Outdoor Play, Hemet, April–May

Cinco de Mayo (Mexican Independence Day), Los Angeles, May

Calaveras Jumping Frog Contest, Gold Country, May

Berkeley Jazz Festival, Berkeley, May

Dixieland Jazz Jubilee, Sacramento, May

National Shakespeare Festival, San Diego, June–September

Carmel Bach Festival, Carmel, July

Festival of the Arts/Pageant of the Masters, Laguna Beach, July

California Rodeo, Salinas, July

Mother Lode Fair, Gold Country, July

California State Fair, Sacramento, August

San Diego National Air Show, San Diego, August

INSIDERS' TIPS

Late summer and fall set the stage for many a harvest festival: pears (Courtland); grapes and wine (Lodi); apricots (Patterson); pumpkin (Manteca); roses (Wasco); garlic (Gilroy); artichokes (Castroville); apples (Mendocino); begonias (Santa Cruz). Not to be forgotten: young Marilyn Monroe was once Artichoke Queen.

Old Spanish Days, Santa Barbara, August
Danish Days, Solvang, September
Harvest Fair, Sonoma, September
Los Angeles County Fair, Los Angeles, September
Monterey Jazz Festival, Monterey Peninsula, September
Valley of the Moon Vintage Festival, Sonoma, September
Grand National Rodeo and Horse Show, San Francisco, October
Oktoberfest, Big Bear Lake, September–October
International Film Festival, San Francisco, October
California Wine Festival, Monterey, November–December

PAMPERING THE BODY BEAUTIFUL

We know we're not alone when we admit that we have pounds to shed, double chins to trim, and bodies that need reshaping. And there's no better place than the Golden State for a little help in firming the flab without much hassle and even with some fun involved. So if you're ready to dust off your Adidas and put away the

Godivas, reserve a spot at one of the following California health spas. Before you know it, you'll be facing the mirror image you've always hoped to call your own.

The Golden Door♛♛♛♛♛, P.O. Box 1567, Escondido, CA 92025; tel. 619-744-5777.

Sonoma Mission Inn and Spa♛♛♛♛, P.O. Box 1447, Sonoma, CA 95476; tel. 707-938-9000.

The Ashram♛♛♛, P.O. Box 8009, Calabasas, CA 91302; tel. 818-888-0232.

Cal-A-Vie♛♛♛, 2249 Somerset Rd., Vista, CA 92083; tel. 619-945-2055.

La Costa Hotel and Spa♛♛♛, 2100 Costa Del Mar Rd., Carlsbad, CA 92009; tel. 619-438-9111.

The Oaks at Ojai♛♛, 122 East Ojai Ave., Ojai, CA 93023; tel. 805-646-5573.

The Palms at Palm Springs♛♛, 572 N. Indian Ave., Palm Springs, CA 92262; tel. 619-325-1111.

Rancho La Puerta♛, 3085 Reynard Way, San Diego, CA 92103; tel. 619-294-8504.

DOING BUSINESS IN CALIFORNIA

The *Wall Street Journal (Western Edition)* has become a standard accompaniment to morning coffee delivered to city hotel rooms in California, certainly on the executive or concierge floors where business travelers congregate.

Other prominent publications focused on California's business scene include *California Business* and *The Executive-Southern California* (monthly magazines); *San Diego Business Journal* (daily magazine); *Daily Commerce* (Los Angeles) and *San Diego Business Transcript* (daily newspapers); *Orange County Business Week* and *San Francisco Business Times* (weekly newspapers). Of special note to entertainment industry participants and spectators are *Daily Variety* and *The Hollywood Reporter*.

Metropolitan daily newspapers carry local and national business news: *San Diego Union* (morning) and *Evening Tribune*; *Los Angeles Times, Los Angeles Herald Examiner*, and *Los Angeles Daily News*, all morning papers; *San Francisco Chronicle* (morning) and *San Francisco Examiner* (afternoon); and, for state government coverage, the *Sacramento Bee.*

Office services for travelers on business in California can range from secretarial support, arranged by a hotel, to rentals of audio-visual and office equipment, available from many specialty stores. In Los Angeles, HQ, The Headquarters Company can provide an office away from the office with staff and essential equipment (213-277-6660).

Teleconference facilities are centered in larger hotels, for example: Los Angeles (Beverly Wilshire, Century Plaza, Hyatt Regency, Sheraton Plaza–La Reina); San Diego (Half Moon Inn, Little America Westgate, Sheraton–Harbor Island, Town and Country); San Francisco (Fairmont, Hyatt on Union Square, Mark Hopkins).

For helpful insight on commercial opportunities and connections in California, the state headquarters of the chambers of commerce has a directory of local chamber offices. Their number and those in the other major cities are:

Sacramento	916-444-6670
Los Angeles	213-629-0711
San Diego	619-232-0124
San Francisco	415-392-4511

Business Hours

Official government and business hours are 9 A.M. to 5 or 5:30 P.M., but people are often at work early—especially stockbrokers, who must keep pace with the East Coast markets—and many stay late, till 6 or 6:30. Entertainment industry types tend to have evening events and thus may not be in their offices till mid-morning.

Banks are generally open from 10 A.M. to 3 P.M. Monday–Thursday, till 6 P.M. on Friday. Savings and loan institutions operate from 9 A.M. to 5 P.M. weekdays and usually on Saturdays from 9 or 10 A.M. till 2 P.M.

Automated teller machines are widely available where travelers move (airports, hotels, office buildings, shopping centers).

Stores and shops can be counted on between 10 A.M. and 5 P.M., and many department and chain stores stay open till 9 P.M. on weeknights—especially in shopping malls. Food markets and drugstores tend to open early, some at 6 or 7 A.M., and close as late as midnight. More and more all-night supermarkets are appearing in the major cities.

PERILS & PITFALLS

Beverly Hills' posh Rodeo Drive can drive shoppers to financial distraction and even destruction. Unless you trust your self-control, stroll these beautiful-people blocks on Sunday when traffic is light and the stores are closed.

Bar hours vary with city liquor laws, San Francisco being the historic winner for bawdy and bustling nightlife. Official closing time in Los Angeles and San Francisco is 2 A.M. weeknights, 4 A.M. weekends (no alcohol after 2 A.M.); in San Diego, 1:30 A.M.

Theater curtains and concert batons rise, most often, at 7:30 or 8 P.M., sometimes with a second "late" show at 10 or 10:30 P.M. Matinees can be found at major theaters, usually at 2 and/or 5 P.M. Movies are screened from midday to midnight.

Museums are rarely open on Mondays. Normal hours are 10 A.M. to 5 P.M. Some have more limited hours in winter. Call ahead.

MAKING FRIENDS WITH CALIFORNIANS

First of all, who is a Californian? Californians come from all over—the U.S., Latin America, Asia, Canada, Australia, Europe, the Middle East, and Africa, in about that order. So they are really people just like you, but they got here first. For all that diversity, a strange California ethos seems to infuse everyone with a warm friendliness, superficially at least. The north can seem more reserved and formal, but there is a certain "sunny-side-up" cordiality throughout the state.

You will think store clerks a personable lot as they offer smiley greetings to you at every cash register. It's actually just an automatic reflex—a nice one, granted, which perhaps seems surprising only because it is so rare these days. If New Yorkers are stereotyped as sincerely insincere, Californians could be accused of being insincerely sincere.

On the other hand, Californians are tolerant, more so as you go north from Orange County, a bastion of patriotic, moral, and economic fervor. No doubt the general live-and-let-live feeling derives from so many types of people having to coexist, many quite eccentric and exotic. Let yourself enjoy and appreciate the colorful mix. There is room here for everyone.

The difference between friendliness and friendship can be attributed to the high mobility of California society. People move on so frequently that real friendships rarely take root; when they do, they take time to do so. But this is the home of the celebrity kiss, where perfect strangers fawn over each other on television talk shows as if they were best Beverly Hills buddies. It's hard to read the signals.

San Francisco has the most evident "old money" with an upper-class society proud of its historic lineage, grand manner, and grand manors elegantly set on Pacific Heights. Los Angeles' old money is new by comparison, and flashy, newer fortunes in Beverly Hills are more visible than the genteel legacies in Hancock Park. Real California gentility rings Santa Barbara, where the Reagan ranch is new money but in grand Western style.

The best way for a visitor to make friends is to find the place or group that caters to your career, hobbies, or interests. That could mean an exclusive city club or a meeting of Alcoholics Anonymous; it could be a surfers' beach or a Sierra Club office, a coffee house or a professional association. Bulletin boards and local, giveaway newspapers are common forums for finding groups and individuals like yourself.

Health clubs are one of the most popular gathering places for meeting people. Bars have their singles scenes, too. The socially adept may do well in hotel lobbies and lounges. "Personals" can be found in numerous, racy newsprint tabloids as well as in glossy city magazines.

INSIDERS' TIPS

"What's your (astrological) sign?" is not the first question a newly met Californian is likely to ask you—or the second. But questions about jobs and rent rates, common elsewhere, are a bit off-putting here. Personal interests, new movies, travel plans, and sporting activities are all more popular topics than one's station in life. That is measured silently by one's car, so rent a Porsche if you wish to impress or pretend.

Longtime Californians regret that their traditionally openhanded and openhearted state has succumbed to modern times with the same caution and distrust found everywhere. It is the way of the West to welcome newcomers because everyone has been one, and not so long ago. The burgeoning of the cities has cost some of the old cordiality. Too many newcomers have come to cash in on California's endless prosperity. Still, you're likely to find a basic friendliness.

Away from the big cities, friendliness is even warmer, but families are also closer and can be more closed. It takes two to three years to build a base of real friends. But in the meantime you'll hear more than often enough, "Have a nice day."

SPORTS IN CALIFORNIA

Spectator Sports

Football. The season runs September to January. In San Diego. The San Diego Chargers play at Jack Murphy Stadium, 619-280-2111. In Anaheim, the Los Angeles Rams play at Anaheim Stadium, 714-937-6767. In Los Angeles, the Los Angeles Raiders play at the Los Angeles Memorial Coliseum, 213-322-5901. In San Francisco, the San Francisco Forty-Niners play at Candlestick Park, 415-468-2249 or 415-771-1149.

Baseball. The season runs early April to early October. In San Diego, the Padres use Jack Murphy Stadium, 619-283-4494. In Los Angeles, the Dodgers play at Dodger Stadium, 213-224-1500. In San Francisco, the Giants play at Candlestick Park, 415-467-8000.

Basketball. The season runs from October to April. In Los Angeles, the Lakers play at the Forum, 213-673-1300. In San Francisco, the Golden State Warriors play at the Oakland Arena, 415-638-6000.

Golf. In San Diego, the Shearson-Lehman Brothers Andy Williams San Diego Open is played at Torrey Pines Golf Club in mid-February, 619-281-4653. The MONY Tournament is held at La Costa Hotel and Spa in mid-January, 619-438-9111. In Los Angeles, the Glen Campbell Los Angeles Open is played at the Riviera Golf Course in late February, 213-482-1311.

Tennis. In San Diego, the National Hardcourt Tennis Championships are played at the La Jolla Beach and Tennis Club in late November, 619-454-7126. The La Jolla Tennis Tournament is played at the La Jolla Recreation Center, 619-454-2071 or 619-454-4434. In Los Angeles, the Volvo Tennis Tournament is held in early September at U.C.L.A., 213-825-2101. In San Francisco, the Transamerica Men's Tennis Championships are held at the Cow Palace in September, 415-469-6065; and the Virginia Slims Women's Tour is held at the Oakland Arena in February, 415-638-6000.

Thoroughbred racing. In San Diego, horses run at the Del Mar Fairgrounds from late July to early September, 619-755-1141. In Arcadia, the Santa Anita Handicap is run at Santa Anita Park, in late April, 818-574-7223. In Alabany, they compete at Golden Gate Fields, 415-526-3020; and in San Mateo at Bay Meadows, 415-574-7223.

Track. In San Diego, the Michelob Invitational Indoor Track Meet is scheduled at the Sports Arena in the middle of February, 619-224-4176.

Boxing. In Los Angeles, matches are held at the Olympic Auditorium, 213-749-5171 and at the Forum, 213-673-1300.

Auto racing. The Long Beach Grand Prix is held in early April in Long Beach, 213-436-9953.

Rodeo. In Daly City, the Grand National and Livestock Show is held in October at the Cow Palace, 415-469-6065.

Participant Sports

Below is a sampling of some of the sporting events that showcase *you* as the participant. In this section, we offer places (or sources for places) where the general public is welcomed. Beyond these recommendations, seek out the facilities in the hotel in which you are staying or through the hotel's concierge. In areas where participant sports are emphasized, we detail what to do and where to do it within that chapter of this book.

Swimming. In San Diego, at Mission Bay Aquatic Park, 1001 Santa Clara Dr., San Diego 92109; tel. 619-488-1036. In Los Angeles, Los Angeles Department of Recreation and Parks, Aquatics Office, 3900 Chevy Chase Dr., L.A. 90039; tel. 213-485-5538 (for the metropolitan area), 213-485-2844 (for the Pacific region), and 818-989-8891 (for the San Fernando Valley).

Ballooning. In San Diego, Pacific Horizon Balloon Tours, 16236 San Dieguito Rd., Rancho Santa Fe 92067; tel. 619-456-2719; and A Beautiful Morning Balloon Company, P.O. Box 2666, Del Mar 92014; tel. 619-481-6225. In Los Angeles, Dann Balloon Flights, P.O. Box 7097, Canyon Lake 92380; tel. 714-244-3511. In Yountville, Adventures Aloft, P.O. Box 2500 Vintage 1870 Complex, 6245 Washington St., Yountville 94599; tel. 707-255-8688.

Windsurfing. In San Diego, Mission Bay Aquatic Park, 1001 Santa Clara Dr., San Diego 92109; tel. 619-488-1036.

Golf. In San Diego, Torrey Pines, 11480 N. Torrey Pines Rd., San Diego 92037; tel. 619-453-8148; and Carmel Mountain Ranch, 14151 Carmel Ridge Rd., San Diego 92128; tel. 619-487-9224. In Los Angeles, Wilson Golf Course, 4730 Crystal Springs Dr., L.A. 90027; tel. 213-663-2555; and Rancho Golf Course, 10460 W. Pico Blvd., L.A. 90064; tel. 213-838-7373. In Encino, Encino Golf Course, 16821 Burbank Blvd., Encino 91316; tel. 818-995-1170. In San Francisco, Golden

Gate Park Golf Course, 47th Ave., Fulton, San Francisco 94121; tel. 415-751-8987.

Hang gliding. In Ignacio, Marin County Hang Gliding Association, #6C, Pamaron Way, Ignacio 94947; tel. 415-883-3494.

Tennis. In San Diego, River Valley Sports Center, 2440 Hotel Circle N., San Diego 92108; tel. 619-297-3391. In Los Angeles, Los Angeles Department of Recreation and Parks, 3900 Chevy Chase Dr., L.A. 90039; tel. 818-246-5613, or Los Angeles Department of Recreation and Parks, 2459 Motor Ave., Los Angeles 90026; tel. 213-837-3087. In San Francisco, Northern California Tennis Association, 645 5th St., San Francisco 94107; tel. 415-777-5683.

Crew. In San Diego, Mission Bay Aquatic Park, 1001 Santa Clara Dr., San Diego 92109; tel. 619-488-1036.

Jogging and walking. In San Diego, Mission Bay Aquatic Park, 1001 Santa Clara, San Diego 92109; tel. 619-488-1036.

Sportfishing. In San Diego, H and M Landing, 2803 Emerson St., San Diego 92106; tel. 619-295-3225.

Hiking. In Los Angeles, California Native, 6701 W. 87th Pl., Los Angeles 90045; tel. 213-642-1140.

Volleyball. In San Francisco, Y.M.C.A., 220 Golden Gate Ave., San Francisco 94102; tel. 415-931-6385.

Bicycling. In San Francisco, Outdoor Unlimited, 245 Millberry Union, University of California San Francisco, San Francisco 94143; tel. 415-476-2078.

Badminton. In San Francisco, San Francisco Park and Recreation Department, San Francisco 94117; tel. 415-558-4268.

Martial arts. A few of the leading martial arts instruction centers in San Francisco are: Aikido with Ki, 1755 Laguna St.; tel. 415-756-6255. Hwa Rang Kwan Center, 3219 Laguna St.; tel. 415-929-0447. Karate USA Academy, 2399 Greenwich St.; tel. 415-552-7283. Shorin Ji Kempo, 1691 Laguna St.; tel. 415-731-0889. Tae Kwon Do-Sun Moo Won, 1712 Divisadero St.; tel. 415-567-2957. Tai Chi Chun Academy, 11 Brenham Pl.; tel. 415-362-4180.

LOS ANGELES
LOS ANGELES IN A HURRY

To hurry in Los Angeles seems a contradiction from the start. One day or two or even three in the Big Orange can only begin to peel the surface of this sprawling megalopolis of 7 million residents. People here think nothing of driving 30 miles "crosstown" to dine with friends. After all, Greater Los Angeles (city, county, and contiguous towns) covers nearly 200 communities and 4,000 square miles. The city alone stretches 64 square miles.

ITINERARIES IN LOS ANGELES

First Day

The beaches (Venice, Santa Monica), Beverly Hills (Rodeo Drive), L.A. County Museum of Art, Hollywood Boulevard, Sunset Strip.

Second Day

Universal Studios, *or* J. Paul Getty Museum and Malibu, *or* downtown walking tour, Museum of Contemporary Art, evening at the Griffith Park Observatory.

Third Day

Queen Mary/Spruce Goose (Long Beach); Marina del Rey boating outing; Los Angeles Music Center evening.

For a fun, not frantic, experience of this exciting area, we suggest a mix of driving tours, walking tours, and stops at certain key attractions. Universal Studios, a top draw for tourists, is an all-day outing by itself. We are not even considering Disneyland here; it's actually in Anaheim, an hour south of Los Angeles, and requires another full day and evening—or more.

But if you must hurry—*very* un-Californian—here are the places we take our friends from out of town who have only a day (or two or three) to taste L.A.

The Beaches (Venice and Santa Monica)

It usually surprises visitors to learn that urban Los Angeles is 15 miles inland from the beach. But beaches are part of Los Angeles' body and soul, and they are the first place to put your toe in the water—literally and figuratively—to feel the city. Venice ♛ ♛ ♛, a seaside community that once came complete with canals and gondolas (a few are left), is considered the Bohemian corner of Los Angeles. The beachfront promenade draws leftover hippies, acrobatic roller skaters, magicians, and musclemen to its carnival-by-the-sand setting of T-shirt, poster, and pizza stands.

The beach is gigantic beyond the winding bicycle path that runs like a 19-mile asphalt ribbon on the beach from Torrance in the south to Santa Monica just north of Venice (and next on this tour). Skate and bike rentals abound along the nearby streets. Famed Muscle Beach is actually a small patch of asphalt with gym weights being hoisted by huge, sun-sweaty beach boys. You must be a member to work out, but everyone can watch—and does. Art galleries represent the more aesthetic side of Venice, home to many artists, actors, and poets. Weekends are the most colorful time to experience the place if you can enjoy the festive crowds.

PERILS & PITFALLS

Parking is a pain in Venice's maze of one-way alleys and strictly monitored streets. Read signs carefully or, safer yet, park a few blocks back from the beach and walk; police are ruthless with tickets and tow-aways.

Santa Monica ♛ ♛ ♛ ♛ exudes more of a family feel—fine shopping, a funky pier, and a long, beautiful beach with a view to Malibu. Main Street's Victorian-style shops and restaurants contrast with modern

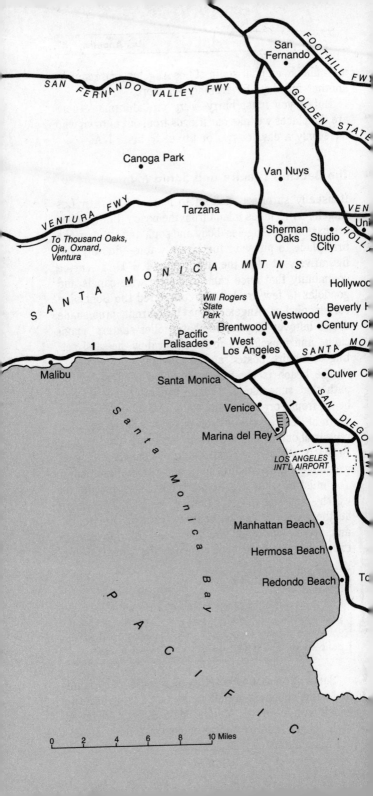

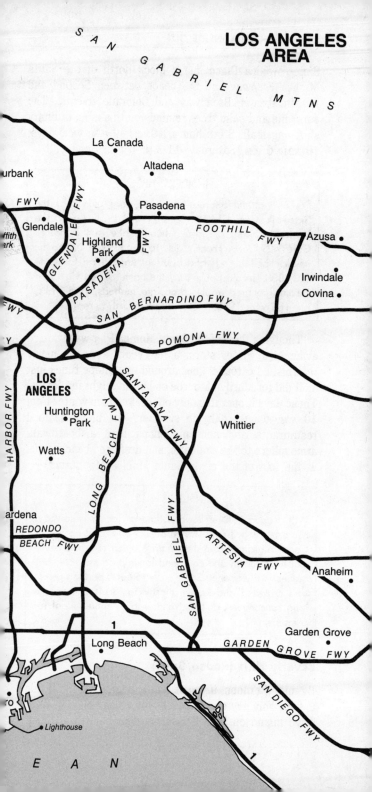

Santa Monica Place just a block north of the Santa Monica Freeway and the beach between Second and Fourth streets, Broadway and Colorado Avenue. The sunshine and palm trees remind you this is no ordinary shopping mall. Store hours, 10 A.M.–9 P.M. weekdays; 10 A.M.–6 P.M. Saturday; 11 A.M.–6 P.M. Sunday.

INSIDERS' TIPS

For a healthful alternative to hot dogs, snack at the Sidewalk Café, 1401 Ocean Front Walk, near the Venice Pavilion, or have a healthshake at the Figtree Café, 429 Ocean Front Walk. To step back in time to the heyday of hot rods and bouffant hair, head for Café 50s, 838 Lincoln Boulevard, the home of red vinyl and chrome counter stools, chocolate malteds, and walls, covered with 1950s memorabilia, worth a read.

Though a third of the Santa Monica Pier was washed away in a winter storm a few years ago, the newly refurbished carousel goes around to calliope tunes just as it did for Marilyn Monroe on her midnight fun forays. These days it operates only on weekends in winter from 10 A.M.–6 P.M., daily in summer. The pier's seafood restaurants and souvenir shops lend a boardwalk atmosphere to the dramatic, sun-drenched beachscape, at the foot of the misty Santa Monica Mountains.

INSIDERS' TIPS

Will Rogers State Beach, named for the cowboy-humorist, is a 3-mile stretch of surf and sand up Pacific Coast Highway from the Santa Monica city beaches—extremely clean and equipped for impromptu volleyball games; just join one. Come early to get a parking place. Less crowded and known mostly to locals is Zuma, a long, uncommercial beach closer to Malibu—ideal for campers.

Beverly Hills (Rodeo Drive)

By mid-afternoon, if you've had enough sun (and if this is your only day on the beach, you've had enough sun), drive inland on Sunset Boulevard just north of the J.

Paul Getty Museum, past the beautiful homes of Brentwood, the tall hedges hiding fabulous estates in Bel Air, and the lush lawns and palm-lined streets of Beverly Hills ♛ ♛ ♛ ♛ ♛.

Jayne Mansfield's Spanish-style mansion (now Engelbert Humperdinck's) is on the corner of Carollwood and Sunset with hearts still etched in its driveway entry and topping its gates. Call Starline Tours ♛ ♛ ♛ for 2-hour tours of movie-star homes—minibuses that can explore where larger motorcoaches cannot; tel. 213-463-3131.

The most lovely glimpses of life in Beverly Hills can be found at Greystone Park ♛ ♛ (905 Loma Vista Drive) and the Virginia Robinson Gardens ♛ (1008 Elden Way). These two private estates are now open to the public after the death of their owners. Greystone is open daily 10 A.M.–5 P.M. for free roaming and spectacular hillside views, the other by appointment only (213-446-8251, ext. 37) for tours of its gorgeous, internationally inspired gardens.

The heart of Beverly Hills, however, is Rodeo Drive ♛ ♛ ♛ ♛ ♛—pronounced *roh-DAY-oh*. Though only 3 blocks long, this stretch of world-renowned designer shops and exclusive, local emporia is the richest concentration of glamour and luxury to be found in the Los Angeles area (Beverly Hills is a city within the city).

INSIDERS' TIPS

Two-hour-free parking structures are well marked, but curbside valet parking is available if you care to indulge yourself. A Free Ride shuttle circuits the Golden Triangle of fine shopping streets every 10 minutes, stopping at all free-parking structures from 7 A.M. on Monday-Saturday. Sunday is a good day for quiet strolls if you don't mind missing the stars. Shops are closed.

Most amusing is Giorgio, recognizable by its yellow-and-white-striped awnings and the atomizer over its door. You may not see it, but every few minutes a spritz of Giorgio perfume is sprayed to tease shoppers with what is allegedly the best-selling fragrance in Beverly

Hills. Like many shops in this fashionable city, Giorgio graciously offers refreshments to shoppers.

Pressure is not part of the sales technique here, so don't be intimidated: Browse freely in Beverly Hills' shops because you may be surprised how affordable some of life's little luxuries can be. Also, explore some of the streets parallel to Rodeo Drive—Canon, Beverly Drive, and Camden—for shops and restaurants frequented by the rich and famous.

A library may not seem much of a tourist attraction in L.A., but the archives of the Academy of Motion Picture Arts and Sciences♕♕—the people who present the Oscars—is a trove of movie-land treasures. Located at 8949 Wilshire Boulevard, the Academy is open Monday, Tuesday, Thursday, and Friday from 9 A.M.–5 P.M. Free.

INSIDERS' TIPS

Few places as small as Beverly Hills can boast so many world-class hotels. *Beverly Hills Cop* filmed its madcap room-service scenes in front of the posh Beverly Wilshire at Wilshire Boulevard and Rodeo Drive. The musical group The Eagles used the classic, pink Beverly Hills Hotel on the cover of their *Hotel California* album. The lobbies of both are worth a walk-through, the latter being home to the famed Polo Lounge where movie moguls breakfast.

Los Angeles County Museum of Art

Farther east approaching Wilshire Boulevard's Miracle Mile of museums, foreign consulates, and fashionable department stores, is the Los Angeles County Museum of Art (LACMA)♕♕♕♕. Its new "front door" (opened fall 1986), the Robert O. Anderson Building, has doubled the exhibition space allowed by the 3 previously existing buildings. As overbearing as it looks from outside, the new building's interior provides pleasingly vast spaces for the museum's rich, 20th-century art collection.

Most notable among LACMA's other holdings are the world's largest collection of German Expressionist paintings, one of the Western world's best collections of Indian, Nepalese, and Tibetan art, and opening in 1988, the Pavilion for Japanese Art, containing the outstanding Shin'enkan collection of Edo-period screens and scrolls.

Located at 5905 Wilshire Boulevard, LACMA is open weekdays except Monday 10 A.M.–5 P.M. and weekends 10 A.M.–6 P.M. Free admission the second Tuesday of the month; other times, $1.50 for adults, 75¢ for children over 5, students, and seniors. Call 213-937-2590 for current special exhibitions and events.

INSIDERS' TIPS

If you fancy primitive biology more than civilized art, a block east of LACMA is the George C. Page Museum and La Brea Discoveries ♛ ♛ ♛. *La Brea* means "the tar" in Spanish, and on this site many ancient animals became trapped in tar pits, their bodies fossilizing for future study—saber-toothed cats, mammoths, sloths. Fantastic for kids and truly fascinating for adults. Hours are Tuesday-Saturday 10 A.M.–5 P.M. Admissions the same as LACMA's.

Hollywood Boulevard

Try to get here after dark. This dowager thoroughfare, while set for a multimillion-dollar overhaul by the city, is still leading the tawdry existence that began as television replaced the high glamour of the movies. Hollywood Boulevard ♛ ♛ ♛, once an avenue of stunning shops, movie palaces, restaurants, and nightclubs, has lost much of its luster. Not to be missed, of course, but it is best seen by streetlight, not daylight. Then imagination can conjure up some of the old magic.

Hollywood and Vine is just an intersection these days, but here at the heart of old Hollywood you can see the bronze stars embedded in Hollywood's Walk of Fame; look up Vine Street at the landmark Capitol Records building, designed in 1954 as the world's first circular office tower (envision a stack of records on a spindle). Stroll west on Hollywood toward La Brea, past a medley of movie memorabilia, poster and T-shirt shops—the bookstores can be especially intriguing for movie buffs—and on to the Chinese Theater (6925 Hollywood Boulevard).

INSIDERS' TIPS

The Hollywood Bowl♔♔♔ sits in a hollow of the Hollywood Hills less than a mile above the boulevard on Highland Avenue. Its tiny museum displays curios from historic concerts and events. Across Highland the Hollywood Studio Museum♔ enshrines the silent movie era in the same yellow barn where Jesse Lasky, Sam Goldwyn, and Cecil B. De Mille made the first feature-length film in Hollywood in 1913, *The Squaw Man*.

Mann's Chinese Theater♔♔♔♔♔, originally Grauman's, draws every Hollywood visitor to its famed forecourt where every star you can think of has come down to earth to plant his or her hand- and footprint in cement. Impressions of Betty Grable's leg and Jimmy Durante's nose are here too. Travelers will find themselves wondering how Judy Garland ever fit in such tiny shoes or Gary Cooper in such large ones.

Sid Grauman, a dark-haired Harpo Marx look-alike, was early Hollywood's greatest showman—a builder of the most exotic movie theaters and producer of extravagant entertainments. His Chinese Theater, built in 1927, resembles a Chinese temple inside and out. It still holds the record for hosting the most movie premieres of any one cinema. His Egyptian Theater farther east at 6712 Hollywood Boulevard held many, too, but does not compare in grandeur these days to the Chinese Theater. To see even a bad movie here is worth the price of admission.

The recently renovated and reopened Hollywood Roosevelt Hotel♔♔, opposite the Chinese Theater, hosted the first Academy Awards dinner in its Blossom Room. Its 1940s, famed Cinegrill once again presents top entertainers of song and dance, and real romantics can book the panoramic, rooftop suite where Gable and Lombard spent their wedding night (tel. 213-466-7000).

INSIDERS' TIPS

Even if you don't stay at the Roosevelt, stroll into its elegant Spanish Colonial-style lobby and upstairs to the free Hollywood history photo exhibit encircling the mezzanine. You will learn more juicy trivia here than in a dozen movie books and feel you are part of it. A drink at the Tropicana Bar brings it all back.

Sunset Strip

Sunset Strip♛♛, a garish streak of neon and night-clubs, cuts a bright swath linking Hollywood to Beverly Hills. This was Los Angeles' late-night action scene before Las Vegas lured away all the top supper-club entertainment with bigger bucks. It then changed to a rock beat, with some clubs still loud and strong like the Whisky, the Rainbow, and Gazzarris. After a downhill decline in the hippie era, this stretch of Sunset Boulevard has begun a comeback with fashionable clothing boutiques, sidewalk cafés, and flashy shops.

INSIDERS' TIPS

All-night eats, a rarity in L.A., can be found at Ben Frank's, a big 1960s-style coffee shop at 8585 Sunset. Lots of Hollywood types and colorful characters show up here after theaters close and parties end. Great fun and little known to out-of-towners. Open 24 hours, 7 days a week.

Today the sights to see are monstrous movie bill-boards, called vanity signs for the way they puff up star egos, and some popular celebrity hangouts: The Comedy Store♛♛♛, part-owned by Steve Martin (8433 Sunset; 213-656-6225); Carlos 'n' Charlies'♛♛ where Joan Rivers often performs and young stars pretend to hate photographers (8240 Sunset; 213-656-8830); and Spago♛♛♛♛♛, a trendy restaurant famed for its goat-cheese pizza and California cuisine, now established as a star mecca (8795 Sunset; 213-652-4025—with an unlisted number for celebrities).

Kids of all ages will get a kick out of Dudley Do-

Right's Emporium ♛ at the very beginning of the Strip (8200 Sunset) and the giant statue of Rocky and Bullwinkle (animated TV-series cult figures) two doors beyond; open Tuesday-Thursday, 10 A.M.–5 P.M.

LOS ANGELES THE SECOND DAY

Now that you have made a whirlwind circuit of the city's highlights—at least those most visitors come looking for—a second day allows time to discover one attraction or area in depth. Here we describe 3 possibilities, each of which will lead to other discoveries in its neighborhood to busy you for a day. Quick stops and good luck on the freeways might get you to two of these, but we would recommend not rushing it; nothing will help you hate L.A. so much as trying to beat the traffic. It's a fact of life, so it's better to scale down your sight-seeing ambitions to a more focused area and enjoy its ambience.

Universal Studios Tour

One of the most-visited attractions in Greater Los Angeles ♛ ♛ ♛ ♛, this 420-acre complex of soundstages, back-lot sets, and simulated movie scenes takes the magic and makes it mundane. The larger-than-life spectacle of the big screen explodes in live shows such as *Conan—A Sword and Sorcery Spectacular* and *King Kong*, and you may catch a movie in the making. The Old West stunt show delivers some corny cowboy roughhousing, and the Screen Test Comedy Theatre puts audience members in costume and makeup for an on-camera sketch with a star, usually of minor magnitude.

Don't get us wrong: This can be a fun-filled day, particularly for families (following the guided itinerary takes 5 hours plus time out for meals and meandering). The tram ride takes visitors from the Colonial American street where Marcus Welby and Beaver Cleaver both lived to the New York street known to Kojak; from the parting of the Red Sea to the parting of Bruce the

Shark's jaws; and past sets for "Knight Rider," "The A Team," and the famed *Psycho* house on the hill.

Located off the Lankershim Boulevard exit of the northbound Hollywood Freeway, the Universal Studios Tour opens Monday-Friday at 10 A.M., weekends at 9:30 A.M., last tour daily at 3:30 P.M. Admission is $14.95 for adults, $10.50 for children over 3, and $11.50 for seniors.

INSIDERS' TIPS

For a more authentic, behind-the-scenes look at moviemaking, the Burbank Studios 👑 👑 👑 👑 👑, dominated by Warner Brothers and Columbia, is the largest studio complex in the world. Located at 4000 Warner Boulevard in Burbank, their daily guided VIP Tours (limit 12 people) require reservations (tel. 818-954-1008). This free and more technical look at filmdom can be followed by lunch in the studio commissary, the Blue Room, if requested in advance.

The J. Paul Getty Museum

The most richly endowed art museum in the world looks, at first, like a movie set itself 👑 👑 👑 👑 👑. Inspired by a 1st-century Roman villa overlooking the Bay of Naples from the slopes of Mt. Vesuvius, this colonnaded court looks out on the Pacific from the cliffs of Malibu. Since the first art collected by oil tycoon Getty was Roman and Greek antiquities, the setting is ideal to display them. By the way, Getty's $1.3 billion bequest on his death has doubled to more than $2 billion since Texaco's 1984 takeover of Getty Oil. Sadly, the benefactor never saw the finished place.

The free, 15-minute docent orientation provides a wealth of facts and trivia about the collection, the eccentric collector, and the incredibly thoughtful details built into the museum, including marble from Italy involving stupendous cost and craftmanship. Upstairs the villa houses its decorative arts collection in period rooms of treasures from French royal households as well as from German and Italian nobility.

PERILS & PITFALLS

Visitors with limited time in Los Angeles are happy to learn the Getty is free but often disappointed to find its limited parking space (a garage under the villa for modern chariots) requires reservations usually a week in advance, more for weekend days. Walk-ins are not allowed unless you are dropped off by cab or private car or come via the RTD bus No. 434 (ask the driver for a museum admission); motorcycles and bicycles can enter anytime. To drive in and park, call 213-458-2003, or write to the Reservations Office, P.O. Box 2112, Santa Monica, CA 90406.

Western art from the late 13th to late 19th century, heavy on the Renaissance and Baroque, occupies more upstairs galleries. The Baroque Painting Gallery has charming concerts on the third Thursday of most months; reservations required (tel. 213-458-2003). Lunch at the indoor/outdoor Garden Tea Room offers light fare at right prices in delightful surroundings.

INSIDERS' TIPS

Across Pacific Coast Highway from the Getty is Gladstone's ♛♛♛, a beachfront indoor/outdoor restaurant of seafood specialties and seductive California milkshakes with exotic liqueurs (like Oreo Vandermint). Crowded and crazed on weekends (you can wait 45 minutes for a table), it is still an "only in L.A." experience.

Before or after seeing the Getty and its peaceful gardens, drive up the coast highway through 27-mile-long Malibu ♛♛♛♛ for a look at some of the most expensive oceanfront real estate in America. Homes of Johnny Carson, Olivia Newton-John, Barbra Streisand, Larry Hagman, and many more dot the Malibu Colony, some along the sand, others in the hills that overlook it. Most beachfront is private, but you can enjoy some of the finest public beaches around at:

Leo Carillo State Beach—caves, scuba coves, good surf, and rock formations sheltering intimate picnic sites

DOWNTOWN LOS ANGELES

GLENDALE FWY

2

GOLDEN STATE FWY

Los Angeles River

110

5

Elysian Park

Police Academy

Sunset Blvd

Pasadena Ave

Dodger Stadium

PASADENA FWY

N. Broadway

1

HOLLYWOOD FWY

Beverly Blvd

Music Center

Civic Center

Hall of Justice

El Pueblo de Los Angeles St. Hist. Park

Olvera

SAN BERNARDINO FWY

Wilshire Blvd

Atlantic Richfield Plaza (Arco Plaza)

Court House

Library

Old Mexico

Union Station

10

Federal Bldg

SANTA

1st St

ANA

ARBOR FWY

Figueroa

City Hall

Philharmonic Auditorium Pershing Square

Japanese Temple

4th St

FWY

101

Convention Center

Whittier

Blvd

5

Olympic

Alameda St

SANTA ANA FWY

Broadway

SANTA MONICA FWY

10

Main St

San Pedro

Central Ave

Washington

Blvd

Los Angeles River

Jefferson

Blvd

Blvd

0   0.5   1   1.5 Miles

Zuma Beach—the largest of all (5 miles long), life-guards, facilities

Surfrider Beach—near the Malibu Pier and appropri-ately named as a surfer's heaven, good for people watching

Paradise Cove—private but accessible for $3, be-neath the red sandstone cliffs of Point Dume, famous (or infamous) nude beach and popular Sandcastle Res-taurant

Topanga Canyon Beach—just across from the Getty, the southernmost Malibu beach, fine for swimming and fishing

Downtown Walking Tour

When Los Angeles boomed earlier this century, fear of earthquakes made it a low-rise city—which is why it spread for miles. A collection of suburbs without a city, pundits had called it. But new antiearthquake construc-tion technology freed architects to reach for the sky, and since the 1970s, L.A. has sprouted a downtown it never had before.

Bunker Hill♛ ♛ ♛, the most exciting part of the redevelopment, had been an elegant neighborhood of Victorian homes that fell into disrepair as the money moved out to the suburbs years ago. Tearing down the whole place and rebuilding from the ground up, Los Angeles has created a "New Downtown," as it is being heralded.

Start at the Westin Bonaventure Hotel♛ ♛ at Fifth and Flower, a mirror-walled complex of 4 cylinders joined in a sky-high John Portman atrium of bubble elevators surrounded by a lake (1974–76), and head for the 35th-floor rooftop lounge. Get your bearings. To one side, the 52-story Atlantic Richfield Plaza (1972), known locally as ARCO Towers (2 of them). To the other side, the hulking World Trade Center complex. Before you, the silvery, sleek, 48-story Wells Fargo Building♛ (1979) with a sharp-angled, red sculpture on an inset roof garden and a plaza of elegant date palms casting playful shadows on a bright Frank Stella mural.

From the hotel, cross a pedestrian skywalk to the Wells Fargo Building and visit its ground-level Wells Fargo Museum—Old West memorabilia of stagecoaches and pony express. Across Fifth Street stands the Los Angeles Public Library♛ ♛ (1923–25) on an island of grass. Squat and fortresslike, this building with its sunburst-tiled pyramid crown is nonetheless graceful and proud—this despite its being tragically torched by an arsonist in 1986 (it is still in recovery).

Now the focus of an expansion program, the library will be the centerpiece of a ring of soaring office buildings. Underway are the 73-story Library Tower from I. M. Pei's design studio, which by the 1990s will be the tallest West Coast building south of Seattle, and Philip Johnson's 67-story Grand Place Tower. Already the new Biltmore Tower looks down on the comparatively little library.

The Biltmore Hotel♛ ♛ (1922–28), on Fifth and Olive, marks another corner of Bunker Hill. Well worth a walk-through, the Italian Renaissance-styled Biltmore has grand, wood-paneled hallways with stunningly rich, coffered ceilings, twisting columns, and stately Palladian windows. Afternoon tea is served in the original lobby, and a more gracious repast you cannot find in all downtown.

Walk up Grand Avenue past the whimsical sculptures of Crocker Court (Crocker is yet another bank which has built a monumental corporate enclave downtown, Crocker Center) and come to the Museum of Contemporary Art (MOCA)♛ ♛ ♛ ♛ ♛ between First and Third. This first American building by Japanese architect Arata Isozaki became an instant hit in L.A., a gem in a concrete forest.

PERILS & PITFALLS

Serious walking may be good exercise, but touristic strolling is not—and workouts seem to be neglected when we travel. Combine sightseeing and exercise at the new Ketchum-Downtown YMCA at Fourth and Hope atop the ARCO Garage. (Call 213-624-2348 for hours.)

Opened in late 1986, this cluster of barrel-vaulted roofs, pyramid skylights, and cubes of red sandstone, glass brick, and enameled walls is an art piece in itself. By 1993, it will be dwarfed by the surrounding towers of California Plaza, the city's biggest development project ever. Half of MOCA's 98,000 square feet is gallery space for exciting new art, much of it Californian. Allow 2 hours to really enjoy it. Open Tuesday–Wednesday and Saturday–Sunday 11 A.M.–6 P.M., Thursday–Friday 11 A.M.–8 P.M. Admission $4 adults, $2 seniors and children, under 12 free. Thursday 6–8 P.M. is free. (Tel. 213-621-2766.)

INSIDERS' TIPS

The Temporary Contemporary ♛ ♛ ♛, a warehouse at First and Central for MOCA exhibits before the museum was built, is still used as a space for more adventurous art shows—same operating hours and admission as MOCA. It's right next to lively Little Tokyo and a Soho-type neighborhood of new art galleries, Cirrus being the most renowned.

Griffith Park Observatory by Night

Its copper domes and monumental white buildings ♛ ♛ ♛ loom up from the Hollywood Hills a mile east of the Hollywood Sign. Its parking lot was the set for a tense scene between James Dean and Sal Mineo in *Rebel Without a Cause*. And its telescope scans the sky (on clear nights) from 7 P.M. (or dark) till 10 P.M. for all to truly stargaze. If you get here in the daytime, you can see to the sea, but it's most fun at night. After a long day on your feet, you will welcome the reclining theater seats in the Planetarium's daytime star show or at the exciting Laserium with its nightly music-and-light shows. The view of city lights stretching forever is unforgettable. General admission is free, but shows cost $2.25 for adults, $1.25 for seniors and children. Call for schedules; tel. 213-664-1191. Access via Western Avenue into Griffith Park.

A THIRD DAY IN LOS ANGELES

If you did the city in the one- and two-day itineraries, you may be ready to do something more relaxing today. You could scratch the sightseeing and treat yourself to a facial (for women *and* men) in a Beverly Hills salon, an acupuncture session at a shiatsu spa, a personalized exercise workout at a body shop (not the kind for cars), or a float in an isolation tank at the Altered States Relaxation Center (where but California?). If the sun has been avoiding you on your visit, you could duck into a tanning salon so everyone back home will think you lived at the beach.

But if your curiosity and capacity for tourism are not spent, we say it's time to go down to the sea in ships—a luxury liner and a charter boat, to be specific.

Queen Mary and Spruce Goose

Long Beach is one of those long drives to a far corner of Los Angeles County but one full of surprise pleasures. For many years a major navy port, Long Beach has also been known for its wide, white, and *long* beach, a popular celebrity resort in the art deco twenties and thirties. Of late, the city is making a dramatic comeback: Landmark older hotels are being refurbished, sleek new ones are now completed (visit the Hyatt's beautiful lounge for cocktails at sunset), and it boasts one of southern California's most unusual attractions.

The *Queen Mary* ♛ ♛ ♛ ♛, once the largest and fastest luxury liner afloat, is docked here in all her glory—12 decks of it open to the public. Built in 1934, the ship carried wealthy aristocrats and World War II soldiers in its elegant spaces. The burnished woodwork, gleaming nickel railings, and hand-cut glass remain. So do the peach-colored mirrors that would make the most seasick society lady look in the blush of health. And so do all the workings of this bygone conveyance from stem to stern. Not dwarfed by history, this venerable ship allows a glimpse at what luxury really meant—sweeping decks, soaring dining rooms, and posh staterooms, now silent with their stories of grand crossings.

The 90-minute tour is recommended to get your orientation before exploring on your own; the tour also visits parts of the ship, like the lavish, first-class swimming pool, which are off limits to visitors today. Open 10 A.M.–6 P.M. daily, the *Queen Mary* holds demonstrations of lifeboat drills, nautical knot-tying, and semaphore signaling to evoke the seamanship of yore. Plenty of souvenir and food outlets to please today's more middle-class crowd. Admission $6 for adults, $4 for children (tel. 213-435-3511).

INSIDERS' TIPS

The *Queen Mary* is a floating hotel as well as an attraction. Check in for the night, and you are given admission-free access to the ship and its companion attraction, the *Spruce Goose*. For reservations, call 213-432-6964.

Inside a 12-story aluminum dome that gleams on the Long Beach shoreline next to the *Queen Mary* is one of Howard Hughes's greatest secrets, the *Spruce Goose* ♛ ♛ ♛. This "flying boat" flew but once; today it floats like a bright, white behemoth in a deep blue space. What is so awe-inspiring about this 8-propeller plane is that it could get off the ground at all. Each propeller is more than 17 feet in diameter; the aircraft weighs 200 tons empty, its 320-foot wingspan longer than a football field. Step up to inspect the cockpit and cavernous interior. Audio-visual exhibits explain the eccentric life of Hughes and how he realized this dream, only to put it under wraps in 1947 forever.

Open weekdays 10 A.M.–6 P.M. and weekends 9:30 A.M.–6 P.M. Caution: The ticket office closes at 4 P.M. daily. Only combination tickets are sold (*Queen Mary* and *Spruce Goose*): adults $13.95 (10 percent off for seniors); children ages 12–17, $9.95; and ages 5–11, $7.95. Wheelchair accessible except in some stairway areas of the ship and plane interiors (tel. 213-435-3511).

PERILS & PITFALLS

Time Voyager, a new attraction under the *Queen Mary/ Spruce Goose* banner, is a bit of a flop. A $25-million audio-visual-effects show that induces queasiness if not awe, it has not even thrilled the kids we have taken; they're jaded from too many space movies. But then, it's part of the main ticket and runs every 15 minutes.

Marina del Rey Boat Charter

No place embodies the stereotypes of southern Califor- nia living more than Marina del Rey♛♛♛. Modern apartments ring a bustling boat haven, and this is where terms like swinging single, yuppy, and hot tub took off. Here people forget the work they must do to pay for their Porsches; here they just play. So head for Rent A Sail♛♛♛ in quaint, clapboard Fisherman's Village (13719 Fiji Way; tel. 213-822-2516), and join the fun. Buy provisions here, too.

With a driver's license, some boating ability, and a $20 deposit, you can captain your own canoe ($10/ hour) or a 14-foot to 25-foot sail- or powerboat ($14– $34/hour). Cash only, please. Drift around the colorful marina itself or sail out to sea.

INSIDERS' TIPS

If you prefer to make a splashier splurge, Charter Con- cepts at 13757 Fiji Way rents some of Los Angeles' grandest yachts for weddings, sunset cruises, or signifi- cant birthdays—complete with helicopter shuttle from the city, if you wish. Call 213-823-2676. With these boats, you can cruise south to Acapulco.

A Music Center Evening

If the Music Center♛♛♛♛ evokes visions of New York's Lincoln Center, no wonder. Both were built in the 1960s style of massive, white marble walls, soaring windows, and stark concrete columns. Here the Dorothy Chandler Pavilion, home of the Los Angeles

Philharmonic in winter, faces the Ahmanson Theater, L.A.'s main stage for touring plays and Broadway try-outs. Between them stands the odd but elegant Mark Taper Forum, a relief-covered theater-in-the-round set in a reflecting pool and host to recitals, lectures, and more experimental productions.

INSIDERS' TIPS

The Dorothy Chandler Pavilion also holds the annual L.A. ritual of the Academy Awards in late March or early April. It's the closest thing to old-fashioned Hollywood premieres—stars, limos, and bleachers for adoring fans. Come at least a day early to get into the strictly controlled seating. Plan to camp out.

There is usually something on at the Music Center—the Los Angeles Master Chorale Group, Los Angeles Civic Light Opera or, in the fall, the Joffrey Ballet season. Call 213-972-7211. For tickets to other entertainments around town, call Ticketmaster, 213-480-3232, or Ticketron, 213-216-6666.

LOS ANGELES WITH PLENTY OF TIME

Most of the world's great cities are older than Los Angeles. Their attractions of touristic interest are often historical or cultural landmarks—stuffy museums, stately homes, tradition-laced restaurants. Nothing is so venerable in sunny L.A., a young city almost consciously erasing things that betray its age.

Los Angeles is a city of the 20th century and its abundance of vintage automobiles is about as classic as it gets. This city, built on entertainment, tends to entertain and amuse more than educate: Museums look like movie sets; houses, grand and modest, are fanciful confections; restaurants are trendy and transient more than traditional. What's true is that L.A. is always new. The trick is making it look old—to watch an empty lot in Beverly Hills become a French chateau with full-grown gardens in a matter of months is to witness history L.A.–style.

Although it is a city with little sense of or respect for its history, Los Angeles has dedicated guardians of its past, who will show you aspects you might not expect. The phrase "Nobody walks in L.A." is a local truism, but walking tours can explore downtown Los Angeles beyond Bunker Hill (previously described on page 60).

Olvera Street♛♛♛, where the original Spanish settlement of Los Angeles was founded, nestles in El Pueblo de Los Angeles State Park in the heart of downtown between City Hall and Union Station. The park's Visitor Center (in 500 block of N. Main Street) holds free walking tours of this landmark of Mexican culture from Tuesdays through Saturdays at 10, 11, 12, and 1 o'clock. Included are the oldest house and firehouse in Los Angeles, as well as enough tacos and souvenirs to save you a trip to Tijuana. Call 213-628-1274.

The Los Angeles Conservancy♛♛, the city's historical society, has volunteer docents who lead walking tours of other downtown discoveries: art-deco L.A.; Pershing Square Landmarks; the Broadway Movie Palace District; Spring Street's "Palaces of Finance"; the Seventh Street "Mecca of Merchants"; and the lavishly art-deco Bullock's Wilshire department store. (Call 213-623-CITY for schedules; tours cost $5 per person.)

Hollywood is worth more browsing for movie fans. Most of the major studios moved out of Hollywood itself, and the town got a bit tawdry as television dimmed the luster of Tinseltown. But a comeback is in progress, and this faded star is rebuilding its reputation for razzle-dazzle.

For guided tours, Hollywood Fantasy Tours♛♛ drives double-deck buses around town from 1721 N. Highland Avenue—5 times daily in summer, once daily off-season—and lets would-be and has-been actors wisecrack your way through a trivial pursuit of old Hollywood, from the Hollywood Sign, once a real estate promotion billboard, to the Warner Brothers studio where Al Jolson filmed the first talkie, *The Jazz Singer,* to the Formosa Café, where Elvis once tipped a waitress a Cadillac and where the "Dynasty" cast and crew may be lunching today. (Call 213-FANTASY.)

INSIDERS' TIPS

Another independent way to find the action is through Hollywood on Location ♛ ♛, a firm that publishes daily listings and maps of movie and TV shoots you can observe in progress on the streets of Los Angeles. Call 213-659-9165 and pick up the information at 9:30 A.M. at 8644 Wilshire Boulevard in Beverly Hills. This service lets you set your own schedule, choosing day or night filmings in whatever part of town you want to be. It is probably the only way to assure yourself of seeing a star or two, short of a chance encounter on Rodeo Drive, or if you get into Spago.

Starline Sightseeing Tours ♛ ♛ ♛ at the Chinese Theater, 6845 Hollywood Boulevard, is best for tours of the stars' homes, unless you want to rely on the outdated maps hawked on every other corner in Beverly Hills. Starline's minivans are the only vehicles allowed to explore the curvy canyons of that tony town and to point out Marilyn Monroe's love nest with Joe Di-Maggio, Burt Reynolds' place a few doors down from Barbra Streisand, and Lucille Ball's unpretentious white-brick home at 1000 Roxbury Drive (the most star-studded street in Beverly Hills). Tours every half hour in summer, every hour off-season. Tel. 213-463-3131. $19 adults, $11 children.

A number of Hollywood exhibitions are in development, but 3 are already open for the starstruck. The Hollywood Studio Museum ♛ is a tribute to the Silent Era, set in the barn rented by Cecil B. De Mille in 1913 to film Hollywood's first feature-length movie (later it was the railroad depot on "Bonanza"), 2100 N. Highland Avenue (tel. 213-874-2276; call for hours and admission). Across the street, the Hollywood Bowl Museum ♛, adjacent to the famed outdoor amphitheater, contains rotating exhibits of costumes, concert clips, and memorabilia of movies made at the Bowl (tel. 213-850-2058 for hours; free admission). The Max Factor Beauty Museum ♛, 1666 N. Highland, displays the makeup breakthroughs of the man "who changed the face of the movies" and its greatest stars in his original Hollywood salon (tel. 213-463-6668; open Monday–

Friday, 9 A.M.–5 P.M., free; cosmetics outlet adjacent).

While movies and television have been a big part of Los Angeles' evolution, legitimate theater has only recently become a burgeoning presence. Though Las Vegas drew away the flashy nightclub acts after World War II, many familiar faces can be seen on stages around town—and we don't mean soundstages. Since 1972, this city has become popular for Broadway tryouts, experimental productions, and shows that let those usually before the cameras do their work with a live audience.

Splashiest of the main-circuit theaters is the Pantages Theater♛♛♛ on Hollywood Boulevard (213-410-1062), extravagantly art deco from its days as a movie palace.

Other houses presenting original productions and Broadway plays include the James Doolittle Theater♛♛♛ and the Henry Fonda Theatre♛♛ in Hollywood, and the Wilshire Theatre♛♛ in Beverly Hills. Midsize houses (300–500 seats) are blooming, most prominently the Gallery, L.A. Stage Company, Solari, Mayfair, Tiffany, Westwood Playhouse, and Coronet.

The Music Center spurred this interest in theater to the point where more than 115 equity-waiver houses (fewer than 99 seats) have sprouted to spawn new talent. Many of these small houses line Santa Monica Boulevard in Hollywood, often staging daring new scripts or popular revivals with enthusiastic casts.

Find details on current performances in the *Los Angeles Times* "Calendar" section daily (and especially its Friday "Weekend" edition), or in two free local papers available in many shops, *Los Angeles Weekly* and *The Reader.* The Los Angeles Convention and Visitors Bureau (213-689-8822) can give more detailed guidance.

One of the oldest visitor stops in Los Angeles is the Farmers Market♛♛ at Fairfax and Third, a 20-acre corner that was an open field where Depression-era farmers sold their produce. Now a gangly collection of

160 souvenir shops and food stalls surrounds the still bustling produce market in the middle where beautiful California fruits and vegetables vie with tempting baked goods like a year-round county fair.

INSIDERS' TIPS

Dupar's Restaurants are all over town, but the white clapboard Dupar's Farmhouse ♕♕♕ at the Farmers Market is a rare local tradition for its hefty, farm-style hotcake breakfasts and its scrumptious pies. Weekend mornings are the most fun—and crowded. No reservations, but call 213-933-8446 to ask how long the wait will be.

Market lovers—purists, that is—may prefer the cavernous Grand Central Market ♕♕ downtown on Third Street. This is fresh-off-the-truck, raucous bargaining and brown bag snapping for an ethnic paradise of provisions—Latino, Anglo, and Oriental commerce side by side from soup to nuts. Early risers can catch the colorful Los Angeles Flower Market on Wall Street near Eighth. Florists come early to stock their shops, so make this a predawn field trip for the main action; if you oversleep, though, it's still fun later on.

The West Side

Far from the hustle of Hollywood and the wholesale scene lies the West Side, the "better neighborhoods" of Los Angeles, and the more refined shops that serve them. Places like Beverly Hills, Bel-Air, Trousdale Estates, and Brentwood are considered West Side. So is Westwood ♕♕♕, the home of UCLA; while very collegiate, it is also very upscale and young-fashion-conscious. Its numerous cinemas flash with megawatts of neon to announce most of Hollywood's premieres these days. Two of the oldest theaters in town, the Fox Westwood Village ♕♕ and the Mann Bruin Theater ♕♕, face each other across the street in art-deco dazzle.

The Westside Pavilion♚♚♚, a multicolored, post-modern shopping mall at Pico and Overland, will inspire awe in the most jaded shopper. Though not the largest mall in L.A., it is the most contemporary, complemented only by the slightly older bastion of the Beverly Center♚♚♚ at Beverly and La Cienega. An advantage of the better-known Beverly Center is its proximity to trendy Melrose Avenue♚♚♚♚, once a worn-down street and now a strip of New Wave boutiques and latest-food-fad restaurants. From La Cienega to La Brea, Melrose Avenue offers funky clothing, hip designer products, and fun foods like Johnny Rocket's Hamburgers♚♚♚ next to the high-gloss Angel City Café♚♚♚ (both places attract young movie faces).

CHILDREN'S LOS ANGELES

We can't think of many kids who wouldn't want to join their parents on a visit to L.A. Even if you do nothing more than spend the day on the beach, dipping into the ocean or flying a Frisbee on the sand, your children will go to sleep at night with smiles on their faces. But elsewhere in this vast playground we call the Big Orange, you'll discover quite a slew of children's activities to keep the little ones busy morning, noon, and night.

One of our favorite diversions for the younger set is to trek downtown to the Los Angeles Children's Museum♚♚♚♚♚, 310 N. Main Street (tel. 213-687-8800). Beyond the brightly painted mural on the face of the building is a wonderland where kids are encouraged to touch, feel, and even wear the exhibits put before them. Make a recording at the museum radio station, write and act in a play that will be videotaped for posterity, and be sure to stop by Sticky City where kids make bright blocks of foam with Velcro strips attached into creations some say resemble bridges and tunnels.

Of course, kids of all ages want to get in on Hollywood's biggest commodity—show business. All over the greater metropolitan area, you'll recognize locations where thousands of films and television shows have been shot. If luck is on your side, you and your troop may even run into some stars in action on location in Los Angeles.

PERILS & PITFALLS

If your child has a favorite television show and his heart set on seeing it filmed while visiting Hollywood, tell him not to hold his breath. Many television programs—particularly sitcoms—invite audiences to share in the laughter, but because of possible disruption, children under the age of 16 are not admitted. If your kids are older and you want to make arrangements in advance of your visit, call the network of your choice (ABC, 213-557-4396; CBS, 213-852-2455; NBC, 818-840-3537; Fox, 213-462-7111). Or call Audiences Unlimited (818-506-0043). This organization can arrange tickets to some 30 programs on all 4 networks.

If a Hollywood studio is on your list, make plans to spend the day at Universal ♛ ♛ ♛. (For details, see Los Angeles the Second Day, page 56.)

If you're seeking sunshine for your kids, head for Griffith Park ♛ ♛ ♛ ♛, the largest metropolitan park in the nation (tel. 665-5188). With more than 4,000 acres of trees, picnic areas, a vast zoo, and an old-fashioned merry-go-round, kids have the space to really let loose. Visit the Griffith Observatory and Planetarium ♛ ♛ ♛—on a clear day (664-1191), and the pony stagecoach and miniature train rides ♛ ♛ ♛ (664-3266).

Beyond Griffith Park, Los Angeles has many more havens of open space, a good number of which are worth checking out. In fact, the Los Angeles City Parks and Recreation Department has special programs for kids in the summer (call 485-5515). We particularly like Will Rogers State Historic Park ♛ ♛ ♛ for the great polo matches on Sundays (call 213-454-8212), and in Pasadena, Brookside Park ♛ ♛ for its hiking trails and volleyball courts (call 818-793-1947).

For the eggheads over 10 years old in your clan, a tour of *Los Angeles Times* building ♛ ♛ ♛ should be on the itinerary (213-972-5000). They'll also enjoy the California Museum of Science and Industry ♛ ♛ as well as the Space Museum♛♛♛ across the street (213-749-0101).

A great source of information on how to keep your children entertained while visiting Los Angeles is *L.A. Parent* magazine. You'll find the free publication at libraries, large food stores, and children's shops, or by calling 818-846-0400. If you need to get away from the kids for a bit, call the Babysitters Guild at 213-469-8246 (closed on Sundays).

EXCURSIONS FROM LOS ANGELES

Within the 4,083 square miles of Los Angeles County lie countless communities nestled side by side as well as vast open spaces rare in an urban environment. While Disneyland, Santa Barbara, and Palm Springs lie within a 2-hour drive, many sights are even closer to L.A. Indeed they are part of it, hard as it is to believe. The metropolitan area stretches 100 miles in every direction—except seaward, and even that goes out 21 miles to Catalina Island.

San Fernando Valley

The San Fernando Valley, commonly called The Valley, has its own attractions. If you drive 22-mile Mulholland Drive♛♛♛♛♛ atop the crest of the Hollywood Hills, you look north to The Valley. If you visit Universal Studios or the Burbank Studios, you're in The Valley. A few miles west on Ventura Boulevard sprawls the 120-shop Sherman Oaks Galleria♛ of Valley Girl fame "fer sure," and here, too, are the largest television studios in the country. Free tours of the NBC Television Studios♛♛♛♛ in Burbank (tel. 818-840-4444) last an hour and a half, including a stop at Studio One, home of the "Tonight" show and an awesome props warehouse.

The San Fernando Mission♛♛, one of the 21 Spanish missions built in colonial California, is actually a replica of the original erected in 1797. Pioneer moviemaker D. W. Griffith filmed his *Custer's Last Stand* on the grounds in the early 1900s. A museum of mission furnishings, including a hand-carved altar, is housed in the thick adobe walls. Located off the San Diego Freeway, 8 miles north of the Ventura Freeway, it is open daily 9 A.M.–5 P.M.; $1 adults, 50¢ children. Call 818-361-0186 for details.

PERILS & PITFALLS

Tickets for the "Tonight" show can be hard to come by on the day of the show. Order them by mail if you live more than 150 miles from Los Angeles and allow 6 weeks for delivery. Write to NBC Ticket Office, 3000 W. Alameda Boulevard, Burbank, CA 91523.

Forest Lawn Memorial Park ♛ ♛ ♛ in Glendale, at 1712 S. Glendale Avenue (tel. 818-241-4151), is where many stars have made their last stand. This cemetery is like a movie set itself with reproductions of famous chapels and art works of the world to sanctify the final rest of Clark Gable, Jean Harlow, a couple of Marx Brothers, and many more. The scenic grounds and stained-glass version of Da Vinci's *The Last Supper* lift Forest Lawn above morbidity to a pleasant place for the living and a pilgrimage spot for Hollywood lovers.

INSIDERS' TIPS

Free tickets for many television tapings are easily available in Los Angeles on the day of the show. Each network has a ticket booth at its studio open from 9 A.M.–5 P.M. Just phone ahead to be sure of availability: ABC, 213-557-4396; CBS, 213-852-2345; NBC, 818-840-3537; Fox, 213-462-7111. Tickets are also given out in front of Mann's Chinese Theater, at the Universal Studios Tour, and by the Greater Los Angeles Visitors Bureau, 213-624-7300.

Six Flag's Magic Mountain ♛ ♛ ♛ in Valencia, less than an hour north on I-5 from Los Angeles (tel. 805-255-4100), could be called southern California's roller-coaster capital. Among its more than 100 rides are the 360-degree-loop, steel "Revolution" and the giant, wooden double coaster called "Colossus." "Roaring Rapids" (avoid it on a chilly day) and "FreeFall" with its

55-mph skydrop are other thrills. Fun for families. Open year-round.

Pasadena

An early favorite in the westward exodus of Easterners seeking sun, Pasadena ♛ ♛ ♛ is one of southern California's most elegant cities. Family roots are deeper here than elsewhere, and a more formal decorum seems to pervade the place. Even its annual Tournament of Roses ♛ ♛ ♛ ♛ ♛ allows no tacky foil on its floats— just flowers. If the Rose Bowl is your goal, plan ahead, for it is the one event in Pasadena that gets crowded— very crowded.

INSIDERS' TIPS

Angelenos in the know watch the New Years' Day Tournament of Roses Parade on television (Channel 5 is the favorite for coverage) and then inspect the floats the next day when they are all on exhibit. For information, call the Pasadena Convention and Visitors Bureau; tel. 818-795-9311.

Ask the bureau as well about concerts in Pasadena Center ♛, a beautiful cultural center in the middle of town with a lively calendar of top talent. Quaint shops and architecture along the main streets reflect the Spanish ambience imitated by Anglo builders in southern California.

The Norton Simon Museum of Art ♛ ♛ ♛ ♛, 411 W. Colorado Boulevard, holds old-world art treasures in a new-age, modern exhibit space of graceful curved walls, uncrowded halls, and a quiet sculpture garden. One of the world's finest private collections of Goya, Rembrandt, Degas, Picasso, and many more was donated by business leader Simon to UCLA. Private day tours are by appointment only; hours are Thursday through Sunday, 12 noon to 6 P.M. Call 818-449-3730.

Ventura County

Some 60 miles north of Los Angeles via the Ventura Freeway are the seaside towns of Oxnard and Ventura, each a boater's haven and gateway to the untrammeled Channel Islands, California's most newly designated national park. Beaches as wide as football fields line this stretch of coast (in between sailboat marinas). Oxnard♛ is known for strawberries and an annual festival thereof. Its Mission San Buenaventura♛♛ (1782) has a fine museum whose lovely gardens hold an archaeological park (tel. 805-643-4318). Call the local tourism office, 805-485-8833, for details.

Ventura♛ is nicknamed the Poinsettia City for its bowers of yuletime flowers, though it is also the winter home of millions of Monarch butterflies starting each October. A sweet scent of lemon blossoms lingers over this area, home to California's largest lemon groves. Call 805-648-2075 for local details.

The rugged terrain of the Channel Islands♛♛♛♛ looms offshore on a clear day. Island Packer Cruises, P.O. Box 993, Ventura, CA 93001 (805-642-1393) is the best means of transport to Santa Barbara, Anacapa, and San Miguel, the three islands open to the public (Santa Cruz and Santa Rosa are privately owned).

Santa Barbara (the island, not the resort city) rises almost vertically from the Pacific waters, its beaches and rocky coves inhabited by funny, flippered marine mammals called pinnipeds. It's an easy hike to 635-foot Signal Peak♛♛, and a wealth of bird life can be spotted along the way. Anacapa, smallest of the islands, has the most impressive views. Hiking trails pass sheer cliffs looking down on hordes of sea lions splashing in the surf, which pounds onto the rocky shore. San Miguel is a wildlife wonderland, a mating ground for seals and sea lions (pinnipeds) and a snapshot paradise.

Santa Catalina Island

More civilized and developed, Santa Catalina Island♛♛♛ "26 miles across the sea" from Los Angeles is also a Channel Island—and it's really only 21 miles despite the Kingston Trio's famous song. Round-trip boat rides cost $20–$25 for adults, $10–$15 for children under 12. The cruise lines to call are:

Catalina Cruise, 213-775-6111

Catalina Express, 213-519-1212

Catalina Passenger Service, 714-673-5245

Formerly owned by the king of Spain and, later, chewing-gum magnate William Wrigley, Jr., Catalina has one main harbor, at Avalon Bay. Here yachters and small pleasure boaters tie up to stay at the Zane Grey Hotel (where the Western writer wrote many of his books), to sip espresso at Café Prego, and to dance, work out, or watch movies at the Casino, home of the Avalon Ballroom, big band entertainment, and much more.

INSIDERS' TIPS

The quickest way to get to Catalina—and without risk of sea sickness—is Island Express's 6-passenger helicopter service. This 15-minute hop from San Pedro or Long Beach (boats take up to 2 hours) costs approximately $80 round-trip. Call 213-491-5550.

Long Beach

"Coney Island of the West" it was called in the 1920s when movie stars would consider a retreat to Long Beach♛ ♛ ♛ ♛ a major jaunt. Today, its *Queen Mary/Spruce Goose* attraction has made it a visitor-must just a freeway away. The city's "long beaches," especially from 55th Street south, still welcome families for all-American fun—no raunchy or even eccentric waterfront scene here. A number of themed shopping centers—Marina Pacifica, the Market Place, Seaport Village—dot the expansive sweep of beach. Shoreline Village♛ ♛ even has a marina for boat-borne shoppers and a ferry shuttle to area hotels.

Sleek, modern office buildings and gleaming, new hotels have given Long Beach a glittering skyline that makes its camouflaged oil derricks even less noticeable. Spanish residential architecture evokes the heritage of the area in handsome, pink and white stucco homes and apartment houses lining Ocean Boulevard. The Casa Rancho Los Cerritos ♛ (1844) is an authentic Spanish ranch house now used as a museum-library with antique furnishings.

A renaissance of good restaurants and popular jazz clubs has enlivened the night scene in Long Beach. Visit Second Street in Belmont Shore ♛ ♛ for an up-and-coming mix of shops, pubs, and restaurants. Broadway and Fourth Streets ♛ ♛ are known for antique shops and cozy restaurants. For what's newest, call the Long Beach Area Convention and Visitors Council, 213-436-3645.

INSIDERS' INFORMATION FOR LOS ANGELES

WHERE TO STAY

**Beverly Hills
(area code 213)**

Century Plaza Hotel ♛ ♛ ♛ ♛ ♛
2025 Avenue of the Stars, Century City 90067; tel. 277-2000 or 800-228-3000
Single room, double occupancy: $130–$195
President Reagan and his press entourage stay at this 1,000-room high rise when they visit. A super-deluxe tower addition is graced with fine museum pieces and antiques. Outdoor Jacuzzi, admission to the Century West health club. La Chaumière (♛ ♛ ♛ ♛ ♛) dishes up superb French fare.

The Four Seasons ♛ ♛ ♛ ♛ ♛
300 S. Doheny Dr., L.A. 90048; tel. 273-2222
Single room, double occupancy: $200–$335
East and West mix at this formal, European-style hotel with great elegance. The location is terrific, just minutes away from world-class shopping on Rodeo Drive. Outdoor pool, concierge. Be sure to visit Gardens Restaurant (♛ ♛ ♛ ♛ ♛) even if you aren't planning to stay at the Four Seasons.

Beverly Hills Hotel ♛ ♛ ♛ ♛
9641 Sunset Blvd., Beverly Hills 90210; tel. 276-2251
Single room, double occupancy: $150–$210
Pink stucco hideaway on 16 acres with private bungalows, tennis courts, and cabanas creates a resort
atmosphere on the edge of Beverly Hills. The landmark
hotel's giant staff outnumbers the guests, so get ready
to be pampered, and don't worry about getting into the
city's best restaurants—just drop by the concierge desk
and Robert Duncan will do his thing. The Polo Lounge
(♛ ♛ ♛) is a must even if you aren't in town to take a
meeting. 200 rooms.

Beverly Wilshire Hotel ♛ ♛ ♛ ♛
9500 Wilshire Blvd., Beverly Hills 90212; tel. 275-4282
Single room, double occupancy: $170–$225
If you want direct access to Rodeo Drive then this is the
hotel for you. Regent International is making this into a
regal place to stay with plenty of pizzazz to impress
even the most jaded traveler. Large rooms and huge
bathrooms. The on-premises French restaurant
(♛ ♛ ♛ ♛) aims to please.

L'Ermitage Hotel ♛ ♛ ♛ ♛
9291 Burton Way, Beverly Hills 90210; tel. 278-3344
Single room, double occupancy: $250–$275
Visiting this lovely hotel is like entering a fine home.
Well-mannered staff are unceasingly accommodating.
All 114 suites feature fireplaces and fully equipped
kitchens. Telephones with up to 5 incoming/outgoing
lines. The intimate Café Russe (♛ ♛ ♛) for hotel patrons and their guests only.

The Beverly Hilton ♛ ♛ ♛
9876 Wilshire Blvd., Beverly Hills 90210; tel. 274-7777
Single room, double occupancy: $120–$195
The 600 rooms at the Hilton are comfortable if not
overly glamorous. You get a low-key feeling about this
rambling place yet the hotel has everything you'll need
during your L.A. stay—like a theater ticket desk, limo
service, a nice pool, underground parking, and 3 major
restaurants including Trader Vic's (♛ ♛ ♛) and
L'Escoffier (♛ ♛ ♛).

Beverly Hills Comstock♛♛
10300 Wilshire Blvd., Beverly Hills 90024; tel. 275-5575
Single room, double occupancy: $95–$125
A 116-suite secret that's nothing amazing—just a comfortable place to stay in a convenient setting. Pool, Jacuzzi.

Downtown Los Angeles
(area code 213)

The Biltmore Hotel♛♛♛♛
506 S. Grand, L.A. 90017; tel. 624-1011
Single room, double occupancy: $110–$185
The biggest draw at this redone grand hotel is an impressive lobby with its hand-painted ceiling. Since the 1,022-room hotel opened in 1923, it has catered to big-name celebrities and regular folk with much success. Don't expect gigantic rooms, but do expect an impressive health club. Bernard's (♛♛♛♛) serves fine Continental cuisine and draws quite a crowd other than hotel guests.

Sheraton Grande Hotel♛♛♛♛
333 South Figueroa, L.A. 90071; tel. 617-1133 or 800-325-3535
Single room, double occupancy: $135–$190
If you like to stay in the thick of a business-oriented downtown, near Dodger Stadium and the Music Center, stay here. All the comforts you'd expect presented in a contemporary setting: limo service, outdoor pool, guest privileges at the Los Angeles Racquet Club. 550 rooms.

The New Otani Hotel and Garden♛♛♛
120 S. Los Angeles St., L.A. 90012; tel. 629-1200 or 800-252-0197 in California, 800-421-8795 nationwide
Single room, double occupancy: $114–$137
The best way to simulate Japanese living, short of flying directly to Tokyo, is to visit this unique 446-room hotel that offers tatami as well as traditional rooms. Beautiful Japanese gardens, health club. Thousand Cranes Restaurant (♛♛♛♛) is a great place to sample sushi and other Nippon imports.

Westin Bonaventure Hotel♔♔♔

404 S. Figueroa, L.A. 90017; tel. 624-1000 or 800-228-3000

Single room, double occupancy: $99–$159

You'll notice this ultramodern, circular, 1,000-room, downtown skyscraper miles before you reach it. Designed by architect John Portman, the 35-story giant has an open lobby atrium surrounding acres of ponds, 5 ascending levels of shopping, and fine restaurants. Zoom up to the top in the glass elevator and have a drink in the revolving lounge.

Eastlake Inn♔

1442 Kellam Ave., L.A. 90026; tel. 250–1620

Single room, double occupancy: $45 and up

If you like your downtown hotel small and private, choose this 8-room Victorian B&B, located away from the mainstream. Robes, breakfast with the *Los Angeles Times*, imaginative weekend packages.

Hollywood
(area code 213)

Le Bel Age Hotel♔♔♔♔

1020 N. San Vicente Blvd., L.A. 90069; tel. 854-1111

Single room, double occupancy: $185–$210

A touch of Europe in West Hollywood, this all-suite retreat has great city views and a lot of original art on the walls. Comfortable and smartly decorated lobby, not too big and not too small. Restaurant (♔♔♔♔) serves Franco-Russian cuisine with class. Try the different kinds of vodka at the bar here.

The Mondrian♔♔♔♔

8440 Sunset Blvd., L.A. 90069; tel. 650-8999

Single room, double occupancy: $130–$185

If you like the work of Dutch artist Piet Mondrian, and if you like to be as current as currently possible, you'll like The Mondrian. This is a hotel for the contemporary set, with all-suites accommodation, uptown decor, and every comfort of a progressive home. Right on Sunset Strip, with lots of original art by Peter Max and others. Building exterior painted by Yacov Agam.

Chateau Marmont Hotel ♛ ♛ ♛

8221 Sunset Blvd., L.A. 90046; tel. 656-1010
Single room, double occupancy: $90 and up
This French Normandy chateau on the Sunset Strip is
offbeat in its charm, offering privacy but few frills. No
dining on the grounds, and no doorman to greet you.
Still, celebrities have always liked to stay here—Jean
Harlow and Billy Wilder in the old days, and Diane
Keaton, and Debra Winger in more recent times. Choose
a bungalow, cottage, or penthouse. 62 rooms.

Le Dufy Hotel ♛ ♛ ♛

1000 Westmont Dr., L.A. 90069; tel. 657-7400
Single room, double occupancy: $123–$160
Residential, all-suite hotel offers comfort and an unpretentious environment. A nice choice if you're in town
on business and have to stay a while. Rooftop pool,
sundeck, and spa. 121 suites.

Hollywood Roosevelt ♛ ♛ ♛

7000 Hollywood Blvd., L.A. 90028; tel. 466-7000
Single room, double occupancy: $100–$120
Right across the street from the footprints at the
Chinese Theater, this beautifully restored hotel op-
erates in an area of town that isn't the chicest, but is
definitely in the thick of things. The first Academy
Awards took place here and quite a few celebrities
honeymooned here during Hollywood's heyday. After a
major renovation, big events may happen at the
Roosevelt once again. Pool decorated by artist David
Hockney, airport bus service, car rentals. 320 rooms.

Sunset Marquis Hotel ♛ ♛ ♛

1200 Alta Loma Rd., L.A. 90069; tel. 657-1333
Single room, double occupancy: $145–$195
The choice of many artists in the music business. It's
convenient to the recording studios and it's casual
enough to not feel conspicuous in. Garden, Jacuzzi. 115
rooms.

San Fernando Valley
(area code 818)

The Registry Hotel ♛ ♛ ♛ ♛

5555 Universal Terrace Parkway, Universal City 91608;
tel. 506-2500

Average double: $150–$180.
From top to bottom, this 455-room, 24-story hotel is a class act. Stay here if you want central access to all aspects of sprawling Los Angeles. Spacious rooms, many amenities including pool and health facilities.

La Maida House ♛ ♛
11159 La Maida St., North Hollywood 91601; tel. 769-3857
Single room, double occupancy: $75 to $155
This B&B is a historic landmark. Near Burbank Airport and Universal City, this 1920s gem is decorated in marble, oak, mahogany, tile, and stained glass. 8 large and airy bedrooms, adorned with oriental rugs and primitive art. In-house travel library.

West Los Angeles/Santa Monica (area code 213)

Hotel Bel-Air ♛ ♛ ♛ ♛ ♛
701 Stone Canyon Rd., Bel-Air 90077; tel. 472-1211
Single room, double occupancy: $195 and up
Swans may be this elegant hotel's trademark, but the hint of total serenity only begins there. Set off the beaten track on a dozen acres of heavily wooded canyon, this hotel is heaven. 92 garden bungalows emphasizing personal service and gracious living. An amazing on-property floral designer. Al fresco restaurant (♛ ♛ ♛ ♛ ♛) serves divine meals under the stars or inside by the fire.

Westwood Marquis Hotel and Garden ♛ ♛ ♛ ♛
930 Hilgard Ave., Westwood 90024; tel. 208-8765
Single room, double occupancy: $160 and up
Tuxedo-clad staff sets the tone for this European-style hotel and its eclectic Continental decor with oriental accents. Second-floor garden, free-form pool, Caribbean-style cabanas. Afternoon tea. Penthouse suites with butler service. Dynasty Room (♛ ♛ ♛ ♛ ♛) with classy Continental cuisine; opulent Sunday brunch in the Garden Terrace (♛ ♛ ♛ ♛ ♛).

Shangri-La Hotel ♛ ♛
1301 Ocean Ave., Santa Monica 90401; tel. 394-2791
Single room, double occupancy: $80–$110

If you like the beach and plenty of nostalgia, then you'll like this hotel. Although this isn't a very luxurious property, it has art-deco decor and ocean views from all 55 rooms.

WHERE TO EAT

Beverly Hills
(area code 213)

Celestino ♛ ♛ ♛ ♛ ♛
236 S. Beverly Dr., Beverly Hills; tel. 859-8601
Average dinner: $25–$30
This popular restaurant's young chef-owner, Sicilian-born and Tuscan-trained, serves some of the best, uncomplicated Italian food in L.A. Pasta is one of his signatures. Impeccable Italian wine list.

La Maison du Caviar ♛ ♛ ♛ ♛ ♛
268 N. Beverly Dr., Beverly Hills; tel. 859-9444
Average dinner: $40
L.A. branch of Parisian house of caviar serves all the de rigueur caviars, and then some. Excellent dinner menu offers an eclectic blend of French fare with Russian, Italian, and Japanese overtones.

The Bistro ♛ ♛ ♛ ♛
246 N. Canon Dr., Beverly Hills; tel. 273-5633
Average dinner: $40
A formal, almost stuffy, atmosphere pervades this Beverly Hills in-spot, the place to see and be seen by long-time celebrities, wealthy socialites, and curious tourists. In addition to the company it keeps, the Bistro is also known for its fabulous souffles and the traditional French fare that is served there.

Colette ♛ ♛ ♛ ♛
9360 Wilshire Blvd., Beverly Hills; tel. 273-1151
Average dinner: $35
Quiet and understated, this dining room could be mistaken for a European restaurant because of its attention to Continental detail. American chef, French feel, California cuisine.

The Grill ♛ ♛ ♛
9560 Dayton Way, Beverly Hills; tel. 276-0615
Average dinner: $30
Often referred to as the unofficial commissary of the
William Morris Agency, this metropolitan, power dining
spot in the heart of B.H. has made its reputation on
simple and straightforward grilled steak and fish. Club-
by atmosphere.

Stellini's ♛ ♛
9184 W. Pico, Beverly Hills; tel. 274-7225
Average dinner: $30–$40
This intimate hideaway is an unpretentious gathering
spot for stars in sports and entertainment. Italian/
oriental/American menu features broiled steaks and
chops.

Ed Debevic's ♛
134 N. La Cienega, Beverly Hills; tel. 659-1952
Average dinner: $11
A nostalgic return to the fifties, this American diner of
the be-bop era serves up hamburgers, meat loaf, and
fried egg sandwiches in a chrome and leatherette setting. Noisy and fun.

**Downtown and Environs
(area code 213)**

Restaurant Katsu ♛ ♛ ♛ ♛ ♛
1972 Hillhurst Ave., Los Feliz; tel. 665-1891
Average dinner: $25 and up
You'll probably drive by this unmarked Los Feliz restaurant if you don't know the address. So make a reservation and make a point of dropping in to taste the best
sushi in the city, artfully presented on breathtaking
one-of-a-kind dinnerware created especially for the restaurant.

Rex il Ristorante ♛ ♛ ♛ ♛ ♛
617 S. Olive, Los Angeles; tel. 627-2300
Average dinner: $50
The food here is very expensive for the paucity of food
on the plate, but the extravagant, art-deco setting in a
former men's haberdashery from the twenties and the
quality of the smallish portions certainly presents an

occasion in dining. The Rolls-Royce set parties in a club in back of the restaurant.

Seventh Street Bistro ♕ ♕ ♕ ♕ ♕
815 W. Seventh St., Los Angeles; tel. 627-1242
Average dinner: $35
Cosmopolitan, art-deco restaurant owned by French-born Laurent Ouenioux offers extraordinary, up-to-the-minute fare for food conscious Los Angeles. Expensive, but special prix-fixe menus are offered for those on a budget. Superior French wine list.

Cardini ♕ ♕ ♕ ♕
930 Wilshire Blvd., Los Angeles; tel. 227-3464
Average dinner: $35
The high-styled, postmodern decor captures your attention upon entering this northern Italian restaurant operating in the downtown Hilton Hotel. Fresh cuisine, capped with some steaming cappuccino and one of Cardini's glorious desserts.

L.A. Nicola ♕ ♕ ♕ ♕
4736 Sunset Blvd., Los Feliz; tel. 660-7217
Average dinner: $18
A neighborhood eatery with an innovative menu featuring American bistro selections. Contemporary art shows are displayed on the white-brick walls and change regularly with a bimonthly party on Wednesday nights. Sultry jazz sounds and an extremely friendly atmosphere make this the perfect place to kick back and have fun.

Cha Cha Cha ♕ ♕ ♕
656 Virgil, Los Feliz; tel. 664-7723
Average dinner: $15
This small café on an unlikely street in an unlikely area doesn't deter Angelenos from dining on the deliciously spiced Caribbean food. Always packed to the gills, including a celebrity here and there. Reservations a must.

Imai Sushi ♕ ♕
359 E. First St., Los Angeles; tel. 617-7927
Tiny, 14-seat sushi bar near the Temporary Contemporary museum is a favorite food-critic haunt. Leave your choices up to the sushi chef, who never fails to delight with impeccably fresh fish.

Hollywood
(area code 213)

Chianti Cucina ♛ ♛ ♛ ♛
7381 Melrose Ave., Hollywood; tel. 653-8333
Average dinner: $25
Stylish Italian restaurant with open cucina. Venetian-born chef Antonio Tommasi has a sure and creative hand overseeing both the modern, trattoria-style offerings (at Cucina) as well as the classic Italian cuisine served in the dark and sedate other half of the restaurant (Chianti). Exceptional wine list.

City Restaurant ♛ ♛ ♛ ♛
180 S. LaBrea Ave., Hollywood; tel. 938-2155
Average dinner: $35
An arty crowd frequents this warehouselike restaurant that has no art on the walls but a video monitor at the bar keeping track of what is going on in the kitchen. The two women chefs have classic French background but add their training in India and Thailand to create an unusual menu that's delicious. Choose the dishes made in the Tandoori oven.

Citrus ♛ ♛ ♛
6703 Melrose, Hollywood; tel. 857-0034
Average dinner: $23
You'll definitely need a reservation at this hopping Hollywood eatery. French-style cuisine, with citrus theme throughout, down to the pale yellow linens. Large patio with white Italian canvas and rosewood umbrellas.

Tommy Tang's ♛ ♛ ♛
7473 Melrose Ave., Hollywood; tel. 651-1810
Average dinner: $16
If you like your Thai food hip and innovative, dine here. There's even a sushi bar should you be turning Japanese for the evening. Simple but fashionable surroundings in the heart of Melrose shopping.

Angeli ♛ ♛
7274 Melrose Ave., Hollywood; tel. 936-9086
Average dinner: $16
Casual Italian bistro that's always busy but worth the wait if there is one. Fresh gourmet pizzas with every conceivable ingredient.

Musso and Frank Grill ♛♛
6667 Hollywood Blvd., Hollywood; tel. 467-7788
Average dinner: $16
The oldest restaurant in Hollywood, New York-style bar and grill complete with waiters that are occasionally less than solicitous.

San Fernando Valley
(area code 818)

Lalo and Brothers ♛♛♛
17237 Ventura Blvd., Encino; tel. 784-8281
Average dinner: $28
The place to eat and be seen in The Valley. Contemporary art changes periodically at this spacious but cozy eatery. Dine alfresco in the garden filled with lemon and orange trees and azalea bushes on tasty California cuisine.

Gourmet Gourmet ♛
19014 Ventura Blvd., Tarzana; tel. 344-7111
Average dinner: $19
Not so special ambience serves some uptown Continental cuisine with a lot of imagination thanks to chef Joey D, a local favorite.

West Hollywood
(area code 213)

Spago ♛♛♛♛♛
1114 Horn, Sunset Strip; tel. 652-4025
Average dinner: $25–$35
The word *glitterati* applies to this landmark California restaurant because of the extraordinary talent of chef Wolfgang Puck and the ambience created by Barbara Lazaroff. Freshest of fresh ideas. Excellent California wine list. Be sure to call and reserve a table before arriving in L.A.

Trumps ♛♛♛♛♛
8764 Melrose Ave., West Hollywood; tel. 855-1480
Average dinner: $35
The quintessential California restaurant with California cuisine created by French-trained Michael Roberts in a

contemporary setting. Try the brie-and-grape quesadilla with sweet pea guacamole or the Chinese roast duck with black beans and pickled pumpkin.

Madeo ♛ ♛ ♛
8897 Beverly Blvd., West Hollywood; tel. 859-4903
Average dinner: $30
Casually formal Italian restaurant serves fish and meats al forno. Calorie-conscious nuova cucina extremely enjoyable. Choice antipasti table.

Marix Tex Mex ♛ ♛ ♛
1108 N. Flores, West Hollywood; tel. 656-8800
Average dinner: $15
Popular L.A. place to try Tex-Mex. Kickass margaritas, great fajitas, and stinging fresh salsa. A great spot for having fun.

La Fabula ♛ ♛
7953 Santa Monica Blvd., West Hollywood; tel. 650-8517
Average dinner: $20
Light and airy dining arena inspired by a trip to Mazatlan. White interior and terra-cotta tables with turquoise inlays are as dramatic as the cuisine, which is classically Mexican.

Mandarette ♛ ♛
8386 Beverly Blvd., West Hollywood; tel. 655-6115
Average dinner: $15
Mandarin Chinese café serves bites of this and that in a plain-pipe-rack Chinese ambience. Cold Chinese beers are the perfect complement to the tasty meals served here.

The West Side and Beach Areas (area code 213)

St. Estèphe ♛ ♛ ♛ ♛ ♛
2640 Sepulveda Blvd., Manhattan Beach; tel. 545-1334
Average meal: $35
Incredibly beautiful food created in the American Southwest mode is so amazing you can't believe it's real, but it's so good you won't want to forgo even a bite. In a shopping center that's hard to find, so ask for explicit directions when you make your reservations.

Camelions♛♛♛♛
246 26th St., Santa Monica; tel. 395-0746
Average dinner: $30
You'll feel as if you've arrived on the French Riviera when you enter this lovely restaurant that serves fine meals with a lot of flair, thanks to the imagination of Elke Gilmore, chef.

Rebecca's♛♛♛♛
2025 Pacific, Venice; tel. 306-6266
Average dinner: $26
Nueva-cocina Mexican food is excellent due to careful attention of chef/owner Bruce Marder and his wife Rebecca. Don't miss the knock-your-socks-off margaritas or the ceviche bar.

BARS AND CAFÉS

Beverly Hills
(area code 213)

The Polo Lounge, in the Beverly Hills Hotel, 9641 W. Sunset Blvd.; tel. 276-2251. *The* official meeting place. Notorious, but somewhat passé.

Downtown and Environs
(area code 213)

Al's Bar, 305 S. Hewitt St.; tel. 687-3558. A small haven for bohemians. Always an interesting crowd.

L.A. Nicola, The Martini Room, 4326 Sunset Blvd., Los Feliz; tel. 660-7217. Mixed crowd of politicians, artists, and neighborhood folk. Changing art shows on Wednesdays. Party atmosphere, contemporary and hip.

The MoCA Cafe, Il Panino, in the Museum of Contemporary Art, 250 S. Grand Ave.; tel. 617-1844. Wonderfully designed, European-style sandwich bar. Linger over a cup of cappuccino in between forays viewing the museum's collections.

The New York Company, 2470 Fletcher Dr., Silverlake; tel. 665-3739. Slick, chic spot catering to gay clientele.

Tiki Ti, 4427 Sunset Blvd., Silverlake; tel. 669-9381. Polynesian-style watering hole specializing in fun tropical drinks.

Glendale
(area code 818)

Jax, 339 N. Brand Blvd.; tel. 500-1604. Homey bar and restaurant is dark and cozy and offers great jazz tunes in an old-world atmosphere.

Hollywood
(area code 213)

Cat and Fiddle Pub, 6530 Sunset; tel. 468-3800. British pub serves jazz on the patio. Good drink prices.

Columbia Bar and Grill, 1448 N. Gower; tel. 461-8800. Hollywood's working actors and behind-the-scenes people drink after a long day's work at this hot spot near major television studios.

Fellini's, 6810 Melrose; tel. 936-3100. Show biz types gather in this nostalgic bar that has R&B music most nights.

Nucleus Nuance, 7267 Melrose; tel. 939-8666. Sophisticated bar draws wheeler-dealers. Art-deco sounds and style.

170 Café, 170 S. La Brea; tel. 939-0170. Contemporary art on the walls and delicious art on the plates of this café hidden in a building full of art galleries with a great bookstore.

San Fernando Valley
(area code 818)

Le Café, 14633 Ventura Blvd., Sherman Oaks; tel. 986-2662. Intimate jazz upstairs, dining downstairs. Popular gathering spot.

The Smokehouse, 4420 Lakeside Dr., Burbank; tel. 845-3731. Convenient spot where studio employees kick back and relax.

Stanleys, 13817 Ventura Blvd., Sherman Oaks; tel.

986-4623. Single spot in The Valley draws mostly yuppies for drinking and dining.

West Hollywood
(area code 213)

Carlos 'n' Charlies, 8240 Sunset Blvd.; tel. 656-8830. You just might find Joan Rivers working out her current act in the cabaret upstairs. If not, the bar is still inviting and always exciting till all hours.

La Masia, 9077 Santa Monica Blvd.,; tel. 273-7066. Spanish-style night spot caters to mid 40s crowd. Live music on occasion.

Mustache Café, 8155 Melrose; tel. 651-2111. French-style café is fashionable, attracting a Hollywood crowd of attractively dressed up-and-comers.

Nicky Blair's, 8730 Sunset Blvd. on the Strip; tel. 659-0929. Ostentatious bar scene draws a very Hollywood crowd of directors, actors, and the like. Paparazzi hang around hoping for some action, and they are never disappointed.

The Palm, 8572 Santa Monica Blvd. tel. 652-6188. A fast crowd of movers and shakers.

The West Side and Beach Areas
(area code 213)

Crayons Bar and Grille, 10800 W. Pico Blvd., in the Westside Pavilion; tel. 475-0970. Lively place with decor that's both futuristic and prehistoric. Local artists have created the ambience. Try the Creature Cooler.

Overland Café, 3601 Overland Ave.; tel. 559-9999. Clean feel, lots of plants, contemporary artwork. Live jazz on the weekends. Continental menu.

Rose Café, 220 Rose Ave., Venice; tel. 399-0711. Cool refreshing patio and indoor setting. Charming and always crowded. You'll be conspicuous without a suntan here.

West Beach Café, 60 North Venice Blvd., Venice; tel. 823-5396. Always a happening scene with a mixed crowd that includes a lot of artist types. Changing art shows, great wine list.

NIGHTLIFE AND ENTERTAINMENT

Theaters

Beverly Hills (area code 213)

Wilshire Theater, 8440 Wilshire Blvd.; tel. 410-1062. Historic house mostly mounts the classics.

Downtown (area code 213)

Los Angeles Theater Center, 514 S. Spring St.; tel. 627-5599. What was once a vintage bank building has turned into a 4-stage theater complex for diverse fare, from works by new American playwrights to well-known classics.

The Music Center, 135 N. Grand Ave.; tel. 972-7211. Los Angeles' premiere theater complex has the Mark Taper Forum for new works, the Dorothy Chandler Pavilion for big stage events, and the Ahmanson for comedies and dramas.

Hollywood (area code 213)

James A. Doolittle Theater, 1615 N. Vine; tel. 462-6666. Nice-sized theater offers a mixed bag of classics, dance, and contemporary works.

INSIDERS' TIPS

If you want to go to the theater in Los Angeles on the spur of the moment, you could save some bucks. Some of the theaters around town offer half-price tickets if you buy them on the day of the performance. Call the individual box office and inquire, or go to May Company ticket booths at the Westside Pavilion, Citicorp Plaza, or in North Hollywood at 6150 Laurel Canyon.

Las Palmas Theater, 1642 N. Las Palmas Ave.; tel. 469-7758. Small theater with hot shows—comedy, drama, musical, or otherwise.

Pantages Theater, 6233 Hollywood Blvd.; tel. 410-1062. Gorgeous art-deco theater with lots of history and some good drama, comedy, and musical fare.

West Hollywood (area code 213)

Matrix Theater, 7657 Melrose Ave.; tel. 852-1445. Catch a musical or a showcase in this intimate house.

Zephyr Theater, 7456 Melrose Ave.; tel. 653-4667. Small theater that offers new works, both comedic and dramatic.

West Los Angeles (area code 213)

Odyssey Theater, 12111 Ohio Ave.; tel. 826-1626. Comedies and dramas by known and unknown playwrights in a small house.

Westwood Playhouse, 10886 Le Conte Ave., Westwood; tel. 208-5454. Legit offerings near U.C.L.A. in a pleasant house with uncomfortable seats, but good sightlines.

Nightclubs

Downtown and Environs (area code 213)

Cache, 2395 Glendale Blvd., Silverlake; tel. 660-6154. Elegant crystal-and-light designs spotlight dressed-up clientele. Each night's dancing is to different themes; for example on Wednesdays the place goes tropical with sizzling salsa sounds from the 12-piece Cache orchestra.

Vertigo, 1024 S. Grand, Los Angeles; tel. 747-4849. Hip underground club with 5 bars and a noisy French bistro done in art-deco black and white. DJs flip new wave and reggae beats. Fashionable dress—you have to pass a test to get in the door.

Glendale (area code 818)

Carnivale, 223 N. Glendale Ave., Glendale; tel. 500-1665. Get set to party at this festive night spot where you'll dance to the latest music and top videos. Entertainment contests, varying cover charge.

Hollywood (area code 213)

Circus Disco, 6655 Santa Monica Blvd., Hollywood; tel. 462-1291. Disco might be dead elsewhere, but here it is still going strong. 3 full bars, light shows, and dance contests. Tuesday and Friday are gay nights; other evenings draw a mixed crowd.

Club Lingerie, 6507 Sunset, Hollywood; tel. 466-8557. Fun and lively crowd congregate at this bilevel nightclub with lots of spunk. Live rock and roll, new wave, and rockabilly tunes, and a very large dance floor. Full bar.

INSIDERS' TIPS

Finding the fun spots of L.A.'s transient nightclub scene is not easy for visitors on their own. The solution is the Party Bus, actually four 44-passenger buses outrageously decorated, which rev up at 10:30 P.M. to make a 2-hour circuit of half a dozen hot and hip clubs. The buses keep going around till 4:30 A.M.; get on and off as you wish for $10, which includes club admission discounts. Meet other tourists and local crazies, too. Call 213-464-5026.

The Comedy Store, 8433 Sunset Blvd., West Hollywood; tel. 656-6225. This is where Steve Martin and Robin Williams first learned how to get a laugh. 3 rooms full of chuckles.

The Groundling Theater, 7307 Melrose; tel. 934-9700. Launching pad for lots of talent like Pee Wee Herman and Elvira to name two of the more off-beat. Comedy and improvisation are costumed with wit.

The Improvisation, 8162 Melrose, West Hollywood; tel. 651-2583. Fabulously funny comedy arena that has launched big names such as Billy Crystal.

The Palace, 1735 N. Vine; tel. 462-3000. Gorgeous place with 5 full bars, an art-deco decor, a large dance floor, and state-of-the-art sound and lighting equipment. Jazz on the upper floor, dancing to rock 'n roll on the lower level. Fashionable attire.

Vine Street Bar and Grill, 1610 N. Vine St.; tel. 463-4375. Intimate supper club books first-class jazz and vocal acts like Nina Simone and Etta James—and on occasion, The Four Tops.

Miracle Mile (area code 213)

Wall Street, 5517 Wilshire Blvd.; tel. 939-3231. A nice mixture of cosmopolitan Los Angelenos gather at this night spot. Full bar, top 40 tunes, 21 and over.

San Fernando Valley (area code 818)

Palomino, 6907 Lankershim Blvd., North Hollywood; tel. 764-4010. Once known worldwide for its country music, now has blues and jazz as well.

Sasch, 11345 Ventura Blvd., Studio City; tel. 769-5555. Trendy night spot features top 40 bands on a nice-sized dance floor. Cover varies.

SHOPPING

Beverly Hills
On Rodeo Drive
Bijan, 420 Rodeo. Designer fashions for men; admittance is by appointment only.

Carroll & Co., 466 N. Rodeo. Traditional clothing for men and women.

Cartier, 370 N. Rodeo. World famous jeweler that needs no explanation.

Chanel Boutique, 301 N. Rodeo. Classy, designer clothing, accessories, and makeup.

Collections, 458 N. Rodeo. High-fashion women's clothing.

David Orgell, 320 N. Rodeo. Silver jewelry and gifts.

Giorgio, 273 N. Rodeo. Yellow-striped awning beckons those who have lots to spend on beautiful clothes and the name-brand perfume.

Gucci, 347 N. Rodeo. The famous G is known to all.

Hammacher Schlemmer & Co., 309 N. Rodeo. Unusual gifts.

Hermes, 343 N. Rodeo. Perfume, soaps, luggage, and scarves.

Lina Lee, 459 N. Rodeo. Stylish uptown women's fashions.

Louis Vuitton, 433 N. Rodeo. Luggage and handbags known the world over.

Pierre Deux, 428 N. Rodeo. Distinctive Provençal furnishings and handbags.

Torie Steele, 414 N. Rodeo. 9 boutiques selling Fendi, Krizia, Maude Frizon, and Valentino.

In the Beverly Center (131 N. LaCienega Blvd.)
Abercrombie & Fitch. Men's and women's clothing, sporting equipment, and unusual gifts.

Atmosphere. High-fashion women's apparel.

Banana Republic. Travel and safari clothing and accessories.

The Broadway. Mainstream Los Angeles department store.

Bullock's. A department store for upscale clientele.

Eddie Bauer. Sporting equipment and accessories.

Futuretronics. Innovative gadgets and such.

Ice. High-fashion women's clothing and accessories.

Intellitoys. A toy store to rival F.A.O. Schwartz.

Laurent David. Fine luggage and handbags.

Tinder Box. Smoke shop.

Williams Sonoma. Kitchenware.

Ylang-Ylang. Fashion jewelry.

Near the Beverly Center
Freehand, 8413 W. Third St. Outstanding collection of crafts, clothing, and jewelry created by California artists. Great for gifts. A store worth seeking out.

Downtown
In the Cooper Building (860 S. Los Angeles St.)
Again Boutique. Clothes for the whole family.

860 Club. Designer fashions featuring Carole Little for Saint-Tropez West at 50 percent or more off.

Fantastic Sportswear Inc. Inexpensive knockoffs of designer sportswear.

Icarus. After-five dresses.

Le Club. Large selection of bags, wallets, hats.

Mom's Gallery and Children's Boutique. Imported European children's clothes.

San Fernando Valley
On Ventura Boulevard
Bud Johnson Design, 12196–98 Ventura. Artifacts from all over the world.

The Collector's Gallery, 12262 Ventura. Movie memorabilia.

Extra Touch. 12180 Ventura. Boutique for the full-figure woman.

Fables, 12260½ Ventura. Victorian-style antiques.

Jewelry Concepts, 12214 Ventura. Large, fine-jewelry selection.

The Victorian Garden, 12184 Ventura. Quality vintage dresses.

Whisper, 12240½ Ventura. Trendy resale shop.

West Hollywood
Melrose Area
All Around the Clock, 7310 Melrose. Antiques and watch repairs.

A Star Is Worn, 7303 Melrose. Secondhand clothing once worn by celebrities.

Betsey Johnson, 7311 Melrose. Women's clothing by New York designer.

Comme des Garcons, 7384 Melrose. High fashion that's a touch eccentric.

Fantasies Come True, 7408 Melrose. Walt Disney collectibles.

Hollywood (Home of the Stars), 706 N. Gardner. Movie nostalgia, sheet music, posters.

Koala Blue, 7366 Melrose. Australiana of all descriptions.

Off the Wall, 7325 Melrose. Antiques and weird stuff (their description).

Territory, 6907½ Melrose. Indian handicrafts.

Texas Soul, 7515 Melrose. Large cowboy-boot selection.

Wacko, 7402 Melrose. Unusual toys and gifts in a colorful environment.

Wild Blue, 7220 Melrose. Functional and wearable art that shouldn't be missed. Great gifts.

Westside Pavilion (at Pico Blvd. and Overland in West Los Angeles)
Alex Sebastian. Men's designer clothing.

Animation Station. Cartoon paraphernalia.

May Company. Moderately priced department store.

Mr. G's for Kids. Educational toy and gift store.

Nordstrom's. Department store with panache.

Sacha. Nifty English shoes for men and women.

La Taste. French gourmet store.

Traveling Light. Accessories of all description.

Westwood

Ann Taylor, 1031 Westwood Blvd. Fashionable women's clothing, shoes, and accessories.

At-Ease, 1001 Westwood Blvd. Traditional clothing for men and women.

The Pigmy Fund, 10967 Weyburn Ave. African jewelry, artifacts, art, and accessories.

The Wilger Company, 10924 Weyburn Ave. Fine traditional clothier for men.

USEFUL TELEPHONE NUMBERS

Emergency Telephone Numbers

911: Emergency dialing to reach police, fire and rescue, highway patrol, and ambulance

Alcoholics Anonymous: In Los Angeles, 213-387-8316
In San Fernando Valley, 818-988-3001

Ambulance: 213-483-6721

California State Automobile Association (AAA): 213-754-2831

Child Abuse Listening line: 213-828-CALL

Dental Society: 213-641-5561

Drug Information and Referral: 624-DRUG

Earthquake Safety Division: 213-485-6177

Lawyer Referral Service: 213-622-6700

Traveler's Aid Society: 213-625-2501

Victim of Crime Assistance: 213-974-7499

Western Union: 213-612-2000

Travel and Business Information

Beverly Hills Chamber of Commerce: 213-271-8126

Highway Condition Information: 213-626-7231

Hollywood Chamber of Commerce: 213-469-8311

Information Line: 213-686-0950

Los Angeles Information Center: 213-689-8822

Los Angeles Visitors and Convention Bureau: 213-624-7300

Rapid Transit Department (RTD) bus: 213-626-4455

Santa Monica Chamber of Commerce: 213-393-9825

Travel Hot Line: 213-466-1053

ORANGE COUNTY

To the visitor, Orange County may mean no more than a vague address for getting to Disneyland—somewhere south of Los Angeles. To Angelenos, Orange County is that vast area luring them away from their urban environs with bountiful beaches and shopping. Both versions are correct, but certainly not the whole picture.

Orange County *is* vast; it is a 782-square-mile area, 42 miles of which are beach. And it is more than just Shangri-la for those seeking that California commodity—a tan. This vital region has an exceptionally strong economic base and rapidly growing residential areas. It is also a vacationer's paradise because it is quintessential California. The weather, no doubt, has a lot to do with this; indeed, Orange County's balmy climes seem to be on automatic pilot most of the year. And then, there are those other aspects . . . world-class hotels, top-notch dining, scores of tiny museums—some worth seeing, some not—and shining examples of California's rich history. Of course, the surfing, lively shopping experiences, and tanned bodies everywhere remain the main stars of this scene.

Bordered to the north by Los Angeles, to the east by the Santa Ana Mountains, to the south by San Clemente and to the west by the ocean, Orange County is a region of great diversity. It is also one of the fastest-growing areas in the country, where natives and visitors go to experience the good life, California-style.

ANAHEIM

Theme park capital of the world, Anaheim is California showmanship at its showiest. Situated inland some 28

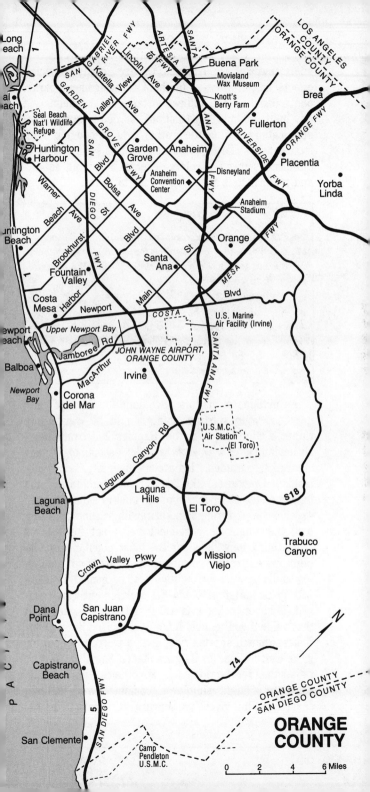

ORANGE COUNTY

miles south of Los Angeles, Orange County's special-effects mecca offers a plethora of amusement parks, odd museums, and offbeat attractions. Anaheim is a city built around its attractions, so don't expect a sophisticated urban center, rather, a hodgepodge of fast-food eateries, large, plush, convention-style hotels in California's primary colors—creme, pink, and aqua—and more motels than you'd care to count.

> ## INSIDERS' TIPS
>
> Besides the few restaurants mentioned in our listings, stick to the dining venues in the major hotels. Anaheim's restaurants tend to be highly gimmicky with little emphasis on food or service.
>
> If you plan to stay here, presumably to be close to Anaheim's most revered attraction, Disneyland, choose from one of the dozens of deluxe chain hotels like the Princess or the Emerald. They offer a soothing respite from the Mickey mania that surrounds you.

As millions of visitors have done for the last three decades, your starting point should be a visit—or rather, a pilgrimage—to the "Happiest Place on Earth." Disneyland♕♕♕♕♕ is a kaleidoscope of fantasy creatures, parades, high-tech ingenuity, and old-fashioned favorites, like Alice in Wonderland and the leader of the rat pack himself, Mickey Mouse. Don't expect to whiz through this sprawling theme park in a day; this might be possible were it not for the excruciatingly long lines for the most popular (translation: fastest) rides. Among them are two of Disneyland's newest attractions which opened in 1987 with great fanfare. *Captain EO,* starring one-glove himself, Michael Jackson, is a 3-D, 18-minute space flick that's fine if you're a sci-fi fan or a Jackson junkie. Star Tours, a much shorter ride, is well worth the hour-or-more wait in line, for its gizmo-laden *Star Wars* setting rather than for the ride itself. Nonetheless, it's a unique concept: A flight simulator, combined with a slick, space-age film, gives "passengers" the liver-jarring experience of careening through space. This ride is not recommended just after consuming a hot dog and a Jungle Julep.

Admission to Disneyland ($20 adults, $15 for ages 3–11) includes unlimited use of all attractions except the Arcade.

PERILS & PITFALLS

If you are at all affected by motion sickness, don't go on Disneyland's new Star Tours ride. Though the standard warning signs are posted, this ride is full of sudden jerks and sharp turns. There's nothing smooth about this ride.

In addition to the rides, the Magic Kingdom offers 7 different themed areas from Main Street U.S.A. to Western Frontierland, from high-tech Tomorrowland to the charming French Quarter of New Orleans Square. Many surrounding hotels offer free shuttle service to the park. It may be advisable to periodically break up your Disney odyssey.

Before the neon and the lasers, Anaheim led a relatively quiet and prosperous existence. First known as California's wine capital until a blight destroyed the crop in the late 1800s, Anaheim became a major center for the orange industry. Much of California's famed citrus fruits came from this area; this, too, came to a gradual end with the opening of Disneyland in 1955. Actually, theme parks invaded Anaheim even before Walt did.

To keep people occupied while they waited in long lines for his wife's famous berry pies, one Walter Knott hit upon the idea of erecting a ghost town for entertainment. It was obviously a hit with the locals and, over the years, theme area upon theme area grew to the present 150-acre Knott's Berry Farm Park ♛ ♛ ♛. This attraction, located in neighboring Buena Park at 8039 Beach Boulevard, is great if you have children. There are 4 theme areas including Camp Snoopy, the newest addition, the Roaring Twenties, Ghost Town, and Fiesta Village. The lines here aren't as long as at Disneyland, and kids do love the 360-degree roller-coaster ride and the so-real-you-can-smell-the-gunpowder Old West area.

While in Buena Park, you might want to take in another attraction, Movieland Wax Museum♛, one block north of Knott's Berry Farm at 7711 Beach Boulevard. While it's no Madame Tussaud's, this museum is known for its over 200 wax reproductions of Hollywood's finest. Celebrity buffs will get a kick out of seeing numerous original props and sets from well-known movies.

There's another lesser-known museum in the area boasting the largest collection of World War I and II souvenirs, medals, uniforms, and weapons found anywhere. Quite a big claim, but the Museum of World Wars♛ at 8700 Stanton Avenue is worth a visit if you're interested in history.

PERILS & PITFALLS

Touted as having so much more than it really does, the Hobby City Collection and Doll Museum are not worth the effort that goes into finding them. Gimmicky is the operative word here.

If it hasn't already become apparent, Anaheim and its adjacent cities subscribe to the bigger-is-best theory. Everything here seems to be billed as the "world's largest" or "the best." Even some of the more mundane structures, like the Anaheim Convention Center and the behemoth Anaheim Stadium, are among the largest of their kind.

And then, there's the Crystal Cathedral♛♛, a monument that defies description and gives impetus to the phrase "only in California." Located in nearby Garden Grove at 12141 Lewis Street, this glass-encased, towering edifice was the inspiration of the Rev. Dr. Robert Schuller of television fame. It seats 3,000 congregation members and has two 90-foot, electronically operated doors behind the pulpit which dramatically swing open to allow drive-in worshipers to be part of the Sunday services. The church, designed by renowned architect Philip Johnson, is open to visitors during the week.

There is one more museum to visit in Santa Ana, a large city slightly to the south of Anaheim. Unquestionably one of the most interesting attractions in this entire area and like an oasis of calm in the midst of Mardi Gras, The Bowers Museum♛ ♛ ♛ ♛ at 2002 N. Main Street is a magnificent hacienda-style building set on lush grounds replete with Spanish tile and statuary. The museum has no central theme (heaven forbid another theme); however, it offers excellent collections of early Spanish and American-Indian artifacts. Also on hand are stunning displays of Pre-Columbian and African art; temporary exhibits are usually worthwhile. While the lack of consistency between the various exhibits seems somewhat disconcerting, each exhibit, in itself, is far too fascinating to miss.

Tourist attractions aside, Anaheim and its surrounding cities, Buena Park, Fullerton, Orange, Santa Ana, and Garden Grove, are primarily Orange County's bedroom communities. Unless unending suburbia is something you particularly want to check out, head toward the coast and travel south along Pacific Coast Highway, which follows the beach all the way down the southern California coast.

PERILS & PITFALLS

Lion Country Safari is no longer open; however, Wild Rivers, a raging-rapids type of water theme park is open during the summer at the same Irvine location. If you must get wet, stick to the ocean—this theme park is filled with the same old mile-long slides and such.

HUNTINGTON BEACH

You'll come first to a speck of a city called Seal Beach; it's a pleasant enough town with a cute main thoroughfare (yes, it's called Main Street), chock-full of shops and cafés. There *is* a small pier at the end of this street, but that's about it; so continue down the coast a bit to the surfing mecca of southern California: Huntington Beach. California's tenth largest city is a laid-back town that loves its beaches and all that goes along with the sand-'n-tan life-style. Indeed, the most impressive aspect of this city is the mile upon mile of clean, wide beach, sloping gently into the ocean—a requisite for perfectly formed waves. This seaside resort is known for its international surfing championships held each year, but any time is opportune for watching agile surfers catch their waves.

INSIDERS' TIPS

Sunday brunch has become a southern California institution. Unfortunately, this means that most restaurants that serve brunch—especially the oceanfront ones like Maxwell's in Huntington Beach—are unbearably crowded. Unless you must indulge, avoid this mid-morning ritual and the hassles with harried waitresses and loud crowds that go along with it.

Named after railroad magnate Henry E. Huntington (who brought the Pacific Electric Railroad to this town), this resort has a rather colorful past, dotted with Spanish settlers and oil barons. Zealous religious groups were so pronounced at the turn of the century that part of the city was nicknamed "Gospel Swamp." But the future of Huntington Beach was sealed forever when oil was discovered in the 1920s. Today, right across the street from the beach, ugly oil derricks ceaselessly pump away at California's energy rich reserves.

As with many of the coastal cities incorporated during the early 1900s, Huntington Beach has both its newer splashier section and its older areas, which surround the famed Huntington Pier ♛ ♛. A well-loved landmark, this lengthy pier was erected in 1914 as the "longest, highest, and only solid concrete municipal pleasure pier in the United States." Though it has weathered California's storms better than others like it, the pier has been periodically restored. A leisurely stroll here is a pleasant way to experience the city and the ocean. Funky, old Main Street♛ just across the main highway is worth a walk-through as well.

INSIDERS' TIPS

The best parking situation for Huntington State Beach can be found near the Beach Boulevard entrance.

Huntington Beach's 28.5 square miles comprise not only beachfront and a few historic points of interest, but also a spanking newer section called Huntington Harbor♛ ♛. Here, elegant homes with their own boat slips share the space with marinas, loaded with restaurants and shops. There's Seacliff Village♛, known for its attractive Cape Cod architecture; Old World♛, desperately trying to be quaint; and Peter's Landing♛, modeled after Port Grimaud in Saint Tropez. The latter marina offers boat rides around its harbor as part of the shopping experience, and the restaurants have thoughtfully provided big windows to maximize the great view.

PERILS & PITFALLS

Huntington Beach might be a nice place to visit, but don't stay at the hotels in the vicinity if you can help it. They're weathered, motel-like establishments and are not up to par with some of the accommodations found in nearby cities.

NEWPORT BEACH

Farther down the coast is the chic, seaside enclave of Newport Beach, home to hundreds of yachts and plenty of Rolls-Royces. This town is more conservative than anywhere else in southern California, a place where you'll likely meet up with more perfectly coiffed, blue-eyed blondes than you're likely to see at a Norwegian ice-carving festival. Home to Orange County's elite and moneyed set, Newport Beach has long been the area's social pacesetter. (On tiny Balboa Island nearby, the grand Balboa Pavilion was fashionable during the Big Band era.)

Today, Newport Beach is the hub not only of social activity but also of new commercial and residential development. Wide boulevards, studded with gleaming high rises and impeccable landscaping, attest to the area's affluence and progress. This new area, called Newport Center, also contains first-class hotels and an exquisite, Mediterranean-style shopping center, Fashion Island♛ ♛ ♛. This attractive indoor/outdoor complex is home to such upscale stores as Neiman-Marcus and Amen Wardy, plus a recently constructed, palazzo-style building, housing even more outrageously expensive shops.

Best of all, there's Irvine Ranch Farmer's Market♛ ♛, a giant food orgy of exotic edibles and better-than-average standard fare. This should be a stop on every hungry tourist's list.

PERILS & PITFALLS

The only annoyance at the farmer's market is that there are too few tables and chairs, and when one is loaded down with a tray bearing 7 different kinds of pasta salad and a yogurt shake, searching for a seat becomes tedious. For this reason, plan to come here during odd hours—and definitely *not* during lunchtime.

A stone's throw away, at 850 San Clemente Drive, is the Newport Harbor Art Museum♛, a modern facility that "concentrates on the art of our time"—a nice way of saying that the exhibits straddle the middle of the road with contemporary art that's neither too daring nor too wacky.

Also in the immediate vicinity (Corona del Mar) is Roger's Gardens♛, at 2301 San Joaquin Hills Road. It's actually a nursery, but strolling through these fragrant gardens under the sunny climes of Newport seems almost like promenading in a park.

Far from the contemporary glitz of Newport Center, the old towns of Balboa Island and Lido Island still draw multitudes to experience their individual charms.

Balboa Island ♛ ♛ ♛ ♛ can still be reached by the 3-car ferry that has operated since the early 1900s; however, the wait is painfully long at times, and the Balboa Island Bridge does just as fine a job—though not as scenic—of getting you there. Walk down Marine Avenue with its bikini shops and ice-cream stands, and make it a point to visit the Victorian-style Balboa Pavilion ♛ ♛, built in 1905 for $15,000. Today, this historic structure is showing its age and is far prettier when viewed from across the harbor.

As you'll notice, houses on Balboa Island are squeezed incredibly close, but with property prices well into the millions, every inch is prime. The same goes for neighboring Lido Island ♛ ♛ ♛ ♛, a prettier town bearing more than a resemblance to a town along the Cote d' Azur. The shopping here is much more spread-out, and boutiques and restaurants have a sophistication not found on Balboa. Definitely plan to walk around and explore the side streets filled with interesting shops.

PERILS & PITFALLS

The houses on Balboa and Lido islands look much better from across the harbor. When you drive around the streets to see these residences up close, they are unimpressive and claustrophobic.

One of Orange County's oldest cities, Newport Beach still retains many historic sites today. One of particular interest is Newport Pier ♛, at Balboa Boulevard and 20th Street. It was rebuilt in the 1940s, and is the site of California's only remaining dory fishing fleet. If you like your fish fresh, you'll love the open-air market each morning featuring the day's catch.

PERILS & PITFALLS

Though you may have heard it somewhere before, here it is again: Do *not* attempt to swim, surf, or anything else at the treacherous Wedge at Newport Beach. It is only for experienced surfers—and then only the daredevils.

Just a couple of miles south of Newport is tiny Corona del Mar, a picturesque town with a few elegant shops and bistros. If you have the time, stop off at Sherman Library and Gardens ♕, located at 2647 Pacific Coast Highway. The beautiful garden setting displays everything from rare cacti to tropical flora. The library itself is also worth a visit.

COSTA MESA

Before heading farther down the coast, travel about 10 minutes inland to Costa Mesa, a town small in size but big in brawn. Though the powers that be in Newport Center are furiously working to change the balance of power, there's no denying that the economic base of the area is in Costa Mesa. A mere 10 years ago, this area was as flat as farmland—in fact, it was farmland with lima beans and strawberries among the produce grown. Though a few green patches occasionally break up the vertical landscape today, Costa Mesa is composed mostly of modern architectural masterpieces, as aesthetically impressive as they are commercially important. It's hard not to be impressed by the monolithic, glass towers bordered by well-tended gardens and outstanding public art displays that make up the South Coast Metro district.

This 3.5-square-mile hub of activity has, as its new crown jewel, the stunning Orange County Performing Arts Center ♕ ♕ ♕, at 600 Town Center Drive. Opened in September 1986, the imposing pink-granite structure is Orange County's first major facility able to handle large-scale productions in its 3,000-seat main theater. An additional 1,000-seat theater is still in the works. This design triumph is highlighted by an enormous architectural sculpture by renowned artist Richard Lippold. A red, gold, and silver aluminum work called *Fire Bird,* it is the center's *pièce de résistance.* Artist Henry Moore's *Reclining Figure* lounges behind the center.

A few blocks away (between the Central Bank and Great Western Savings Tower on Anton Boulevard), the artistic landscape of South Coast Metro changes with

California Scenario ♛ ♛ ♛. This outdoor sculpture by Isamu Noguchi is a serene retreat framed by the two glass buildings. Six areas represent 6 vital elements of California's environment, from the forest to the desert to the ocean. Off to one side, 15 granite rocks that seem to be precariously perched are fitted together to create *The Spirit of the Lima Bean,* Noguchi's tribute to the Segerstrom family which owned (and still does) the land when it was, pardon the pun, full of beans.

The largest, most profitable shopping center in southern California, South Coast Plaza ♛ ♛ ♛ at 3333 Bristol Street, draws throngs of shoppers on weekends. Definitely a place to visit and shop, a favorite California pastime. Skip visiting neighboring Irvine; just continue back to the coast and head south.

LAGUNA

You'll soon come to California's answer to European chic: Laguna Beach, a lovely, gentle seaside resort. Thankfully, there's much more to this town than bikinis and boogie boards. A walk along the main thoroughfare, which winds through town, will yield numerous charming bistros, sophisticated boutiques, and more art studios and galleries than you can shake a brush at.

INSIDERS' TIPS

The well-known Pottery Shack on Pacific Coast Highway is filled with handmade items plus a large housewares section. You'll discover some real bargains here, along with pottery-making demonstrations if you hang around long enough.

Since the early 1900s, Laguna has been home to artists, due in large part to the breathtaking scenery found here. Views of the jagged coastline are among the most spectacular anywhere, and vantage points overlooking the beach should not be missed. Stop off at Heisler Park ♛ ♛ ♛ ♛, at Cliff Drive and North Coast Highway, where beautiful gardens mesh with the panoramic views of the cliffs and ocean.

Laguna has long been a favorite of many of Hollywood's screen legends—among others—and beautiful houses in the hills make for delightful tours. Though it was a hippie hangout in the sixties, today funk has been replaced with casual elegance. And everywhere, Laguna's heritage as a major repository of California art seems evident.

PERILS & PITFALLS

Art festivals abound here during the summer, but the Sawdust Festival is one that you could easily skip. Held in a dusty canyon, the gathering smacks of Laguna's earlier hippie days.

Stop off at the bright pink, palm-treed Laguna Art Museum ♛ ♛ ♛ ♛ at 307 Cliff Drive, to view the 1,100-piece permanent collection of California art from the beginning of the century to today. This airy, postmodern building is a work of art itself and should not be missed.

Perhaps the one thing for which Laguna is most famous is the unusual art spectacle held each July and August, known as the Pageant of the Masters ♛ ♛ ♛ ♛. This magical event is a superbly executed "performance," where live models painstakingly (and, it appears, painfully) re-create major works of art in *tableau-vivant* style. Giving new meaning to the still-life concept, the pageant and its sister event, the Festival of the Arts (which features a huge collection of art by California artists—all for sale) sound almost tacky but draw upwards of 250,000 people annually to the Irvine Bowl location in Laguna and are actually presented with good taste. Since parking problems may be even more legendary than the main attraction, we advise you to take the shuttles provided from town if you choose to attend.

All in all, a visit to Laguna is not one you're likely to forget. The bougainvillea-draped paradise is cooled by ocean breezes and frequented by all who truly want a slice of California's reputed "good life." Though some find it hard to leave this town, the pretty, private community of Laguna-Niguel beckons slightly south of Laguna.

DANA POINT

The next town south of Laguna-Niguel is tiny Dana Point. If this area looks like a coastal suburb, that's because it is. Veer off the highway and take Golden Lantern to Dana Point Harbor Drive, where you'll happen upon one of the coast's loveliest marinas. This shady road offers a relaxing drive flanking the harbor. At one end, by the Orange County Marine Institute, is the *Pilgrim II*, a replica of the square-rigged ship that brought Richard Henry Dana to the area in 1835. He immortalized the area in his book *Two Years Before The Mast*. The town, in return, took on his name. A bronze statue of Dana can be seen farther down the marina.

Though a haven for boat lovers, the Dana Point Harbor and Marina is for those with appetites as well. Several seafood restaurants are on hand as are a few gift shops.

One museum is worth a stop if you're a seafaring sort. The Nautical Heritage Museum♥, at 24532 Del Prado, is located in an old lighthouse and filled with excellent scale models of tall ships, whalers, and U.S. flagships, plus antique navigational instruments, and even a cozy alcove in the back stocked with tales of the sea.

PERILS & PITFALLS

Despite its impressive sounding name, the Orange County Marine Institute is an ill-conceived, loose compilation of a few whale bones and a couple of sad-looking aquatic specimens. In fact, the name of this place has more letters in it than the institute has fish.

SAN JUAN CAPISTRANO

From Dana Point, it's on to San Juan Capistrano, a town known for its faithful swallows and for its shining examples of early California (that means Spanish-style) architecture. Capistrano, partly situated along the coast but mostly inland, will send you back in time. Hacienda-type buildings, gardens, and an older area will allow you to envision what California used to be like during its pre-Anglo days.

When we were there, we half expected to see a couple of padres crossing the street; instead, we were among zillions of tourists and some very friendly town folk. The big draw in this town is the famed Mission San Juan Capistrano ♛ ♛ ♛ ♛ ♛, located at Camino Capistrano and Ortega Highway. This mission has reason to be called the "Jewel of the Missions"; most of the old buildings have been left untouched so that the mission stands in its original, though harshly weathered state. Large inner courtyards, planted with giant calla lilies and shade trees, add to the natural beauty of this place, founded in 1776 by Father Junipero Serra. Some adobe buildings have been restored, and also Father Serra's exquisite stone chapel.

Besides the historic significance of this site, the return of the swallows is an annual event that intrigues visitors and is good for at least two local events. It is said that, each year, on March 19, the square-tailed cliff swallows return to Capistrano for the summer and leave for Goya, Argentina, some 6,000 miles south, on October 23. While you might miss the swallows, you're certain to see many white pigeons hanging around the mission waiting for the birdseed that tourists dole out.

Around the back side of the mission is a stunning postmodern building, the San Juan Capistrano Library ♛ ♛ ♛ ♛, at 31495 E1 Camino Real. This updated, mission-style structure, designed by architect Michael Graves, is surprising in that it is able to blend in gracefully with the old Spanish buildings around it.

Back along Camino Capistrano, take a walk and stop off at some of the pretty restaurants for Mexican food. At El Peon, a large shop featuring overpriced Mexican handicrafts (right across the street from the mission), visitors congregate each Saturday and Sunday at 1 P.M. for a guided walking tour of the town.

Farther south along the coast, San Clemente is a

bucolic little town with a few offbeat shops but nothing of significant interest to induce a stop; Richard Nixon no longer lives there.

INSIDERS' INFORMATION FOR ORANGE COUNTY

Anaheim
(area code 714)
Where to Stay
Anaheim Marriott ♕ ♕ ♕
700 W. Convention Way, Anaheim 92802; tel. 750-8000
Single room, double occupancy: $128
High-rise hotel attracts lot of convention biz. Fitness center, 2 pools, saunas, game room. Cable car trolleys go to Disneyland. JW's(♕ ♕ ♕ ♕) is an excellent Continental-cuisine restaurant on the premises.

Disneyland Hotel ♕ ♕ ♕
1150 W. Cerritos, Anaheim 92803; tel. 778-6600
Single room, double occupancy: $130
A sprawling, multithemed complex, a stone's throw from Disneyland, with 1,200 rooms and 8 restaurants—Granville's(♕ ♕ ♕ ♕) serves American cuisine that's some of the best in the area. This place is a mini-Disneyland in itself, great for kids of all ages. Monorail to the park, marina with pedal boats, puppet theater, dancing waters.

Emerald of Anaheim ♕ ♕ ♕
1717 S. West St., Anaheim 92802; tel. 999-0990
Single room, double occupancy: $95
Contemporary hotel with twin towers, situated across from Disneyland. Pool, whirlpool spa, tennis, and health spa facilities available nearby. The Third Floor Continental restaurant(♕ ♕ ♕ ♕) is worth checking out.

Travelodge at the Park ♕
1221 S. Harbor Blvd., Anaheim 92805; tel. 758-0900
Single room, double occupancy: $75
Archways and tiles give a Spanish flavor to this terracotta hotel situated next door to Disneyland. Pleasant, if uninspired accommodations. 260 rooms. Pool, spa, complimentary Disneyland shuttle.

Where to Eat
The Catch ♛
1929 S. State College, Anaheim; tel. 634-1829
Average dinner: $20
In proper 19th-century, Victorian style, this restaurant offers hearty American fare but is especially adept at seafood entrées. A good family place.

The Overland Stage and Territorial Saloon ♛
1855 S. Harbor Blvd. at the Inn at the Park Hotel, Anaheim; tel. 750-1811
Average dinner: $17
Rip roarin', Western-themed restaurant is a crowd pleaser. Interesting specials like buffalo and quail. Mediocre service.

Shopping
Anaheim Plaza, 500 N. Euclid St. One of California's sprawling malls with 3 department stores and 75 specialty shops. Shuttles operate between major hotels and this mall. Fine if you need something in a pinch.

**Buena Park
(area code 714)**

Where to Eat
Medieval Times ♛
7662 Beach Blvd., tel. 521-4740
Average dinner: $25
Relive Camelot during a 4-course meal. This 11th-century faux castle gets you in the jousting mood as knights on horseback whiz past. An unusual place to eat.

**Costa Mesa
(area code 714)**
Where to Stay
Westin South Coast Plaza ♛ ♛
666 Anton Blvd., Costa Mesa 92626; tel. 540-2500
Single room, double occupancy: $80–$160
Modern high rise is large and airy. 394 rooms. Service is decent. Enjoy cocktails in the atrium lobby. Best feature: It's close to some of the best shopping in southern California. Pool, tennis, putting green.

Where to Eat
Ambrosia♛ ♛ ♛ ♛
695 Town Center Dr., Costa Mesa; tel. 432-7559
Average dinner: $45
Elegant establishment serves some of the finest French food around. Good wine list, discreet service, and 18th-century romantic ambience.
Copa de Oro♛ ♛
633 Anton Blvd., Costa Mesa; tel. 662-0798
Average dinner: $28
This is a Mayan imitation and very creative. Some Southwestern cuisine. Friendly service, well-dressed patrons.
Grand Teton Chalet♛ ♛
695 Town Center Dr., Costa Mesa; tel. 432-7791
Average dinner: $30
Unique dining in lodge serving very exotic Continental and American fare, like black bear and alligator. Slow service, striking atmosphere.
Shopping
South Coast Plaza, 3333 Bristol St. More than 250 upscale stores in this shopping mall plus 8 major department stores.
Swap Meet (Anything and Everything)
Orange County Swap Meet, 88 Fair Drive between Fairview and the Newport Freeway; on Saturday and Sunday from 7 A.M. to 4 P.M.
Theater
South Coast Repertory, 655 Town Center Dr., Costa Mesa; tel. 957-2602. 500-seat main stage features comedies and dramas. Experimental plays on smaller second stage.

**Dana Point
(area code 714)**
Where to Stay
Marina Inn♛
24800 Dana Point Harbor Dr., Dana Point 92629, tel. 496-1203
Single room, double occupancy: $70
Modern, low-slung, motel-style accommodations. 135 rooms. Great harbor location. Pool, redwood sauna.

Where to Eat

Delaney's ♛ ♛

25001 Dana Dr., Dana Point; tel. 496-6195

Average dinner: $18

For fish lovers. An oyster bar, plus specialities like shrimp Rangoon and abalone. Harbor view.

Cannons ♛

34344 Green Lantern, Dana Point; tel. 496-6146

Average dinner: $24

Incredible view and nicely prepared seafood.

Beaches

Doheny State Park Beach, 25300 Dana Point Harbor Dr.; tel. 496-6171. Large park, surfing, grassy areas, picnic areas, and a campground with 120 spaces. Book at least two months in advance; specify oceanfront lots.

Fountain Valley
(area code 714)

Nightlife

The Hop, 18774 Brookhurst; tel. 963-2366. Orange County's most popular rock-and-roll club with live bands and dancing to fifties and sixties music. Special concerts as well.

Fullerton
(area code 714)

Where to Eat

The Cellar ♛ ♛

305 N. Harbor Blvd., Fullerton; tel. 525-5682

Average dinner: $32

Located in the original cellar of the former Villa del Sol hotel. Traditional French fare, extensive wine list.

Garden Grove
(area code 714)

Where to Stay

Hyatt Regency Alicante ♛ ♛ ♛

100 Plaza Alicante, Garden Grove 92640; tel. 971-3000

Single room, double occupancy: $100

Giant, pink-flamingo statues stand in the fountains at

the entrance to this 17-story hotel near Disneyland. Impressive, ultramodern place to stay. 400 rooms. Concierge, popular lobby café. Landscaped roof garden. Pool, tennis, health spa.

Huntington Beach
(area code 714)
Where to Stay
Huntington Beach Inn ♛
21112 Pacific Coast Highway, Huntington Beach 92648; tel. 536-1421
Single room, double occupancy: $75
Located across the highway from the ocean with modern furnishings, pool, and a 9-hole golf course. Sandpiper(♛ ♛), glass-enclosed café, is pleasant with a nice view.

Where to Eat
Maxwell's by the Sea ♛ ♛ ♛
317 Pacific Coast Highway, Huntington Beach; tel. 536-2555
Average dinner: $26
Large seafood selection and fantastic ocean view. Glass-enclosed patio. Crowded Sunday brunch.

MacArthur Park ♛ ♛
16390 Pacific Coast Highway, Huntington Beach; tel. 846-5553
Average dinner: $18
A typically California restaurant. American food, great barbecue. Quick and pleasant, and a super harbor view.

Tibbie's Music Hall ♛
16360 Pacific Coast Highway, Huntington Beach; tel. 840-5661
Average dinner: $22
Old-fashioned, all-American eatery is the setting for this musical dinner theater. Servers perform the best of Broadway and old favorites.

Beaches
Bolsa Chica State Beach, between Warner Ave. and Huntington Beach Pier; tel. 846-3460. One of the best-known beaches in the area offering a bike path, excellent clamming and fishing, and great surfing.

Huntington State Beach, off Pacific Coast Highway, near Beach Blvd.; tel. 536-1455. Very long, wide beach; very clean, excellent for surfing. Fire rings, snack facilities. Parking is easier by Beach Blvd.

Irvine
Where to Eat
Morell's (in the Irvine Hilton and Towers) ♛ ♛
17900 Jamboree Blvd., Irvine; tel. 863-3111
Average dinner: $33
Pastel dining room offers fresh California cuisine, a good wine list, and intriguing desserts.

Laguna-Niguel
(area code 714)
Where to Stay
The Ritz-Carlton ♛ ♛ ♛ ♛
33533 Ritz-Carlton Dr., Laguna-Niguel 92677; tel. 240-2000
Single room, double occupancy: $250
Magnificent, classic, Mediterranean structure, perched atop a 150-foot cliff overlooking the Pacific. Fine art and antiques grace the sprawling property. 393 spacious rooms, full resort facilities. Jogging and bike trails, golf course, tennis, 2 pools, complete fitness center. The Dining Room(♛ ♛ ♛ ♛) presents delectable Continental cuisine. Average dinner: $60.
Eiler's Inn ♛ ♛ ♛
741 South Coast Highway, Laguna 92651; tel. 494-3004
Single room, double occupancy: $100
Charming B&B on Laguna's main street, 12 rooms. Lovely courtyard and fountain is the setting for breakfast, afternoon wine and cheese. Cozy, filled with antiques. Popular, so reserve well ahead.
Hotel San Maarten ♛ ♛
696 South Coast Highway, Laguna 92651; tel. 494-9436
Single room, double occupancy: $100
Caribbean style with tastefully decorated rooms, facing

a lush inner courtyard. 55 rooms. Private, tropical. Pool, sauna, suites with Jacuzzis.

Surf and Sand Hotel♛ ♛
1555 South Coast Highway, Laguna 92651; tel. 497-4477
Single room, double occupancy: $130
Spacious rooms with separate sitting areas on the beach. All have private lanais. Longtime area favorite. The Towers(♛ ♛ ♛ ♛) is an exquisite art-deco restaurant at the top of the hotel offering sophisticated French fare. Great for romantic repasts.

The Carriage House♛
1322 Catalina St., Laguna 92651; tel. 494-8945
Single room, double occupancy: $95
New Orleans-style B&B on a quiet shady street. Each of the 6 suites is decorated differently.

Where to Eat

Las Brisas♛ ♛
361 Cliff Dr., Laguna; tel. 497-5434
Average dinner: $24
One of the best views of the coast can be had here while enjoying some very good nouvelle Mexican and American cuisine. Try the seafood specialties. Always crowded.

The Cottage♛ ♛
308 North Coast Highway, Laguna; tel. 494-3023
Average dinner: $17
Down-home, hearty fare is dished up at this Hansel-and-Gretel-style establishment—everything from ribs to lasagna. Famous for omelettes and buttermilk blueberry pancakes.

Tortilla Flats♛ ♛
1740 South Coast Highway, Laguna; tel. 494-6588
Average dinner: $16
Pretty hacienda-style restaurant, chock-full of Laguna's under-30s set. Very good Mexican fare.

Partners Bistro♛
448 South Coast Highway, Laguna; tel. 497-4441
Average dinner: $24
Utterly charming, antique-filled bistro serving French cuisine. Nothing fancy.

Theater

Laguna Moulton Playhouse, 606 Laguna Canyon Rd.; tel. 494-0743. Longtime local favorite. Good comedies, dramas, and musicals.

Beaches

Aliso Beach County Park, 31000 block of Pacific Coast Highway; tel. 661-7013. Fishing pier, grassy areas, dramatic rocky beach. Tidepools make this spot great for snorkeling.

Salt Creek State Beach, Pacific Coast Highway and Niguel Rd. in front of the Ritz-Carlton; tel. 661-7013. Very large beach surrounded by bluffs. Good surfing.

Newport Beach
(area code 714)

Where to Stay

Four Seasons Hotel ♛ ♛ ♛ ♛

690 Newport Center Dr., Newport Beach 92660; tel. 759-0808

Single room, double occupancy: $205

Impressive tower set on a hill overlooking Newport Beach and the ocean. The epitome of California elegance; 296 spacious, well-appointed rooms. Many amenities. Serenely landscaped pool. Health club, massage, tennis, whirlpool, weight room. The Pavilion(♛ ♛ ♛ ♛) is a lovely dining experience. Features nouvelle cuisine and low-fat alternative fare. Good wine list. Average dinner is $35.

Hotel Meridien ♛ ♛ ♛ ♛

4500 MacArthur Blvd., Newport Beach 92660; tel. 476-2001

Single room, double occupancy: $145

Concrete and smoked glass form an imposing structure less than a mile from John Wayne/Orange County Airport. Deluxe, with art and antiques for decoration. Health club, tennis, extensive business center.

The Newporter Resort ♛ ♛

1107 Jamboree Rd., Newport Beach 92660; tel. 644-1700

Single room, double occupancy: $150

Rambling pink villa has 26 landscaped acres with an

emphasis on the outdoors. Tennis is big here. 9-hole golf course, 3 pools, spas, and a fitness center.

Where to Eat
Amelia's ♛ ♛
311 Marine Ave., Balboa Island; tel. 673-6580
Average dinner: $18
Don't expect great ambience, but do come for a cozy evening and some good Italian fare. Skip dessert.

Bubbles Balboa Club ♛
111 Palm St., Balboa; tel. 675-9093
Average dinner: $26
Authentic, thirties supper club with original art, fresh fish, and live jazz. Mellow, memorable way to spend an evening.

The Cannery ♛
3010 Lafayette Ave., Newport Beach; tel. 675-5777
Average dinner: $25
Seafood and steak house enhanced by historic waterfront location. Rock 'n roll on the weekends. Great brunch, also supper cruise with champagne.

Shopping
Fashion Island, Newport Center. Beautiful Mediterranean-style complex with exclusive stores like Ellesse and Fiorucci, great places to lunch like Irvine Ranch Farmer's Market.

Nightlife
Promises, 3333 W. Pacific Coast Highway; tel. 642-0506. Casual night spot overlooking Newport Harbor. Top forties music.

Beach
Newport Beach, runs the length of Balboa Peninsula. Great surf, including the famous Wedge, for highly experienced surfers only. Central location, crowded.

San Clemente
(area code 714)
Where to Stay
San Clemente Inn ♛
2600 Avenida del Presidente, San Clemente 92672; tel. 492-6103
Single room, double occupancy: $80
Nicely landscaped inn, bordering the State Park and

near the beach. Traditional decor, spacious condominiums, gourmet(♕ ♕) restaurant. Pool, spa.

Where to Eat
Andreino's ♕ ♕
1925 S. El Camino Real, San Clemente; tel. 492-9955
Average dinner: $28
Andreino De Santis is famous for his very fresh pastas. Beautiful stained glass, antique-filled restaurant.

San Juan Capistrano
Where to Stay
Capistrano Surfside Inn ♕ ♕
34680 Coast Highway, San Juan Capistrano 92624; tel. 240-7681
Single room, double occupancy: $150
Casual white-and-blue hotel, tastefully furnished, contemporary style. 37 rooms. Local shuttle service. In-room spas, full kitchens. Sauna, exercise room.
Capistrano Edgewater Inn ♕
34733 Pacific Coast Highway, San Juan Capistrano 92624; tel. 240-0150
Single room, double occupancy: $70
Wood-beamed, rustic inn with Jacuzzi and sauna. 30 rooms. Across from the ocean.
Where to Eat
L'Hirondelle ♕ ♕
31631 Camino Capistrano, San Juan Capistrano; tel. 661-0425
Average dinner: $20
Diners swear by the pepper duck, but there are other tempting French entrées to choose from. This quaint, lace-curtained, French/Belgian restaurant has only 12 tables, so reservations are a must.

Santa Ana
(area code 714)
Nightlife
Crazy Horse Saloon, 1580 Brookhollow Dr.; tel. 549-1512. Famed country-and-western watering hole. Live bands.

Seal Beach
(area code 213)
Where to Stay
The Seal Beach Inn ♛ ♛ ♛
212 Fifth St., Seal Beach 90740; tel. 493-2416
Single room, double occupancy: $105
One of southern California's most charming country inns. Near the ocean, with rooms named for flowers. 22 rooms. Worth seeing even if you don't stay overnight. Pool, library, tea room.

SAN DIEGO COUNTY

SAN DIEGO

Name the two biggest cities in California. Los Angeles and San Francisco, right? Wrong. Quiet and somewhat unsung (until San Diegan Dennis Conner recaptured the America's Cup in 1987), California's second largest, oldest, and southernmost city is suddenly coming into its own.

It's hard to go wrong if you choose a vacation destination where the average year-round temperature is 70 degrees. But San Diego, 120 miles south of Los Angeles and 15 miles north of the Mexican border, offers that and plenty more. There's a healthy abundance of sports (try 72 golf courses within a 30-minute drive), culture (more than its share of museums and excellent theater), and scenic beauty.

But we are getting ahead of ourselves. First things first. This is how it all began: San Diego was discovered by Portuguese explorer João Rodrigues Cabrillo, who claimed the area for Spain in 1542. The Spanish followed Cabrillo in 1602 and named the area San Diego in honor of a Spanish patron saint San Diego de Alcalá. A Franciscan mission bearing his name was the first of 21 missions begun along the California coast by the Spanish and Mexican missionaries. Since then, a town best known for its zoo, has largely been playing second fiddle to other unmentionable California cities. But in the past few years, underdog San Diego has matured, acquiring the kind of savvy sophistication worldly visitors demand, yet managing to maintain an untainted presence.

Atypical of a large California city, San Diego can be pleasant to explore by foot. Its friendly and compact feel, the ocean-scented air, clean streets, and an artist's

palette of pastel-colored, squat buildings make one almost eager to tie up the old shoelaces and set out. Almost—because there's also an excellent transportation system. In addition to the familiar San Diego transit buses, there's the red San Diego trolley system which runs through town all the way to the Mexican border. A more expensive service called the Molly Trolley caters to hotel tourists who want their tours of the city guided. Both trolley services offer discounts for visitors who plan frequent use.

This city's number-one attraction remains the world-renowned San Diego Zoo ♛ ♛ ♛ ♛ ♛. As home to the finest collection of exotic wildlife in the world, it is easy to spend hours or even a full day attempting to see the 3,200 animals. The 100-acre facility, which backs onto Balboa Park, includes a children's zoo and petting kraal and is home to popular koala bears and a two-headed snake. Some of the gardenlike areas around the zoo aren't just for looks. San Diego's climate creates a thriving environment for tropical vegetation, and some of those not-so-common plants provide native food for the animals.

INSIDERS' TIPS

Even though the all-encompassing bus tour is not the only way you should experience the zoo, we recommend you take it upon arrival just to get a feel for this giant place. After the tour, go back on your own to see the enclosures that most interested you. For a behind-the-scenes tour, which lasts 3½ hours, you'll need reservations and additional funds. Tel. 619-234-3153. Regular admission $8.50 adults, $2.50 children. Behind-the-Scenes Tour, $16.75 adults, $7.50 children.

After the zoo, head a few blocks west and turn south down Fifth Avenue. This is the beginning of the Gaslamp Quarter ♛ ♛ ♛, a 16-block, 38-acre stretch that runs from Broadway to the waterfront. The Gaslamp Quarter was created by Alonzo Horton, a Wisconsin entrepreneur who purchased 960 acres of land for $265 in 1869 and built a wharf at the bayside. Horton encouraged businesses to move away from the original city center—now Old Town—inland to the north and into a new town by giving away parcels of his land to those who promised to develop it. Today the area, identified by its now electric, candelabra-style lampposts, has some of the best Victorian-style commercial buildings in the West.

PERILS & PITFALLS

The Quarter, like much of San Diego, is mostly safe for walking, but we do warn you to use common sense and to leave your best jewelry in the hotel safe. A number of winos and street people claim the Gaslamp Quarter as their stomping grounds, and although they are not as aggressive as in other cities, the rule of thumb is to steer clear of their antics.

The area isn't consistently Victorian, though, but rather a checkerboard of architectural and social statements, with historical sites and new hotels on some blocks, X-rated cinemas and red light activity on others.

Among the Italian-Baroque, Victorian, Romanesque, and Baroque-Revival structures in the Gaslamp Quarter, one building in particular will interest the visitor. It's the William Heath David House♛ on Island Avenue. A prefab built on the East Coast and shipped around the Horn, the somewhat homely structure is the oldest surviving building in what is now referred to as New Town. Victorian furniture and artifacts are displayed on the ground floor.

INSIDERS' TIPS

The Gaslamp Quarter Foundation offers a guided tour, on Saturdays only, around the William Heath David House as well as some of the other 153 historical buildings in the Quarter.

Across the street on Island Avenue is the Horton Grand Hotel♛♛♛ which once provided lodging for the likes of Wyatt Earp and President Benjamin Harrison. The hotel is actually two hotels, dismantled and rebuilt on the present site—which formerly contained a brothel—using 85 percent of the original brickwork and some of the original balconies. Walk through the glass atrium, ask to see the restored $200,000 staircase, and take a look at the small Chinese Museum which recognizes the role of the Chinese community in San Diego.

Several blocks northwest on the original site of the Horton Grand Hotel is the mecca of shopping-center enthusiasts, Horton Plaza ♛ ♛ ♛ ♛. This 4-story, pastel-colored edifice suggests a retail Disneyland. Visual to the point of distraction, with such a confusing layout that you could use a map to get around, you'll soon forget how much money you're spending. Still, it doesn't cost anything to enjoy the outdoor entertainment (they have plenty of buskers that stroll around on most days), or to take a look at the Jessops Street Clock on the ground floor. The 20-dial timekeeper is jeweled with topaz, jade, agate, and tourmaline—all stones native to the area. It took 15 months to craft.

Five or so blocks to the southwest is the more tourist-oriented Seaport Village ♛ ♛. This winding, bayside site with its 65 red-roofed stores is a popular place if you don't mind paying a bit extra for San Diego memorabilia and other trinketry. There are some charming shops like the Upstart Crow, a bookstore which offers up cappuccino with its Christies and Conrads; there's also the Broadway Flying Horses Carousel—a Coney Island attraction a century ago—and a half-mile-long walkway by the bay. Horse-drawn carriage rides depart from here for a tour of a small section of the city.

Directly across San Diego Bay from Seaport Village is Coronado ♛ ♛, the bulbous end of a finger of land which encloses the bay. Coronado is largely given over to the U.S. Navy's North Island Naval Air Station, the departure point for the first leg of Charles Lindbergh's famous Paris flight in 1917.

Those who venture across the Coronado Bridge usually do so to visit the turret-topped Hotel del Coronado ♛ ♛ ♛. The Del, as it is locally known, was completed in 1888 and attained a unique status thanks to Thomas Edison and his electric light system. But don't drop by with the hope of finding that watering-hole atmosphere enjoyed by the celebrities who once flocked here, or romance on the scale experienced by Edward, Prince of Wales, and Wallace Simpson (this is where they met). The hotel has turned to group business in recent years, and although the setting is as lovely as ever, the property itself is somewhat disappointing. Still, do make the crossing to Coronado, dine at the Del's outdoor restaurant, and then spend the day at the beach. We like Silver Strand State Beach♛♛♛ and the nearby Imperial Beach♛♛♛, which runs down to Mexico.

If you have time to explore the San Diego area a little farther afield, follow Harbor Drive up from Seaport Village and along to the Embarcadero♛. Nautical types will want to stop and look at the 3 ships in the Maritime Museum♛♛, including the Star of India, a British-built, iron-hulled merchant vessel which is the oldest one afloat.

PERILS & PITFALLS

Watch your timing if you plan a visit to Coronado. The 2.2-mile-long toll bridge gets very busy at rush hour and can take some 20 minutes to cross. A foot-passenger ferry began operation to Coronado Island from the Broadway Pier at the Embarcadero in the summer of 1987, $1 one-way. We think this is the way to go.

The nearby Broadway Pier♛ is an added bonus on weekend afternoons when the U.S. Navy usually docks a ship and invites the public on board as guests of the commanding officer. The adjacent pier is for the cruise ships. In between, a smaller dock area is where boat companies offer to show off the bay.

Harbor Drive takes you past Lindbergh Field, with the U.S. Navy Training Facility on your right. (As you cross the small bridge by the training center, look at the vessel on which most new recruits get their first taste of shipboard life. The ship is called the U.S.S. *Neversail* for obvious reasons.)

On the bayside of the curved drive are Harbor and Shelter islands♛♛, man-made islands created when the U.S. Navy dredged the bay to make room for larger carriers. Both offer marina facilities and bayside walkways. A few tuna boats still operate from this part of the bay, though the fleet has been reduced drastically in the past few years.

From here, follow the road signs out to Point Loma and the Cabrillo National Monument ♛ ♛ ♛ ♛. Point Loma is largely owned by the U.S. Navy, but don't be put off by the forest of antennae and military buildings you'll pass on the drive. Cabrillo is well worth the visit, especially when the weather is clear.

INSIDERS' TIPS

Cabrillo National Monument is a good place for landlubbers to watch migrating California gray whales from December through February. Don't forget your binoculars.

The monument offers a wonderful view of most of San Diego and Coronado, as well as a small museum and a number of documentary film presentations. California's first lighthouse—a quaint, wooden structure—is just a few steps up the hill and is open to public view.

Heading away from the monument and Point Loma, go northwards to Mission Bay Park. Along the south shore of this 27-mile, largely beach-lined inlet is San Diego's second major attraction: Sea World ♛ ♛ ♛ ♛. The 80-acre marine park offers displays and shows with trained killer whales, dolphins, and seals. Our favorite place in Sea World is the Penguin Encounter, the $7-million Antarctic home to 300 penguins for which the park's staff make 12,000 pounds of ice a day. On a conveyor belt you'll pass all the different kinds of penguins.

Sea World has also added a nonanimal entertainment show called City Streets, and there is the Places of Learning facility with an acre-sized floor map of the U.S. The nearby store is staffed largely by teachers, who can advise on educational books, toys, and games. But the animals of Sea World remain the number-one attraction there, with Shamu, a 3-ton killer whale, heading the popularity list. For a closer look at Sea World, ask to sign up for the behind-the-scenes tour when you enter.

INSIDERS' TIPS

Sea World opens at 9 A.M., but for those wanting to get a head start, a small section near the new main-gate complex opens at 8 A.M. Visitors can check with the information booth, see the show schedule for the day, and avoid some of the usual opening crush. Ticket prices are $17.95 adults, $11.95 ages 3–11. Tel. 619-226-3901.

On the way into San Diego, stop off at Old Town♕♕, the original heart of San Diego circa 1820, when California was under Mexican rule. Now a State Historic Park, Old Town was the original site of the Mission San Diego de Alcalá, built on the commanding Presidio Hill. The mission has been moved 6 miles north to Mission Valley, and the hill is now a 40-acre park with lovely views. The Serra Museum♕♕ is worth a visit, but much of the lower part of Old Town has become the tourist version of a Venus's-flytrap.

From here it's a short and easy drive southeast to San Diego's cultural and museum jugular vein—Balboa Park♕♕♕♕. Named for Vasco Núñez de Balboa, the Spanish explorer who discovered the Pacific, the 1,400-acre park has 11 museums, 3 art galleries, a Botanical garden (closed Fridays), and the Simon Edison Center for Performing Arts♕♕♕♕♕ (aka the Old Globe Theater, one of southern California's finest theaters).

The museum buildings date back as far as 1915, when the first of two expositions was staged in the park, and include the Natural History Museum♕♕♕, the Aerospace Historical Center♕♕♕♕, and the Hall of Champions♕♕♕♕, which highlights San Diego's sporting history. The Reuben H. Fleet Space Theater and Science Center♕♕♕♕ houses one of the nation's most impressive Omnimax theaters, with a dome-shaped screen that surrounds viewers and a multichannel sound system. The Science Center is full of eye-tricking gimmickry that the whole family will enjoy.

As you walk through Balboa Park, listen for the bells in the California Tower, a building that houses the Museum of Man.

INSIDERS' TIPS

For outstanding theater, go to the Globe or the La Jolla Playhouse; but for something a tad unusual, catch a performance at the park's Starlight Bowl, an open-air theater located directly under the flight path of San Diego's Lindbergh Field. An early-warning noise-detection system alerts actors and musicians to freeze in mid-stride for a few seconds each time a plane flies over. They then resume on the very note they left off—usually to audience applause. The novelty can quickly wear off if you're a season-ticket holder, or if there's a busy flight schedule that night.

The romantically inclined may stop for suggestive sustenance at the Cafe del Rey Moro near the main cluster of buildings in Balboa Park. Suggestive because this is a popular place for weddings with up to 5 taking place in a single day.

INSIDERS' TIPS

Balboa Park is the sort of place that can take a few hours or all day, depending on interest. There really is something for everyone, and the park's information center offers a special pass into several of the park's museums that could save some bucks. Check with the center first, however, as the pass is not recommended for seniors or children, who receive discounts anyway.

TIJUANA

Some 15 miles south of San Diego is the Mexican border and Tijuana♛. You don't need a passport to go across the border if you're an American, if you plan to stay less than 72 hours, and if you don't go south of Ensenada. However, you *do* need identification, and in case of some problem, a driver's license doesn't prove you're an American citizen. Customs duties permit you to return with up to $300 worth of merchandise duty-free each month—but you can only bring in one quart of liquor in that period.

PERILS & PITFALLS

With its begging throngs and hazardous food and drink, Tijuana should really be treated as nothing more than a tourist-trap and is hardly representative of the real Mexico. Visit only if you have a compelling urge to be able to tell people you've crossed the border. Those in the know strongly advise people who are driving into Mexico to stop and purchase Mexican car insurance from one of the agencies on the U.S. border. A car accident in Mexico is treated as a felony, and the driver must be able immediately to prove financial capability—either with cash on hand or with a Mexican (*not* an American) insurance policy. If you take the family pet across, U.S. Customs will want to have proof that the animal has had a rabies innoculation within the last 6 months.

Heading north is by far the best option if you're visiting San Diego. From Sea World, follow W. Mission Bay northward toward Mission Beach♛♛. As with any beach town, if you don't want your journey to progress at a snail's pace, stay off the main beach boulevard.

LA JOLLA

Parts of Mission Beach are pleasant for everyone, but some of it is more appealing to the beach and surf-rat characters. Some liken the place to Los Angeles' Venice Beach. But La Jolla♛♛♛♛♛, just a few miles up, is southern California's beauty spot. Art galleries, stores, boutiques, and restaurants are neatly crowded in to take advantage of the sea views. If there are blemishes to the place, they are the traffic and the prices, which reflect the somewhat snobbish air of some of the residents and are as steep as some of the cliffs overlooking the bay. Parking is also at a premium.

La Jolla, southern California's answer to Carmel, is a favorite destination for divers, who like exploring the deep-water canyon just offshore. Be warned that none of the plant or sea life can be removed from the San Diego–La Jolla Underwater Park. Those who prefer staying dry can explore the Sunny Jim Cave♛, a 133-stair descent, which leads into a natural ocean cave. Otherwise, hang tight to your wallet as it quickly lightens during your visit.

The Jacques Cousteaus of the world will want to continue around the bay to the Scripps Institute Aquarium♛ ♛ ♛, which has a doughnut-shaped, 22-tank display, containing about 200 species of sea life that can be found off the West Coast and Mexico. An inner display area illustrates oceanographic concerns and some of the projects on which Scripps Institute is working.

INSIDERS' TIPS

Try to visit Scripps Institute (open 9 A.M. to 5 P.M. daily) during feeding times on Sundays and Wednesdays at 1:30 P.M. Museum staffers advise this is the best time to see the fish when they are most active. The museum is open all year. No charge, but suggested voluntary contribution (for nonprofit activities) is $2 adults, $1 children.

Beyond La Jolla is the north country which includes Del Mar♛ ♛ ♛ ♛ and its famous thoroughbred track that comes alive with the sound of hoofs meeting turf near the surf from late July to mid-September. To the east is Escondido—31 miles north of San Diego—with several nearby wineries to visit.

INSIDERS' TIPS

The Wild Animal Park offers a special photo safari 2 days a week from May to September. These 2- and 4-hour tours let you get close to zebras, gnus, impalas, and gazelles. Just think—you can save the cost of that long-imagined safari to Africa, or better yet, you may be inspired to save, so you can go and experience the real thing.

A few miles east of Escondido is the San Diego Wild Animal Park♛ ♛ ♛—a 1,800-acre nature preserve in the San Pasqual Valley. Open daily, hours vary by season, so call ahead, 619-234-6541. Admission $12.95

adults, $6.20 ages 3–15. The park features animals and vegetation from Africa, Australia, and Asia. There is a 5-mile-long tour around the park on the Wgasa Bush Line Monorail, elephant rides, the Nairobi Village, an Australian rain forest, and aviary complexes.

If you wish to push on even further, there's Palomar Observatory♛♛♛♛ to the north of the park (65 miles from San Diego). Palomar houses America's largest telescope and boasts some beautiful countryside views. To the east of the park is the gold mining town of Julian♛♛ and some re-creations of its days of glory. On the way back, stop at the Mission San Diego de Alcalá♛♛♛ in Mission Valley. A small museum at the mission contains some historical records and artifacts from the local community.

INSIDERS' TIPS

Also north of San Diego, but not on the prime list of tourist spots, is the Miramar Naval Air Station. The military base is home to the U.S. Navy's Top Gun squadron popularized by the movie of the same name. Base officials are reluctant to book tours, but try writing them several months in advance of your trip at the Public Affairs Offices, NAS Miramar, San Diego, CA 92145. State that you'd like to tour the Top Gun Squadron and ask for an appropriate date.

San Diego, now the seventh largest city in America, has yet to become a jaded attraction in tourist terms, although it's not hard to envisage it happening once the new downtown Convention Center is built in 1989, and if the America's Cup is hosted there. The best travel advice is to become a second Cabrillo and set out to discover what's best about today's San Diego.

INSIDERS' TIPS

For up-to-date information on events in downtown San Diego, contact the 24-hour Event Line at 619-239-9696. Additionally, there is an arts hot line at 619-234-2787. For accommodation suggestions, contact the International Information Center at 619-236-1212 or visit the helpful agency in Horton Plaza.

INSIDERS' INFORMATION FOR SAN DIEGO COUNTY

San Diego
(area code 619)
Where to Stay
Hotel del Coronado ♛ ♛ ♛ ♛

1500 Orange Ave., Coronado 92118; tel. 435-6611
Single room, double occupancy: $105–$425
A little over a century ago, railroad tycoon Elisha Babcock wanted to build a hotel that would be the "talk of the Western World." Steeped in tradition, the rambling, white, Victorian landmark is known all over the globe. The Del sits on an incline overlooking the Pacific on the Coronado peninsula. Fascinating castlelike architecture, tranquil setting. Of the original 5-story building and 2 newer sections, the older portion of the hotel has the most character. The Prince of Wales(♛ ♛) offers haute cuisine; the Ocean Terrace(♛ ♛ ♛ ♛ ♛) is an outdoor eatery with a tremendous view.

San Diego Marriott ♛ ♛ ♛ ♛

333 W. Harbor Dr., San Diego 92101; tel. 234-1500
Single room, double occupancy: $160
Nicely located high rise with a lot of panache, this hotel caters to the business traveler. Extensive fitness facilities, good restaurants. Tennis, swimming pool.

Sheraton Grand on Harbor Island ♛ ♛ ♛ ♛

1590 Harbor Island Dr., San Diego 92101; tel. 291-6400
Single room, double occupancy: $145
All rooms at this 12-story, 350-room hotel have a view. Many special features like butler service for the suites on the top 2 floors. Swimming pool, Jacuzzi, sauna, gym, bike rentals, running paths. Great place for families.

U.S. Grant Hotel ♛ ♛ ♛ ♛

326 Broadway, San Diego 92101; tel. 232-3121
Single room, double occupancy: $135
Perfectly located in the newly emerging downtown, this midsize hotel (283 rooms) has a big hotel's personality and plenty of charm. On the National Register of Historic Places and across the street from fun-filled Horton

Plaza. Helpful concierge service, plus concierge floors. Fitness facilities, larger rooms. Many suites have Jacuzzis. The Grant Grill(♕ ♕ ♕ ♕ ♕) is a great place for a power lunch.

La Valencia ♕ ♕ ♕ ♕

1132 Prospect Ave., La Jolla 92037; tel. 454-0771

Single room, double occupancy: $118

This large, pink, Spanish-style hotel overlooking the La Jolla Bay was built in 1926 and has retained its graceful ambience to this day. Pool, sauna, Jacuzzi. 100 rooms. The Whaling Bar(♕ ♕ ♕ ♕) is popular with the locals.

Horton Grand ♕ ♕ ♕

311 Island Ave., San Diego 92101; tel. 544-1886

Single room, double occupancy: $106

Tucked into the lower Gaslamp Quarter, the 110 rooms in this quaint hotel are warm and welcoming, each with its own fireplace. To learn of your experiences in the hotel, and to tell you about what others have experienced, there is a diary in each room to read and to fill out. A delightful place to stay.

Sheraton Harbor Island East ♕ ♕ ♕

1380 Harbor Island Dr., San Diego 92101; tel. 291-2900

Single room, double occupancy: $140

This hotel is 12 stories high and has its own boat marina. 712 rooms. Good bay views. Comfortable, near the airport. Two pools, Jacuzzi, children's pool, sauna, tennis courts, game room.

The Westgate ♕ ♕ ♕

1055 Second Ave., San Diego 92101; tel. 238-1818

Single room, double occupancy: $124–$144

This grand dame is located downtown, with 223 rooms—no two of which are alike. Elegant and stately, with a wonderful 18th-century French lobby. Fine art throughout the property.

Heritage Park Bed and Breakfast Inn ♕

2470 Heritage Park Row, San Diego 92110; tel. 295-7088

Single room, double occupancy: $95

Gray Victorian house with 9 rooms, 6 of which share bathrooms. Turret room, named for its tower, has great views of Old Town and Mission Bay.

Hyatt Islandia on San Diego's Mission Bay♛
1441 Quivira Rd., San Diego 92109; tel. 224-1234
Single room, double occupancy: $100
Setting is what you'd expect to find in San Diego. Accommodations are sleek and spacious; 260 of the 350 rooms are located in a tower with balconies for perfect views of the Pacific, the marina, and the city's skyline. Near the zoo, swimming pool. Complimentary airport transportation. We like the garden rooms the best.

Where to Eat

La Gran Tapa♛♛♛♛♛
611 B St., San Diego; tel. 234-8272
Average dinner: $17
Feast on a selection of 30–40 different tapas choices at this European bistro. Specialities include the gambas al ajillo, which is shrimp with garlic and hot peppers in olive oil. Big and boisterous.

Gustaf Anders♛♛♛♛♛
2182 Avenida de la Playa, La Jolla; tel. 459-4499
Average dinner: $35
The Swedish chef, Ulf Standberg, is another European producing exquisite California cuisine with a classic flair. Sleek setting, contemporary art for sale. Caviar bar. Attentive service. Excellent wine list.

Rainwater's on Kettner♛♛♛♛♛
1202 Kettner Blvd., San Diego; tel. 233-5757
Average dinner: $40
Located in a restored warehouse, this place has been hailed by critics as "San Diego's number-one steak house," but it's much more—great Maine lobster and veal, plus an oyster and caviar bar. Exhibition kitchen, wine room.

Dinis-by-the-Sea♛♛♛♛
3290 Carlsbad Blvd., Carlsbad; tel. 434-6000
Average dinner: $17
Known for fresh abalone and Mexican specialties. Panoramic views of the ocean. Soothing, comfortable, and always fun.

Top o' the Cove ♛ ♛ ♛ ♛
1216 Prospect St., La Jolla; tel. 454-7779
Average dinner: $35
Ask for a front window seat at this Continental, nouvelle restaurant. The highlight of your meal will probably be dessert. Ask to try the chocolate box.

Celadon ♛ ♛ ♛
3628 Fifth Ave., San Diego; tel. 295-8800
Average dinner: $15
Thai cuisine served in an exquisite, pink dining room. Taste the Pad Talay or Chicken Kaprao.

Papagayo ♛ ♛ ♛
861 W. Harbor Dr., San Diego; tel. 232-7581
Average dinner: $13
In Seaport Village, elegant dining overlooking the bay. Fresh fish specialties and a large assortment of shrimp preparations.

Piret M Bistro Gallery ♛ ♛ ♛
The Lumberyard, 897 First St., Encinitas; tel. 942-5146
Average dinner: $20
California and French cuisine served in a contemporary, arts-and-crafts-gallery setting. Second, more informal dining room, with first-class gourmet food and fresh flowers, for dining in or taking out.

Piret's ♛ ♛ ♛
8697 Villa La Jolla Dr., La Jolla; tel. 455-7955
Average dinner: $18
Bistro food in a pleasant setting. Prix-fixe, gourmet dinners are popular on Saturdays. Vintage wines, good buys.

The Polo Cafe ♛ ♛ ♛
Rancho Santa Fe Plaza, 3790 Via de la Valle, Del Mar; tel. 259-POLO
Average dinner: $14
Hosted by John Moriarty, this traditional café is a local meeting place. Market-fresh menu, salads and seafood. Open courtyard faces the New Polo Grounds in Rancho Santa Fe. Eat indoors or out. California wines and champagnes.

Fallbrook Grocery Café ♕ ♕
321 Alvarado St., Fallbrook; tel. 723-0588
Average dinner: $15
Out-of-the-way country café nestled in the heart of the green and rural avocado country. French-style country cooking, fresh and local ingredients. Culbertson champagne (that's the owner's winery just up the hill), by the glass, or by the bottle.

Fat City ♕ ♕
2137 Pacific Highway; tel. 232-0686
Average dinner: $22
Unique eatery uses bowling balls as flower vases and stacks of tennis and Ping-Pong balls as dividers. Always lively, there are even neon murals on the walls. But, the ambience overshadows the Continental cuisine, which is only mediocre.

Kansas City Barbecue ♕
610 W. Market St.; tel. 231-9680
Average dinner: $7
Not the greatest food, but a place where the locals hang out. Used as a location for the film *Top Gun.*

Theaters

Gaslamp Quarter Theater Company, 444 4th Ave.; tel. 234-9583. What once was a 1920s dance hall is now home to this 96-seat, nonprofit theater producing original, young playwrights' works. Second 250-seat theater houses classic and contemporary plays as well as musicals.

La Jolla Playhouse, P.O. Box 12039, La Jolla 92037, the corner of North Torrey Pines and La Jolla Village on the U.C.S.D. campus; tel. 534-3960. Legit theater that's bold and innovative. Classics with a twist. Operating during summer months and drawing big-name Hollywood and Broadway talent.

San Diego Repertory Theater, 1620 Sixth Ave., San Diego; tel. 235-8025. Admirable quality theater troupe gives care to productions.

San Diego State Open Air Theater, College Ave., San Diego; tel. 265-6947. Primarily, rock performance theater, but some classics and some comedies from April through October.

Simon Edison Centre (Old Globe Theater, Cassius Carter Center Stage, Old Globe Festival Stage), Balboa Park, San Diego; tel. 239-2255. More than 50 years of fine presentations of the classics and Shakespeare. In the winter, contemporary new works are presented.

Nightlife

Comedy Store, 916 Pearl St., San Diego; tel. 456-9176. Many well-known comedians appear here as well as top local artists. Sunday is amateur night—so come prepared.

Confetti, 5373 Mission Center Rd., Mission Valley; tel. 291-8635. There's always a party at this bilevel night spot with confetti thrown on the floor and streamers flown through the air. 3 bars, 2 dance floors, top-40 tunes. Cover charge.

Corvette Café, 3946 Fifth Ave., Hillcrest; tel. 542-1001. Take a trip back into the fifties and sixties when you visit this lively night spot. There's even a '59 Corvette in the place for all of you car buffs. Full bar.

Earthquake Café, Mission Center Road at Mission Center Court, Mission Valley; tel. 297-3603. What's shakin' is the motto here at this fifties diner with an eighties flair. All prices are based on the Richter scale. Full bar, very happening.

Elario's, 7955 La Jolla Shores Dr., La Jolla; tel. 459-0541. Sit back and watch the waves roll up to the shoreline and listen to the sultry, jazz sounds performed by local musicians.

Halcyon, 4258 W. Point Loma Blvd., Point Loma; tel. 225-9559. Dance to top-40 tunes on the weekends in this large, noisy disco.

Improv, 832 Garnet Ave., Pacific Beach; tel. 483-4520. Comedy showcase in cabaret setting.

Mandolin Wind, 380 University Ave., Hillcrest; tel. 297-3017. Home of rhythm and blues. Local bands like King Biscuit Blues Band entertain during the week.

Spirit, 1130 Buenos Ave., Bay Park; tel. 276-3993. Experimental club for live new-wave and rock bands.

Shopping

Horton Plaza, 1st Ave. and Broadway, San Diego. You might need a guide to get around this enormous postmodern mall with 132 shops (4 of which are major department stores), 35 restaurants, 7 movie theaters and one legit. Minstrels and jugglers stroll around the mall to entertain those who are just window-shopping.

If you're actually looking to buy, of particular interest to the vacationer is Le Travel Store with a full travel agency, bookstore, and many terrific compact travel items.

Kite Country has all kinds of kites costing from a couple of bucks to a couple of thousand dollars.

Dudenhoeffer is a family owned jewelry shop in the business for more than a century.

Chocolate Carousel makes chocolate business logos, hand-made candies, and European truffles.

For more information on Horton Plaza, call 239-8180.

Seaport Village, West Harbor Dr. at Kettner Blvd., San Diego. This remake of a small fishing village is crammed with shops that carry just about everything.

Apple Box Wooden Toys sells playthings that can be personalized.

Bazaar del Mundo is filled with Mexican crafts and knickknacks.

Fascination is a fun shop stuffed with surprises.

For more information on Seaport Village, call 235-4013.

Useful Telephone Numbers

911—Emergency dialing to reach police, fire and rescue, highway patrol, and ambulance
Arts and Crafts Council Calendar: 619-465-6833
California State Automobile Association (AAA): 619-560-1811
La Jolla Town Council: 619-454-1444
Poison Control: 619-294-6000
Recorded Information on Attractions: 619-239-9696
San Diego Visitor and Convention Bureau: 619-232-3101
Traveler's Aid: 619-232-7991
Visitor Information: 619-236-1212
Western Union: 619-232-5164

PALM SPRINGS, THE DESERT RESORT COMMUNITIES, AND THE INLAND EMPIRE

Not long ago, if you heard the words "mystical, magical oasis," one name would spring to mind: Palm Springs. But in recent years a whole string of sister resorts—places like Rancho Mirage, Palm Desert, and Indian Wells—have grown up in southern California's Colorado Desert, each one intent upon earning the same title. Now known as Greater Palm Springs, the area stretches east from Palm Springs for 20 miles along Highway 111 through the Coachella Valley (between the San Jacinto and San Bernadino mountain ranges), ending in Indio and La Quinta (home of the PGA West).

In fact, the competition for attention begins even before you hit Palm Springs. A bit more than a half-hour east of Los Angeles, off Interstate 10, you encounter a cluster of little cities known as the Inland Empire, each one winking in its own unique way, beckoning its distinctive attractions.

The best way to explore—and enjoy—the desert and inland "empires" is to select a central base. Plot day trips from there, or better still, devise a series of weekends based on different activities: golf in Palm Desert perhaps, or horseback riding in the Indian Canyons in Palm Springs, even water sports and hiking at Lake Arrowhead. The area's greatest attraction—a warm, dry climate—makes Greater Palm Springs a tempting destination for all sorts of health buffs and adventure-seekers.

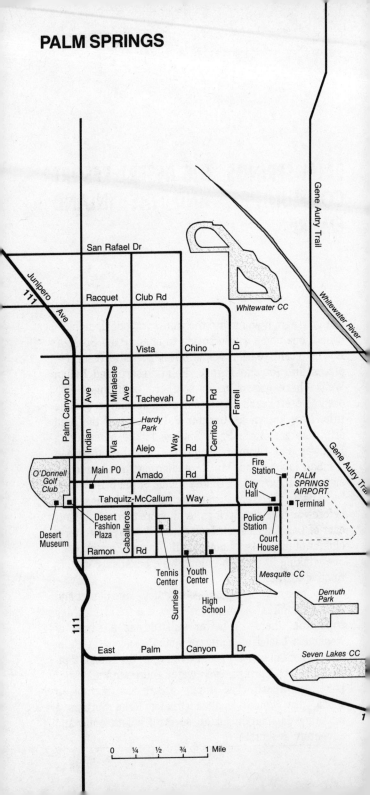
PALM SPRINGS

PALM SPRINGS

Palm Springs itself, 110 miles east of Los Angeles, is still the best-known resort in the area—and the most popular. Once upon a time Palm Springs was so exclusive few ordinary mortals were even sure exactly where it was. This was the most idealized small town in America, the place movie stars went to be just ordinary people, where Johnny Weissmuller practiced his strokes in the pool (at the Hotel El Mirador), Spencer Tracy played chess, and Clark Gable played golf. It was here in Palm Springs that Greta Garbo could truly be alone. While movie stars, princes, and presidents still frolic in Palm Springs in large numbers, what was once a little village has grown into a sophisticated resort with Beverly Hills–style shopping and hotels for everyone.

PERILS & PITFALLS

Desert heat is deceptive and even dark-skinned first-timers should listen to locals who warn about sunburn. A strong sun block is absolutely necessary to prevent blisters and burns.

There are signs of change everywhere in Palm Springs. New hotels are under construction, there are better restaurants, and all around there's a sincere effort to anticipate the needs of a wider range of visitors. One major renovation is an expensive update of the health facilities at the Spa Hotel, the place that first made Palm Springs famous.

PERILS & PITFALLS

Stay clear of Palm Springs during Easter weekend and college spring breaks, when students flock here like Monarch butterflies to Pacific Grove. Restaurants, theaters, and hotels are crammed with partying students and the streets are bumper-to-bumper teenagers.

One of the best ways to explore the desert cities is to take an organized tour available through many of the local companies. A standard, half-day bus tour will give you the lay of the land as well as point out many movie stars' homes. An even more thrilling way to see the sights is by hot-air balloon. Several companies operate out of Palm Springs, Palm Desert, Rancho Mirage, and Thermal. Flights range from a simple soar to an extravagant champagne picnic. If you like your flying motorized, there are ultralight sight-seeing flights and helicopter tours, too.

PERILS & PITFALLS

Valet parking is the rule rather than the exception, so make sure you have a pocketful of dollar bills when you step out at night for dinner or entertainment. Don't count on parking the car yourself—spots are rare.

Unlike the other desert resort cities, Palm Springs is a walking town. A stroll up Palm Canyon Drive—the main drag—is still a number-one pastime. The street is gently illuminated by lights recessed in palm trees that stretch from one end of town to the other. Tucked between chic boutiques, you'll find an assortment of art galleries and patio restaurants—the perfect spots for people-watching. The city's two major shopping centers, The Desert Fashion Plaza♕♕♕♕ and The Courtyard♕♕, are a few blocks from each other. Both feature such internationally recognized names as Yves Saint Laurent, Rodier, and Laura Ashley.

PERILS & PITFALLS

From December through March temperatures may be balmy during the day, but bring something warm for evening, when the mercury has been known to drop below zero. At gala balls and social events during "the season," fur coats are as common here as they are in New York.

Just behind the Desert Fashion Plaza is the Palm Springs Desert Museum♕♕♕♕, an architectural showpiece tucked into the mountain. The museum's permanent collection includes paintings, drawings, graphic arts, and photography. The Denney Western American Art Wing contains some of the finest art of the American West. The Annenberg Art Wing presents major trends in contemporary art, emphasizing the works of California and Southwestern artists. The museum's natural science section focuses on the desert environment and an Indian collection of weaving, baskets, pottery, and jewelry. The small—but almost perfect—Annenberg Theater in the museum hosts internationally known performing artists throughout the winter season.

PERILS & PITFALLS

Throughout high season in the desert, dinner reservations are an absolute must, particularly when weekenders from Los Angeles flock to town. Without a reservation, even some out-of-the-way spots will channel you into the bar for a two-hour wait.

For history buffs, Miss Cornelia White's House♛, built of railroad ties in 1894, now sits on the Village Green at 223 South Palm Canyon Drive amid a collection of pioneer artifacts. Cornelia was one of the three pioneering White sisters who came to the desert in 1912. Next door, the McCallum Adobe♛, once the home of the John Guthrie McCallum family, now contains a major portion of the Palm Springs Historical Society collection.

PERILS & PITFALLS

Dress warmly if you take the aerial tramway in winter—that means hats and gloves! The temperature is always much lower in the mountains than it is at sea level.

The Palm Springs Aerial Tramway♛♛♛♛♛, 15 minutes from downtown Palm Springs, puts visitors in touch with snow and a refreshing pine forest year-round—in case you get homesick. It also provides a cooling break from the saunalike summer of the desert floor below. The tramway, the world's largest, double-reversible, passenger-carrying vehicle of its kind, takes visitors through five climatic zones up some 12,800 feet of the steepest slopes of any mountain in North America. In winter, cross-country skis are available for rent. In summer, campers, hikers, nature lovers, and photographers hike through the wilderness of Mt. San Jacinto State Park, which is usually 40 degrees cooler than the desert floor below. Special events, such as the annual Moosehead Championship Sled Dog Races held each year in January, are scheduled throughout the year.

THE DESERT RESORT COMMUNITIES

The Indian Canyons ♛ ♛ ♛ ♛ provide another lush get-away from the desert. You can reach the canyons by a toll road at the end of South Palm Canyon Drive, 5 miles south of Palm Springs. Take a picnic lunch into Palm Canyon—a 15-mile-long gorge—where you can sit under native Washingtonia filifera palms. Andreas Canyon, with its magnificent fan palms and Cahuilla rock art, is best explored on horseback, and Murray Canyon, home to a band of renegade horses, also has the spectacular Tahquitz waterfall, though keep in mind that entry to this canyon is by special permit only.

For cactophiles and other plant lovers, the Moorten Botanical Garden ♛ ♛, at 1701 South Palm Canyon Drive, is on the way to the Indian Canyons. Here, more than 2,000 varieties of cacti and desert birds are on exhibit.

PERILS & PITFALLS

Never take off for overnight camping into the San Jacinto Wilderness area without alerting park rangers stationed at the top of the aerial tramway. The park is vast and confusing, and even the most intrepid hikers can lose their way. The rangers also have maps of the area for day hikers.

At the Living Desert Reserve ♛ ♛ ♛ ♛, just off Highway 111 in Palm Desert, you can walk through 8 different desert environments in a 1,200-acre park full of indigenous plants and animals. In addition to a walk-through aviary, rare endangered species, such as the slenderhorn gazelle, Arabian oryx, gila monster, and other huge birds of prey, call this place home.

Joshua Tree National Monument ♛ ♛ ♛ ♛, 50 miles

northeast of Palm Springs, is an unforgettable day trip for photographers and nature lovers. The monument covers more than 870 square miles of high desert, rich with distinctive wildlife, massive rock formations, and panoramic views of the desert. Children love the Jumbo Rocks, a bizarre collection of boulders (one is actually a giant skull) that resemble something from the *Land Of the Giants*. For photographers, sunset in the Joshua tree forest is a must.

> ## PERILS & PITFALLS
>
> If you choose to explore the desert during the summer months, make sure you advise someone staying behind of your plans, and take along proper headgear and ample water. Temperatures can soar to 120 degrees during the day, bringing on serious dehydration, even among robust hikers.

You probably never thought of surfing in the desert, but the Oasis Water Resort ♛ ♛ ♛, 1500 Gene Autry Trail, is to water parks what Maxim's is to dining—and the perfect relief from desert heat. In addition to an immense wave pool for surfers, there's a lushly landscaped, white-water river for tubing, family flumes, and freefall and tube slides. This Rolls-Royce of water fun also features a full spa and gymnasium, excellent spa dining, and even a private "beach," complete with cabanas and telephones.

While we're on the subject of unlikely desert attractions, snowbirds pining for the north can don ice skates and dream of Chicago at the Ice Capades Chalet ♛ in the Palm Desert Town Center. The ice rink features a full-time disc jockey and offers group classes for all ages. Occasionally an Ice Capades star joins the circle of skaters, too.

Fishing is another activity we don't easily associate with the desert, but Rainbow Ranch ♛ ♛, 12 miles northwest of Palm Springs in Whitewater Canyon, guarantees trout for supper for a small admission charge. You can buy bait and rent tackle, but the bonus is that the fish are cleaned for you. There are even facilities for grilling freshly caught trout.

Baseball fans can catch the California Angels ♛ ♛ ♛ in spring training and preseason exhibition games during March and April at Angel Stadium in Palm Springs. The Class-A, farm affiliate of the team uses the stadium as home base for its entire season.

Golf still tops the list of activities in the desert. At last count the total number of golf courses in the valley was over 100. Little wonder the area is called "the winter golf capital of the world." Many courses are private, but some of these allow members of other accredited country clubs playing privileges. The ultimate challenge course is the PGA West–TPC Stadium Course ♛ ♛ ♛ ♛ ♛ in La Quinta. This is also the site of the Skins Game and the 1987 Bob Hope Chrysler Classic. The Tournament Player's Course, an undulating links-type course similar to its Scotch cousin, has been called "the toughest course in the world from the back tees."

INSIDERS' TIPS

While everyone thinks of the desert as a winter resort, the best weather often falls in October and April when crowds are lighter. While temperatures can hit 110 degrees and above in the summer, the air is extremely dry and not enervating. Summer prices fall to rock bottom. Even top hotel rooms are available for $50 or less. Bonus during these hot days: Many restaurants now have outdoor air-conditioning!

At one time, the desert social season began with the Bob Hope Desert Classic in January and ended in April, but that's no longer so. More and more, the desert cities are year-round resorts, if the staggering list of events they host—tournaments, parades, balls, circuses, festivals, and races—is any indication. The Greater Palm Springs Convention and Visitors Bureau publishes a calendar of events with details and dates for visitors who want to participate. A great many celebrities usually appear at the benefit events throughout the year. In addition to golf and tennis tournaments, there are balloon, road, and cross-country-ski races; jazz and date festivals, Indian powwows, and the Concours d'Elégance, an auto race.

The annual Date Festival♛♛♛, staged each February in Indio, is one of America's most unusual expositions. It honors, what else, the date. Why? Between 70 and 90 percent of the world's supply is produced nearby in the Coachella Valley. The festival includes an Arabian Nights pageant, a horse show, and ostrich and camel races.

INSIDERS' TIPS

If you take in the Indio Date Festival, don't go home without a package of Medjool dates. These plump, melt-in-your-mouth delicacies are the emperors of the date world and bear no resemblance at all to anything found in your local supermarket.

THE INLAND EMPIRE

If any area in southern California has suffered an image problem, it's this collection of 66 communities known as the "Inland Empire." It used to be that stressed-out Angelenos would jump in their cars and drive nonstop for 2 hours for a weekend of relaxation in the desert, unaware of the mountain getaways and other delights that lay unexplored on either side of them. But the charms of this area—now under the Inland Empire umbrella—are being discovered by more and more people all the time.

RIVERSIDE

As the largest city in the area, Riverside has often been overlooked, considered merely an industrial center. But you may find it lives up to its slogan, "Riverside . . . a nice surprise!" The city first jumped into prominence in 1873 when a resident named Eliza Tibbets planted two small Washington navel orange trees, thereby launching California's citrus industry. The navel orange trees, brought by missionaries from Brazil, were unique because they produced oranges without seeds. Of the two original trees, one known as the Parent Navel

Orange ♛ still remains in a small park across the street from the Tibbets homestead at Magnolia and Arlington avenues.

Once the center of the lucrative citrus industry, Riverside was left a legacy of fine Spanish mission-type buildings, including the Mission Inn Garden Hotel ♛ ♛ ♛ ♛, now a state historical monument and landmark. The inn is undergoing a multimillion-dollar renovation intended to revive it as a world-class hotel— its antique windows, bells, and clocks in place, and all its turrets, towers, and enchantment intact. It's scheduled to reopen in mid-1988.

The inn began as a 12-room adobe and grew over 65 years into a veritable castle, covering an entire city block. Its guest register has included crowned heads of Europe, artists, writers, movie stars, and even U.S. presidents. Richard and Pat Nixon married in the presidential suite, and Ronald and Nancy Reagan honeymooned here. Take a walking tour of the area to see other fine examples of Spanish mission architecture. Don't miss the Riverside Art Center and many of the city's churches.

Riverside's numerous museums specialize in local history and Victoriana. Check out the March Field Museum ♛ ♛ ♛ on the March Air Force Base, where 50 years of vintage aircraft, World War I memorabilia, uniforms, and photographs are displayed. The Botanical Gardens ♛ ♛ on the campus of the University of California, Riverside has some 2,000 species of plants on 37 acres of rolling terrain.

LAKE ARROWHEAD

The county calls it "our Switzerland," and there *is* a strong smack of the Alps in this year-round mountain retreat. In winter, the 35 downhill runs at Snow Valley ♛ ♛ ♛, 20 miles up the hill from Lake Arrowhead, offer skiers the largest such area in southern California. Cross-country skiing is popular at Green Valley Lake. In Lake Arrowhead, ice skaters can whirl and spin at the Blue Jay Ice Castle ♛ ♛ ♛, an Olympic-size, indoor/outdoor rink, open year-round. Santa's Village in Skyforest—complete with Mrs. Claus, the Lollipop Lady, elves, pixies, amusement rides, and a petting zoo with reindeer—is a favorite among children.

In summer, Lake Arrowhead becomes a lake resort where waterskiing, regattas, sailing, and fishing compete for attention with wilderness adventure. There are self-guided walks through Heap's Peak Arboretum ♛ ♛ to see mountain plants, animals, and a 20-acre National Children's Forest ♛ ♛. The Forest Service has also mapped out dozens of hiking trails. A good way to get the feel of the lake and its history is on a cruise aboard the *Arrowhead Queen*, a 60-passenger paddle wheeler that also hosts private parties.

BIG BEAR

Just southeast of Arrowhead lies another mountain resort that combines the charm of Vail with the magnificence of Lake Geneva. Big Bear Lake ♛ ♛ ♛, a lively alpine community just 2 hours from Los Angeles, is a winter and summer playground in the clouds. At 7,000 feet, this place provides the perfect weekend high for the smog-breathing, traffic-crazed city dwellers who crave crystal-clean air, mouthwatering international cuisine, and enough sports and recreational activities to satisfy even the most hyperathletic vacationer.

If you've heard anything about Big Bear at all, it probably had to do with the spectacular winter ski scene. And understandably so! In addition to nearby Snow Forest and Goldmine, Snow Summit, located in the heart of Big Bear, is the largest ski resort in southern California. With 10 chair lifts, 3 lodges, and stadium lights that ignite the mountain for night skiing, who needs Mammoth? And with the best artificial snowmaking facilities in the state, you'll find plenty of sun-worshipping ski bucks and snow bunnies swooshing down the slopes in shorts clear into spring. If you're not that proficient on skis, however, there are other ways you can get around Big Bear. Vacationers can rent everything from snowmobiles, to horses, mountain bikes, small fishing boats, or romantic horse-drawn carriages that wind through downtown and along the lake. But however you choose to scoot around in this mountain paradise, be sure to pack a camera with lots of film. You never know when you might spot one of the many bald eagles, bear, deer, or other wildlife indigenous to the area.

During the summer months, Big Bear goes through a mild transformation. Snow skiers become water-skiers, lumberjacks become tennis pros, and trout and bass become hungry! Thrill seekers can explore the placid waters of Big Bear Lake via jet skis, aerial tours offered at Big Bear's Municipal Airport, or even by parasail. But if you'd rather enjoy a view with both feet on the ground, the Big Bear Solar Observatory ♔ ♔ ♔, the largest solar observatory in the world, offers tours to the general public. And if that's not enough, every August the great gold rush is celebrated during a big shindig called Old Miners Days ♔ ♔. Among the events in this celebration is a 43-mile, no-holds-barred burro race! But if riding a jackass doesn't interest you, then visit Big Bear in the fall when the annual Bavarian Oktoberfest ♔ ♔ turns this mountain into a huge alpine celebration with several other species of party animals.

PERILS & PITFALLS

Be careful when making reservations to stay up here. Many of the roadside motels are overpriced and look much better from the outside than they do on the inside. Contact the Chamber of Commerce at 714-866-6190 for tips on the availability of the best hotels. Also, if you visit Big Bear during the winter, don't plan on arriving or departing from the mountain at night. Cold evening temperatures are known to cause slick, icy road conditions.

REDLANDS

Once a favorite health resort, Redlands ♔ ♔ ♔ ♔ gets its name from the iron-streaked soil in the area. College students and those interested in California history are drawn here to see the wealth of turn-of-the-century Victorian homes. The local chamber of commerce publishes a driving guide to many of them. The San Bernardino County Museum♛♛♛, just off Interstate 10, has the world's largest bird-egg and local bird-life collection. The Lincoln Shrine♛♛♛♛, the most comprehensive collection of Lincoln memorabilia in the country, contains 100,000 volumes, 46,000 documents, 12,000 pictures, and 2,000 recordings on and about Lincoln and the Civil War.

Special events in Redlands include the Great Y Circus♛♛, the oldest community circus in the world, and the annual Chili Cook-Off/Fireman's Muster♛♛♛ in the spring, which attracts thousands of firemen and spectators from all over the state. The Memorial Weekend Bicycle Classic♛♛ draws riders from all over the world.

TEMECULA

One of the notable events in this community's history was a visit in 1879 by Helen Hunt Jackson that inspired her to write her famous romantic novel *Ramona*. Performed as a play, it's now a traditional annual event♛♛♛ and includes a massive cast. Temecula, 40 miles south of Riverside on Interstate 15, was a strategic point along the old Butterfield Overland Stage route. Because of this, the town has figured in many historical events. It remains a good example of a turn-of-the-century Western American town; much of its story is told in the Old Town Temecula Museum♛ through original documents, photographs, and other artifacts of the Old West.

The area is also thriving wine country. There are tours, tastings, and lectures available at most of the 13 vineyards and wineries in the area. During the fall crush, local wineries invite visitors to watch the winemaking process as well as taste some of the previous vintages. White wines are the specialty—Zinfandels, Rieslings, and Sauvignon Blancs—but many also produce a good Cabernet Sauvignon. Some wineries are only open for tasting on weekends so call ahead for hours.

VICTOR VALLEY

This little-known collection of high-desert communities, 100 miles northeast of Los Angeles, is at the cross-roads of southern California's major cities. Until recently, the desert beauty of these towns was explored by few, even though its location on the southeastern edge of the Mojave Desert gives the area a choice climate and lots of Joshua trees—hallmarks of high-desert terrain. The Roy Rogers–Dale Evans Museum ♛ in Victorville contains souvenirs from the stars, models of western vehicles, a large gun collection and, yes, a stuffed Trigger, the smartest horse ever to appear on celluloid. At Calico Ghost Town ♛ ♛ in Yermo, you can roam the tunnels of Maggie's Mine, climb aboard a railroad car, or wander along wooden sidewalks to catch a glimpse of the silver mining town as it was in its heyday.

CLAREMONT

Often called "the city of trees and Ph.D.s," Claremont ♛ ♛ ♛ is 30 miles east of Los Angeles at the foothills of the San Gabriel Mountains. The town almost looks as though it belongs in New England because of its tree-arbored streets, ivy-covered college campus, and old Victorian homes. Walking tours are popular here; detailed guides are available for the village, the colleges, and Memorial Park. The Raymond M. Alf Museum ♛ ♛, devoted to geology, has the largest and most diverse display of fossil footprints in the United States. The Kenneth G. Fiske Museum ♛ ♛ has one of the most comprehensive collections of rare historical and ethnic musical instruments in the West, and the Rancho Santa Ana Botanic Gardens ♛ ♛ ♛, one of the top 8 botanical collections in the United States, has 83 acres devoted entirely to native California plants.

GLEN IVY HOT SPRINGS

Just an hour out of Los Angeles, Glen Ivy ♛ ♛ ♛ ♛ is nestled, just as its name implies, in a secluded glen, completely removed from urban stresses. Glen Ivy Hot Springs has the only red-clay mud bath in southern California. Pools, baths, whirlpool tubs, and spas are filled with soothing mineral water at temperatures that range from 85 to 108 degrees.

OAK GLEN

Year-round, this high-altitude getaway is the place to go for cool temperatures and the best apple pie and cider in southern California. Visitors can watch cider being pressed at apple ranches such as Linda Vista ♛ ♛. Check out the antique and gift shops or relive the area's pioneer days at the Old School House ♛, an authentic, country schoolhouse museum.

PERRIS

Named after a local pioneering railroad engineer, Perris's main attraction is the State Recreation Area where boating, camping, fishing, swimming, windsurfing, and jet- and waterskiing—or any other water sport—is possible. The Orange Empire Railway Museum ♛ ♛ ♛ is a must for train buffs.

INSIDERS' INFORMATION FOR PALM SPRINGS AND AREA

**Inland Empire, Big Bear
(area code 714)**
Where to Stay
Knickerbocker Mansion ♛ ♛ ♛ ♛ ♛
869 S. Knickerbocker Rd., Big Bear 92315; tel. 866-8221
Single room, double occupancy: $80

A large, log-cabin B&B, tucked away in the pines but within walking distance of downtown. Built by Bill Knickerbocker in 1920 with just an ax. Warm setting, friendly hosts. 10 rooms.

Big Bear Inn ♛ ♛ ♛

42200 Moonridge Rd., Big Bear 92315; tel. 800-BEAR-INN

Single room, double occupancy: $70

Large Swiss chalet near the base of Snow Summit. Slightly overdecorated, but terrific service, good food, and nightly entertainment. Pool, aerobics room, juice bar, bakery. 80 rooms.

Where to Eat

George and Sigi's ♛ ♛ ♛ ♛

41456 Big Bear Blvd., Big Bear; tel. 585-8640

Average dinner: $20

Gingerbread house with friendly waitresses, serving hefty portions of rich, authentic German fare. Huge homemade cakes for dessert.

The Iron Squirrel ♛ ♛ ♛ ♛

646 Pine Knott Blvd., Big Bear; tel. 866-9121

Average dinner: $21

Excellent French restaurant with early American atmosphere. Food rivals big city eateries, and the wine list is more than adequate.

Palm Springs and Desert Resorts (area code 619)

Where to Stay

Grand Champions Resort ♛ ♛ ♛ ♛ ♛

44-600 Indian Wells Lane, Indian Wells 92210; tel. 341-1000

Single room, double occupancy: $125–$175

A desert hotel done in the grand European style. Private butler service, 22 pools and spas, health and fitness center, sauna, steam baths, 12 lighted tennis courts, and two 18-hole golf courses. The Jasmine Restaurant (♛ ♛ ♛ ♛) has a California-cuisine menu designed by Los Angeles superchef Wolfgang Puck.

Marriott Desert Springs ♛ ♛ ♛ ♛ ♛
74-855 Country Club Dr., Palm Desert 92262; tel. 341-2211
Single rooms, double occupancy: $210–$270
Marriott's flagship hotel; the desert's Venice, with 23 acres of lakes and gondolas to take visitors to their rooms. 18-hole golf course, world-class health spa, a beach by a freshwater lake. 892 rooms.

Maxim's de Paris Suite Hotel ♛ ♛ ♛ ♛ ♛
285 N. Palm Canyon Dr., Palm Springs 92262; tel. 322-9000
Single room, double occupancy: $125 and up
Designed by Pierre Cardin, this 194-suite hotel brings 19th-century ambience with 20th-century comfort to downtown Palm Springs. Stunning 6-story atrium lobby blends hotel into the Desert Fashion Plaza. Formal dining room (♛ ♛ ♛ ♛) with superb wine cellar.

La Quinta Hotel ♛ ♛ ♛ ♛ ♛
Eisenhower Dr. & 50th Ave., La Quinta 92253; tel. 564-4111
Single room, double occupancy: $80–$100
Originally opened in 1926, these Spanish-style cottages on 26 acres are special. Set among olive groves and date palms, La Quinta was a favorite retreat for the stars of Hollywood's Golden Era—and still draws quite a few celebrities today. 38 holes of championship golf, 11 lit tennis courts.

Marriott's Rancho Las Palmas Resort ♛ ♛ ♛ ♛
41-000 Bob Hope Dr.; tel. 568-2727 or 800-228-9290
Single room, double occupancy: $210–$225
California, mission-style architecture in lush lake setting. Lots of sports activities at this resort: 25 all-weather tennis courts, 27 holes of golf, 2 hydrotherapy pools. 456 rooms. Three restaurants including Cabrillo (♛ ♛ ♛) with a touch of Spanish flair.

The Palm Springs Marquis ♛ ♛ ♛ ♛
150 S. Indian Ave., Palm Springs 92262; tel. 322-2121
Single room, double occupancy: $120–$140
Luxury hotel within steps of shopping and restaurants. Some fireplaces, complete kitchens. Al Fresco restaurant (♛ ♛ ♛ ♛) serves northern Italian cuisine. Poolside dining and bar.

INSIDERS' TIPS

During the height of summer, when temperatures soar upwards to 115 degrees, rooms in the desert go for next to nothing. So if you're inclined, check in at a fraction of the price you'll pay during high season—then quickly jump into your swimsuit and spend the day keeping cool in your hotel pool.

The Spa Hotel and Mineral Springs ♛ ♛ ♛ ♛
100 N. Indian Ave., Palm Springs 92263; tel. 325-1461
Single room, double occupancy: $95
An original, Indian hot-water spa in the heart of Palm Springs. Now a deluxe resort with 230 rooms, all with private balconies. The total spa experience with eucalyptus steam and Roman tubs, beauty salon, one freshwater and two mineral-spring outdoor pools. Rennick's (♛ ♛ ♛ ♛) serves good French cuisine.

Desert Princess ♛ ♛ ♛
Vista Chino at Landau, Palm Springs 92263; tel. 322-7000
Single room, double occupancy: $150–$180
A country-club setting, offering full resort amenities: 18-hole, championship golf course, racquetball courts, pool, 10 tennis courts, hydrotherapy pools, men's and women's salons. 300 pleasantly decorated rooms.

Ingleside Inn ♛ ♛ ♛
200 W. Ramon Rd., Palm Springs 92262; tel. 325-0046
Single room, double occupancy: $95 and up
A favorite getaway spot for the famous (and not so famous), tucked behind a high wall within walking distance of shops and restaurants. Melvyn's restaurant (♛ ♛ ♛ ♛) is a big favorite with celebrities. Each room has a distinctive decor.

La Mancha Private Club and Villas ♛ ♛ ♛
444 Avenida Caballeros, Palm Springs 92262; tel. 323-1773
Single room, double occupancy: $127–$190
A Mediterranean-style resort within walking distance of Palm Canyon Drive with lots of extras like large-screen televisions, VCRs, and lots of movies to view. Complimentary use of Chrysler LeBaron convertibles. A good number of the 54 accommodations are actually

tile-floored villas with their own pools, Jacuzzis and/or tennis courts that look as if they belong on the European Riviera.

The Plaza Resort and Racquet Club♛♛♛
400 E. Tahquitz Way, Palm Springs 92262; tel. 320-6868
Single room, double occupancy: $135–$155
Conveniently located steps away from shopping, this relaxing resort offers a giant pool, and 4 restaurants, including the award-winning Tapestry Room (♛♛♛♛) preparing fine gourmet cuisine.

Two Bunch Palms♛♛♛
67425 Two Bunch Palms Trail, Desert Hot Springs; tel. 329-8791
Single room, double occupancy: $115 and up
Legend has it that this place was once owned by Al Capone as a secret hideaway. We don't know if that's true but we do think this is the perfect place to hide. It is a big favorite with the film crowd. A hot-water pool resembles a lagoon from a Dorothy Lamour film. No frills like room service or porters.

Villa Royale♛♛
1620 Indian Trail, Palm Springs; tel. 327-2314
Single room, double occupancy: $65–$95
Owners are passionate travelers and have decorated each of the 30 units in the motif of a different country. Some suites have fireplaces, and all are warm and friendly. Continental breakfast.

Where to Eat

Ristorante Mamma Gina♛♛♛♛
73-705 El Paseo, Palm Desert; tel. 568-9898
Average dinner: $28
Excellent northern Italian cuisine made famous at Mamma Gina's of Florence.

Bono♛♛♛
1700 N. Indian Ave., Palm Springs; tel. 322-6200
Average dinner: $31
Singer Sonny Bono may not carry the best tune, but he does know how to cook. Popular southern Italian dishes. Local hot spot.

Las Casuelas Terrazas♕♕♕
222 S. Palm Canyon Dr., Palm Springs; tel. 325-2794
Average dinner: $18
A touch of Mexico with the best people-watching patio
in the desert. Great margaritas.

Eveleen's♕♕♕
664 N. Palm Canyon Dr., Palm Springs; tel. 325-4766
Average dinner: $27
Intimate New Orleans-style eatery with only 12 tables
and a loyal word-of-mouth clientele.

Presette♕♕♕
777 E. Tahquitz Way in The Courtyard, Palm Springs;
tel. 322-1311
Average dinner: $32
Fresh ingredients blended in imaginative ways in the
French/Continental style.

Rennick's♕♕♕
Palm Springs Spa Hotel, 100 N. Indian Ave., Palm
Springs; tel. 325-1461
Average dinner: $25
Excellent spa cuisine attractively presented and a low-
calorie dessert selection that can't be matched.

Le Vallauris♕♕♕
385 W. Tahquitz Way, Palm Springs; tel. 325-5059
Average dinner: $36
Charming patio setting in a French-style home, excellent food—but pricey. Only desert restaurant winner
of Travel/Holiday award.

Lou Calen (The Vineyard)♕♕♕
265 S. Palm Canyon Dr., Palm Springs; tel. 327-1196
Average dinner: $30
Traditional, Provençale cuisine with new entrées daily.

Billy Reed's♕♕
1800 N. Palm Canyon Dr., Palm Springs; tel. 325-1946
Average dinner: $20.50
Always a lineup, but Billy Reed's remains a favorite for
good food at fair prices.

Zorba's ♛ ♛
Las Palmas Shopping Center, 42-434 Bob Hope Dr.,
Rancho Mirage; tel. 340-3066
Average dinner: $20
Warm, family atmosphere, good food, live Greek music
and dancing—belly and otherwise.

Shopping

The Alley, Palm Springs Mall & 180 N. Palm Canyon Dr., Palm Springs. A favorite soup-to-nuts stop for gifts, greeting cards, and just about anything else.

The Courtyard, 777 E. Tahquitz Way, Palm Springs. Features top European names in a collection of boutiques.

Desert Fashion Plaza, 123 N. Palm Canyon Dr., Palm Springs. Elegant shopping complex featuring exclusive boutiques, such as Gucci and Laura Ashley, plus major department stores, such as Saks Fifth Avenue.

Elaine Horwitch Galleries, 1090 N. Palm Canyon Dr., Palm Springs. The biggest of the desert's many, many art galleries.

The Forgotten Woman, in The Courtyard, Palm Springs. Catering to the large lady with very fashionable styles.

Glas von Marion, 191 S. Indian Ave., Palm Springs. The finest selection of Bavarian, lead crystal vases, bowls, glasses, chandeliers, and clocks in the desert.

Loehmann's, 2500 N. Palm Canyon Dr., Palm Springs. Best bargains in quality clothes in the desert.

Manufacturing Furriers Outlet, 120 Tahquitz Way, Palm Springs. Designer furs at discount prices.

Palm Desert Town Center, 72-840 Highway 111, Palm Desert. Biggest shopping area in the desert with 5 major department stores, boutiques, restaurants, theaters, and ice rink.

Roger Dunn Golf Shop, Date Palm & Highway 111, Cathedral City. Desert's largest golf shop.

THE CENTRAL COAST

Whether or not you agree with Ronald Reagan's politics, you'll probably appreciate his choice of residence in California in the hills above Santa Barbara. Located between Los Angeles and San Francisco, this stretch of coast blends the best of both—the beaches of the south and the rolling hills of the north, sunshine with comfortable temperatures. Everything in moderation—except for extravagant San Simeon Castle, the pink fantasy-roomed Madonna Inn, and ruggedly dramatic Big Sur and—oh, well, so much for moderation.

The Pacific Coast Highway, the "Main Street" of this oceanside ribbon, will mesmerize you with endless views of shoreline beauty. Then it will wend through elegant but unpretentious towns—Danish Solvang, mystical Ojai, old-moneyed Santa Barbara (enlivened by its university campus crowd), artistic Carmel (even the golf courses are masterpieces), and quaint Monterey, making an exciting comeback John Steinbeck would enjoy.

The drive between San Francisco and Los Angeles takes about 12 hours on the Coast Highway (Route 1) and 8 or less on the Golden State I-5 more inland. If saving time is your goal, go inland; but if having one of the most memorable times of your life is more important, take the coast—and count on 3 days to do it at all right, more if you can.

SANTA BARBARA

A diminutive size and a more reserved character bring Santa Barbara into striking contrast with Los Angeles,

2 hours to the south. Calm is pervasive here, encouraged by the stolid, California mission architecture and the abundance of sunshine and sea air that remain strangers to smog. For some, Santa Barbara is a tonic for the urban frenzy that is L.A.

Spilling toward the Pacific from the Santa Ynez mountains on its northern flank, the town of Santa Barbara presents a slate of year-round activities that exploit its uncrowded beaches and maximize its cultural savoir faire. But there's more to Santa Barbara than just a pretty face. She wears the intelligence of history behind her palm-treed, bougainvillea-ed facades.

Immerse yourself in Santa Barbara's atmosphere at the area's most famous landmark, Mission Santa Barbara ♛ ♛ ♛ ♛, often called the "Queen of the Missions" for its well-preserved, regionally representative design. The garden must have been styled by angels. Founded in 1786, the Franciscan mission is still a parish church. Spend a dollar and take a self-guided tour. Children under 16 admitted free.

INSIDERS' TIPS

Remnants of the mission's original water system, or aqueduct, are still visible from the hill just north of the mission.

Spanish design influences contemporary buildings downtown, which have been built to conform with their older established neighbors. White or pastel plaster walls topped by red-tiled roofs remain as au courant today as they were when Charles III reigned over the mother country.

Santa Barbara wants you to relax. Board the Santa Barbara Trolley ♛ ♛ ♛, which runs along central State Street and the wharf, and also stops at the mission. The downtown "Red Tile Walking Tour" ♛ ♛ ♛, outlined in a free sight-seeing guide available at the Santa Barbara Conference and Visitors Bureau, is 90 minutes' worth of architectural insight into the community's Hispanic heritage. One of our favorites is the Presidio Real (royal fortress), 122 East Canon Perdido Street. Founded by Imperial Spain, its 20th-century incarnation supports adobe homes, a chapel, and El Cuartel (the barracks).

Nearby, the rambling adobe home (1827) of the Presidio commandante serves as the core of El Paseo, a picture-book shopping arcade whose demeanor recalls Old Spain, if not her prices. Lunch in the center courtyard at a sidewalk café to the music of shoes clacking on the terra-cotta tiles. Beware! Antique, specialty shops and art galleries will try to charm you right out of your budget.

Occupying an entire downtown block, the Spanish-Moorish Santa Barbara County Courthouse♛♛♛ remains one of the nation's most beautiful public buildings. Resembling a castle more than a courthouse, the interior is elegance itself—painted ceilings, wrought-iron chandeliers, giant murals, carved doors, and imported tiles. From the observation deck of El Mirado, the 70-foot clock tower, breathtaking views of the city, mountains, and sea reaffirm what's really important.

PERILS & PITFALLS

Four infamous traffic lights intersect Highway 101 in central Santa Barbara—at Santa Barbara Street, Anna Capa, State Street, and Chapala—each requires *at least* a 4-minute wait. Patience is rewarded: by 1990, all 4 will be just a memory.

Santa Barbara beaches, known as the South Coast, face the sun in winter and draw mild temperatures in summer. The miles of clean, uncrowded sand are occasionally interrupted by tall palm trees, picnic tables, and barbecue pits. Twenty miles offshore the Channel Islands loom in handsome detail. If the sand isn't hot enough for you, heat up your own action on a dozen volleyball courts and a giant soccer field. Take a windsurfing lesson.

Is nothing less than beautiful here? Santa Barbara Harbor does not disappoint. Rent a boat for a shoreline cruise, fishing expedition, or whale-watching excursion. On Stearns Wharf, we shopped, fished, dined (not, we hasten to add, on our own personal catch of the day), and strolled in perfect peace. Take advantage of the mile-long bike path that hugs the shore. Two-wheelers and the increasingly popular mini-surreys are for rent.

At the east end of the trail, the Andree Clark Bird Refuge♛, a beautifully landscaped water lagoon, is home to some 220 varieties of birds and waterfowl.

Next to the Bird Refuge, the Santa Barbara Zoological Garden♛♛ features a small zoo, an animal petting area, a sea lion exhibit, a miniature-train ride encircling the estate, botanic gardens, a children's play area, a snack bar, and a large picnic area. Open daily.

Long a center of southern California art and culture, Santa Barbara hosts 3 institutions of higher learning, its own symphony orchestra, and more than 85 performing and visual arts groups. Plays, concerts, dance performances, and lectures crowd the schedules of several area theaters. Every Sunday from 10 A.M. until dusk, local artists exhibit and sell their work at an arts and crafts show along oceanfront Cabrillo Boulevard, although a lot of this "work" appeals to few but the mothers of those who made it. Information about performances and events is available through the Santa Barbara Arts Council, 805-966-7022.

OJAI

Check out *Lost Horizon*, the 1937 Ronald Coleman classic, and see how much of the town of Ojai you recognize. If your idea of Shangri-la is music wafting through the heavily orange-blossomed air, or playing tennis until the happily-ever-after, book your trip now. Inside the village of Ojai, 90 minutes north of Los Angeles, and about 40 minutes from Santa Barbara, we discovered other means to a glorious end—like dining, golf, hiking, biking, and horse riding. Ojai Trail♛♛♛ takes honors as one of the premier diversions, half paved for hiking and biking, half covered with wood chips for the horsey set. With oaks and eucalyptus spreading their great arms through the pristine air, Ojai is loveliness itself.

Those mystically inclined will want to explore another aspect of Ojai. Traditionally this town has attracted occultists who claim the setting has strong spiritual energies and magical magnetism. Tourist development of Ojai is more recent than its reputation for welcoming what out-of-staters might regard as California's fringe element—artists, UFO fanciers, and the cosmically connected. But we find these Ojaians add to the specialness of the place. Shirley MacLaine would feel right at home.

Ojai is also the site of the nation's oldest, collegiate tennis tournament. Every spring, athletes from colleges across the West converge here for a long weekend of top competition. If you plan a visit at the end of April, be sure to make reservations in advance as the town fills up with spectators.

SOLVANG AND THE SANTA YNEZ VALLEY

Alas, poor Yorick would have found peace in Solvang. Forty-five miles north of Santa Barbara in between the Santa Ynez and San Rafael mountain ranges, Santa Ynez Valley offers sanctuary not only to mad Danes but to ranchers, winegrowers, and movie stars. (Not to mention former movie stars, like the one whose other house is a big white affair in the center of the nation's capital.)

The Spanish ranchers of early California prized the valley, much of whose quietude survives today. Cattle graze under oaks, and thousands of acres of vineyards dot the countryside.

Tucked in the heart of the Santa Ynez Valley is Solvang ♛ ♛, a touch of Old Denmark transplanted to California. Literally, "sunny valley" in Danish, Solvang was founded in the 1900s by a group of Danish educators from the midwest in search of a site for a school.

They copied the architecture of their homeland, a style sweetly preserved today. Windmills, thatched roofs, gas streetlights, and the ubiquitous scent of freshly baked pastries define life here among the craft and antique shops. Danish "Honen Streetcars," pulled by blond, Belgian draft horses, ferry visitors through the village streets.

Buy a few Danish pastries or head for more serious

gastronomic pursuits at any of the valley's 16 wineries, cellars, or vineyards. The Firestone Vineyard 👑 👑 (805-688-3940) and Austin Cellars 👑 👑 (805-688-9665) are recommended.

Old Mission Santa Inés 👑 👑, created in 1804 and located on the eastern outskirts of Solvang, appeals to us for its turbulent history clearly depicted in murals on the chapel wall and in an impressive, on-site museum of Indian Mission-Era artifacts. Guided tours are conducted daily. Call 805-688-4815 for information on touring hours.

If you travel through the area during the summer, consider attending the Solvang Theatrefest 👑 👑 👑. Held outdoors, performances are nightly, except Mondays. And Solvang's Scandinavian heritage is celebrated on the third weekend of September, when townspeople don traditional costumes of their homeland, maybe in celebration that they don't have to spend the upcoming winter in Denmark.

PERILS & PITFALLS

Despite these attractions, Solvang has sacrificed most of its old-world charm to the tourist trade. Expect some fairly crass commercialization, big crowds, and scant parking space. This place is cute, maybe *too* cute. We only stop here when we crave a butter cookie or need to stretch our legs during the drive from Santa Barbara to destinations north.

Within minutes of Solvang, 4 secluded towns mimic the area's pioneer past. Ballard, the valley's oldest town, sports the proverbial little red schoolhouse. Founded in 1883, the school is still in session. On Highway 101, Buellton's thoroughbred horse trade competes for the town's identity with the Andersen family's split-pea soup. Los Olivos, once a major stagecoach stop and southern terminal for the narrow-gauge Pacific Coast railroad, still attracts tourists with restored buildings like Mattel's Tavern and the old Stage Coach Inn.

More than 11 parks throughout these rolling hills beckon. Among the best: Nojoqui Falls Park, and its

164-foot-high falls; Gaviota Beach Park, with excellent beach and bathing facilities; and Lake Cachuma Recreation Area, ideal for fishing, camping, boating, horseback riding, swimming, and picnicking.

SAN LUIS OBISPO

San Luis Obispo captures a lot of California qualities in one setting—sand dunes, meadows, lakes, forests, and high desert all share one county. Victorian homes, weathered barns, and old country stores characterize this town of 40,000.

Home to California Polytechnic University at San Luis Obispo (famous for its fine agriculture and architecture schools), San Luis Obispo is an old-fashioned place where the pace is slow and the folks are friendly. The gentle climate encourages visitors to town and to the nearby wine country and Pacific coast.

In the heart of town, Mission San Luis Obispo de Tolosa ♛ ♛ ♛ reigns as one of those founded by the only Californian on the acknowledged track to sainthood, Father Junípero Serra. Unlike most California missions, Mission San Luis Obispo—with its whitewashed walls, marble altars, and high, cross-beamed ceilings—remains the center of town activity as it has since 1772. (For more information, contact the mission at 805-543-6850.)

The delightful Mission Plaza surrounds the mission and is a lively center of art exhibits, music, and dance. One warm spring day, we saw a horse-drawn carriage here, whisking newlyweds off to a secret honeymoon retreat.

Mission Plaza also sets the stage for La Fiesta, a yearly May celebration during which the town salutes its Spanish heritage. The plaza is intersected by San Luis Obispo Creek, a cool, refreshing brook meandering through town with footbridges to link the plaza with shop-lined San Luis Obispo streets.

Mission Plaza is within walking distance of the community's Historical Museum, and it's the ideal starting point for walking tours of the town's gabled Victorian homes♛, as well as for the San Luis Obispo Path of History♛ ♛. A descriptive guide to the Path of History Tour is available at the San Luis Obispo Chamber of Commerce, located at 1039 Choro Street. (For information, call 805-543-1323.)

San Luis Obispo claims a more offbeat notoriety: To wit, "Gum Ball Alley," the authoritative repository of locally chewed gum; the Motel Inn, reputed to be the world's first motel; and the Madonna Inn, a garish spectacle of unleashed imagination that's renowned for its individually themed rooms.

Traveling west of town, wine aficionados will appreciate more than 20 wineries in San Luis Obispo country, ranging from mom-and-pop shops to full-production plants. South of San Luis Obispo, Avila Beach and Avila Hot Springs call to the swimsuited crowd, and Point San Luis Obispo plies the angler trade with daily deep-sea fishing charters. Water-skiers might consider Lake Lopez, which also hosts windsurfing, boating, fishing, hiking, and camping.

If poetry is in your soul, and what you fancy is the perfect flower or a memorable sunset, head with picnic basket in hand to Montana de Oro State Park (Spanish for "Mountains of Gold")♛ ♛. For spectacular views spanning the country's inland valleys and coastline, take the 10-mile See Canyon Drive; nowhere affords a better panorama of the region. Hit this trail in autumn and you can buy hand-picked apples, apple cider, and other harvest fruits along the way.

INSIDERS' TIPS

Above all, enjoy San Luis Obispo leisurely. Its pace is its charm and patience is rewarded.

CAMBRIA

Two and a half hours north of Santa Barbara, you will be in northern California. In Cambria, where the pines meet the sea, two distinct villages are bridged by Cambria Square, a residential and commercial complex. The east village was originally downtown, its first buildings erected in the late 1860s. Today it is a mishmash of shops, food outlets, and lodging. For some reason, Tudor is a popular architectural conceit.

The newer west village is decidely upscale—art galleries, gourmet restaurants, specialty shops, and inns abound. Try the Allied Arts Schoolhouse♛♛♛ where hundreds of local artists exhibit and sell their work.

What you really need to do in Cambria is to get small. The Lilliputian miniatures—knights in shining armor, Alices in Wonderland, and Mad Hatters—populate the Cambria Soldier Factory♛♛♛, turning out an astonishing 25,000 figurines each month.

Working ranches, farms, and vineyards surround Cambria. Don't miss the wonderful beaches to the west.

INSIDERS' TIPS

Take a ride—by car or by bike—along Santa Rosa Creek Road, an idyllic country lane that bisects cattle ranches, orchards, and farms selling fresh produce and homemade goodies.

Since it opened in 1958, Hearst San Simeon State Historical Monument♛♛♛♛ (north of town in San Simeon) has put Cambria on the map. The magnificent estate of the late newspaper publisher William Randolph Hearst, Hearst Castle (as it is commonly known), is open for tours daily, except on Thanksgiving, Christmas, and New Year's Day.

San Simeon is ostentatious and eccentric, like a dotty, rich aunt, who is both the life and the embarrassment of the party. The mansion is bizarre; its gold-gilded towers flaunt an architectural melting pot of styles. This monument to wealth and immediate gratification, which took decades to build, is an equally mixed bag of interior design. The whole estate offers a 360-degree view of the lush Santa Lucia Mountains to the east and the Pacific Ocean to the west. Four different walking tours are available; reservations are highly recommended. (In California call 800-446-PARK; from outside the state call 619-452-1950.)

INSIDERS' TIPS

Be prepared to walk at least half a mile and climb 150 steps on these tours. Visitors in wheelchairs may make special arrangements and reservations by calling the castle at 805-927-4622.

While in Cambria, take a walk along Moonstone Beach ♛ ♛ ♛, spectacular public parklands that run for miles of rugged coastline along Highway 1. It's a beachcombers' paradise—polished pebbles of jade, agate, and quartz. Tide pools host the ocean's microcosmic population. Enjoy rock and surf fishing. Trails for hiking, walking, or jogging appeal to the energetic. Day-use picnic grounds are available at Leffingwell's Landing at the north end of the beach. Keep your eyes peeled for sea otters and sea lions frolicking near the large rocks at Piedras Blancas, north of Cambria.

BIG SUR

South of Carmel, along Highway 1, lies Big Sur ♛ ♛ ♛ ♛ ♛. Stark mountains jutting up on the right for hundreds of feet loom above the Pacific Ocean. The occasional promontory, sprinkled with wildflowers and grazing cattle, softens the jerky terrain where the atmosphere is a pleasing blend of fresh mountain and tangy sea air. Slip into visions of early California along this 90-mile stretch. Bring lots of film.

We join many others in voting the Cabrillo Highway (better known as Coast Highway 1) as one of the world's most scenic routes. Sweeping vistas distract one's attention from what is an astonishing piece of highway engineering, remarkable for its bridges and winding byways that were carved out of the western slopes of the Santa Lucia Mountains flanking the coast. The highway took 16 years to build (at a cost of $10 million) and opened in 1937. It's worth every penny. More, in fact.

Big Sur itself may be a land of drama, but the life-style of its residents is committedly low-key. Many of its 1,200 inhabitants are direct descendants of the original pioneer families who settled the area in the 1860s to ranch or log the towering redwoods. Today, many are stuck in the sixties—the 1960s, that is—by choice.

PERILS & PITFALLS

When driving along this serpentine highway, don't expect to find grocery stores, banks—or great radio reception. Big Sur residents travel to the Monterey Peninsula cities, so provision yourself ahead of time.

Big Sur may be simple, but dull it isn't. Its natural beauty inspires art, so plan to browse through the several fine art galleries along the highway. California food and wine are amply supplied in a number of singular eateries. Lapidarians may opt to search for nuggets of jade along Jade Beach.

Camping, hiking, fishing, and swimming at Garipata Beach, a local favorite, are all fine methods of getting to know this incredible chunk of real estate. Big Sur State Park (2,944 acres) is open daily and contains 80 miles of hiking trails, serving also as the hub for 500 miles of trails through the national forest.

Campsites are available at Pfeiffer-Big Sur State Park (our favorite), J. P. Burns and Molera parks, and Ventana Wilderness Inn Campsite Area. (For more information on the Big Sur area, call the Big Sur Chamber of Commerce at 408-649-1770.)

INSIDERS' TIPS

There is one exception to the above warning. Large signs on the Coast Highway point to a place that's one hour forty-five minutes north of San Simeon and at mile marker 46 from the Monterey County line. It's called Nepenthe (408-667-2345), a great resting/dining/shopping/viewing spot that sticks up on a hill over the craggy cliffs on the oceanside of the thoroughfare. If you pass Restaurant Lucia, you've gone too far, but it's worth it to backtrack. Be sure to try out Nepenthe's great fries and to pick up a few gifts, many of them works of art created by local craftsmen and women.

POINT LOBOS

Back on the road again (Highway 1), immediately south of Carmel, a jetty of land described by Robert Louis Stevenson as "the greatest meeting of land and water in the world" introduces Point Lobos State Reserve. Stevenson was so enchanted by this rocky headland that it became the inspiration for his classic novel *Treasure Island.*

Point Lobos State Reserve's ♛ ♛ ♛ ♛ ♛ 1,276 acres of land harbor a treasure trove of discoveries, from delicate beaches and intimate coves to sea creatures, great and small. For a small entrance fee, visitors should wander the trails winding among cypress groves. The slate-blue waters of China Cove beckon bold swimmers to take a crisp plunge.

Other living creatures enjoy Point Lobos as well. More than 178 species of vertebrates and 88 species of marine life inhabit the area, from the odd mollusks that make lace out of seashore stone, to the sea lions that give the point its name—Spanish explorers christened the land *Punta de los Lobos Marinos,* or "Sea Wolves' Point."

INSIDERS' TIPS

Given the size of Point Lobos, plan to spend an afternoon or even a day to appreciate the area fully.

SAN JUAN BAUTISTA, CASTROVILLE, AND SALINAS

A 40-minute drive northeast of Carmel on Highway 156 (off Highway 101) brings you to the quiet old mission town of San Juan Bautista. Evocative of a sleepy Latin American village overlooked by the passage of time, San Juan Bautista inspires creative sloth. A lazy afternoon stroll along the peppertree-lined streets offers antique stores and specialty shops stuffed with quilts and handmade toys. Several art galleries decorate the scene as well.

Within San Juan Bautista is one of California's finest culturally preserved compounds, San Juan Bautista State Park♕♕♕. Amid the park's 6 acres, discover this preserved Mexican town in which colorful buildings—restored as house museums—depict life as it was in the mid-to-late 1800s.

INSIDERS' TIPS

For a closer glimpse at ages past, visit the park on the first Saturday of every month for "Living History Day," when Civil War soldiers flirt with hoop-skirted ladies, blacksmiths practice their trade, and dance-hall girls deal cards to a variety of bandits.

On the western edge of the park, the largest of California's 21 missions dominates a ridge overlooking the Salinas Valley. Mission San Juan Bautista's♕♕ whitewashed walls, red-tiled roof, hand-hewn benches, and pastel reliefs typify the simple beauty of the early missions for which the Golden State is known. The mission and the park are open year-round. (For information on the park, call 408-623-4881.)

The artichoke capital of the world, Castroville♕♕, lies just west of San Juan Bautista along Highway 156. This agricultural town of Italian heritage prides itself on its famous horticulture. Test that product during Castroville's annual Artichoke Festival each September. (For information on the festival, call the Castroville Chamber of Commerce at 408-633-2465, or write the California Artichoke Advisory Board at P.O. Box 747, Castroville, CA 95012.)

South of Castroville, the abundant cropland of Salinas includes vineyards, whose 33,000 acres of wine grapes produce some of the state's finest wines.

Salinas is also the heart of Steinbeck country. Steinbeck House♕♕♕, birthplace of California's most lauded author, John Steinbeck, complements the Steinbeck home (now part restaurant) and the John Steinbeck Library. Fans should examine the Steinbeck memorabilia and some of the author's original manuscripts.

The Boronda Adobe and Harvey Baker House have

19th-century artifacts chronicling Salinas's lively past. Historic Old Town is worth a look. (For information on Salinas's historical home tours, as well as details on the valley's wine district with its many wineries that are open for touring, contact the Salinas Chamber of Commerce at 408-424-7611.)

Thirty-one miles south of Salinas, the spectacular spires and caves of Pinnacles National Monument♛ ♛ ♛ ♛ puncture the sky. Amid these remnants of an ancient volcano, picnicking and hiking present opportunities to explore the formation a bit more intimately. (For information, call 408-389-4578.)

CARMEL

The southernmost gate of 17-Mile Drive ushers drivers into what some perceive as the "perfect" village of Carmel♛ ♛ ♛ ♛. The name itself means "at rest," and if you can abide the sometimes sanctimonious attitudes that prevail here, the serenity and romance of this resort is seductive. Artists, writers, and musicians like it here, and some even make a living.

Carmel is a scant square mile; it takes only a few hours of rubbernecking to fully take in the fountains and the flowers of this Hansel-and-Gretel town. Fairy-tale cottages, each with their own name (there are no house numbers), line Carmel's shaded avenues; small, European-style cafés glow in harmony with their setting; a Mediterranean market tempts the palate with a cornucopia of food and wine from around the world.

A shoppers' delight, the avenues and alleyways of Carmel closet more than 90 art galleries, antique stores, tea shops, designer boutiques, and specialty stores. Along Carmel's cobblestone pathways, consuming interests override sensibility. Buy chocolate and French handbags and exquisitely crafted jewelry and Scottish tartans. Why not?

Determined to keep as much of its natural beauty as possible, city fathers and mothers (including current Mayor Clint Eastwood) have prohibited gaudy signs, hot-dog stands, and billboards.

PERILS & PITFALLS

Inevitably, the presence of Carmel's movie-star mayor has attracted a gaggle of often intrusive stargazers to the quiet town. Expect to see and hear a lot about Mayor Eastwood, who's gamely tried to shun most of the hype.

A trip to Carmel isn't complete without a stop at Mission San Carlos Borromeo del Rio Carmelo ♕ ♕ ♕. Fountains, a flower-filled courtyard, a lovely basilica, dusty-rose-colored bell towers, and a poignant cemetery (Father Junípero Serra is buried here) all bring distinction to this Spanish gem—it's the loveliest of California's 21 missions.

Carmel's landmark stone castle—Tor House, built by Robinson Jeffers in 1918, is worth a look. Docent tours through Tor House are available Friday and Saturday, 10 A.M. to 3 P.M. (Reservations are required, for information call 408-624-1813.)

Choose an off-the-main-road itinerary, and take a leisurely drive inland down Carmel Valley Road. Meander past wineries, photogenic old barns and farms, a bubbling brook, noisy with the frogs of Steinbeckian lore, and even a Buddhist temple. Tassahara Hot Springs here purports to bring peace of mind to a hassled urban populace.

PEBBLE BEACH

At the western edge of Pacific Grove, one of 4 gates leads to California's famed 17-Mile Drive ♕ ♕ ♕ ♕. If you like homes that look like hotels, whose lobbies front the lapping Pacific, spend the 5 bucks per car for entry. Inside the gates, 5,300 acres of the world's most photographed seascapes and 7 world-class golf courses (4 public), known internationally for their beauty and difficulty, share space with the lucky homeowners. Groves of fog-shrouded, wind-sculptured Gowan and Monterey cypresses dress this perfect set.

This circuit can be driven in an hour, an afternoon,

or a day—depending on how all this . . . abundance affects you. We do recommend a thorough inspection of the many rock outcroppings if you like the sight of sea life in its element.

The Lodge at Pebble Beach dominates the golf-course perspective. With its array of restaurants, tony shops, and manicured grounds, the Lodge serves as host year-round to a passing parade of celebrities.

Golf—almost a religion here—reigns 365 days a year. From the spectacular oceanside bluffs at Pebble Beach to the quiet, forest fairways at Spyglass Hill, the royal and ancient game enjoys no finer setting in the world. For a real touch of history try 90-year-old Del Monte Golf Course, or maybe the new challenge of Poppy Hills, home of the Northern California Golf Association.

PERILS & PITFALLS

Be warned: It *is* expensive to play golf on the Monterey Peninsula—up to $125 a round. But, it may be worth it, due to the quality of the courses, their wondrous natural beauty, and the tremendous memories of your visit to this golfer's mecca.

Cycling, equestrian sports, jogging, and hiking are other outdoor pursuits in the neighborhood. Watch for the perennial Lodge events: The AT&T Pebble Beach National Pro-Am in January, the Concours d'Elégance in August, and the California Cup Polo Challenge in September.

Spanish Bay, a second resort in Pebble Beach, opened in late 1987, complementing the services of The Lodge from its oceanfront perch along 17-Mile Drive.

PACIFIC GROVE

Five minutes west of Monterey, Pacific Grove's most prominent residents know how to light up the skies. Millions of orange and black Monarch butterflies wing their way from lands as distant as Alaska each October in a mysterious sojourn that culminates in the pine trees of Pacific Grove. They hang in great clusters, fluttering lazily about town on warm days, until their March departure.

In addition to the seasonal beauty of the butterflies, Pacific Grove embraces a 3-mile stretch of coastline rich with tide pools, sand dunes, and rocky beachheads. Its environmental amenities attract easel-toting artists, walkers, and scuba divers. One coastal community here dates back to 1875, when it was a Methodist summer retreat. Its collection of gabled, Victorian homes sport brightly colored turrets, porches, and belfry gazebos, exuding an old-fashioned charm, rich in romance and relaxation.

Along the waterfront Ocean View Boulevard ♛♛♛♛, a magic carpet of mesembryanthemum (pink, purple, and lavender ice plants) unfolds in profusion from May through July. The drive from Lover's Point along the ocean is spectacular at any time.

MONTEREY

The Monterey Peninsula is a land of rainbow-hued sunsets, sugar-white beaches, and a cacophony of sounds. Here, listen to the music of the sea and the notes of jazz and Bach. The land reverberates with echoes of a hearty past. Vacationers to the peninsula follow in the steps of many illustrious ghosts, from the Spanish conquistador Sebastián Vizcaíno, the first white man to set foot on the peninsula in 1602, to such literary heroes as Robinson Jeffers and John Steinbeck. Today, artists, writers, painters, and poets remain drawn to a land Henry Miller called a "place of grandeur and eloquent silence."

Monterey's personality today is reminiscent of some peaceful Mediterranean coastal communities. But tranquility hasn't always been Monterey's style: up to the mid 19th century, Monterey was California's liveliest settlement, the Spanish capital of Alta California until its population saw the raising of the Stars and Stripes in 1846.

The Monterey Walking Path of History ♛♛♛ is a leisurely 3-mile stroll, a self-guided route leading visitors past some 45 historic adobes. Attractions include California's first theater, the Larkin House, perhaps the most striking example of Monterey colonial-style architecture, and the Custom House, where the United States flag was first officially raised over California by Commodore John Drake Sloat on July 7, 1846. Together, these structures form the finest group of 18th- and 19th-century buildings in the state. Many of the adobes are open for guided tours. (A walking map and information on tour times can be obtained at the Monterey Peninsula Chamber of Commerce, located at 380 Alvarado Street, or by calling 408-649-1770.)

Since Monterey's settlement by the Spaniards in the 18th century, the city has drawn its sustenance from the sea. Traditionally, the hub of the seafaring village's activities was Fisherman's Wharf and Cannery Row, now two of Monterey's best-known attractions. They're a bit overdone for our taste—we wish we had walked the wharves alongside Steinbeck.

Fisherman's Wharf♛ ♛, once the domain of salty fishermen, originally served was a pier where trading schooners unloaded cargo and was the center of the booming sardine and whaling industries. Today, the wharf is dominated by seafood restaurants, with menus offering freshly caught delicacies. Sea lions provide their own entertainment as they frolic in the pierside waters.

PERILS & PITFALLS

Give a miss to the many junky shops hawking jewelry and nautical wood carvings along the waterfront. Rather, seek out the antique shops a couple of blocks inland on 17th Street or Lighthouse, where you're sure to find some lovely bargains from another era.

From 1921 to 1946, Monterey's Cannery Row was known as the sardine capital of the western hemisphere. At the peak of its activity, this raucous strip, immortalized by John Steinbeck in his 1945 novel *Cannery Row*, boasted no less than 16 canneries where more than 240,000 tons of sardines were packed yearly. In its heyday, the area throbbed with a lively pack of eccentrics, from fishermen to hucksters. But by 1948, the prolific sardines had disappeared, and the Row as Steinbeck knew it died.

Today, however, Cannery Row—thanks largely to Steinbeck's enduringly popular novel—is enjoying a mini-renaissance. Rotting buildings and brothels have been replaced by antique shops, art galleries, cafés, wine gardens, hotels, and bookstores. Another catalyst to this revival is the Monterey Bay Aquarium ♛ ♛ ♛ ♛, a state-of-the-art underwater complex which opened in 1984.

PERILS & PITFALLS

Parking is a *big* problem at the Aquarium; in fact, the attraction draws so many people, and cars, that the ensuing congestion interferes with all of the businesses in the vicinity. Play it safe and park a few blocks away on nearby side streets. Everyone will be happy you made that extra effort.

The wonders of a hidden world come to light at this internationally acclaimed aquarium that emphasizes indigenous flora and fauna. Nearly a hundred innovative habitat galleries and exhibits plunge visitors into Monterey Bay and its deep shale reefs, its rocky shores, and turbulent tide pools, sloughs, sandy seafloors, and even its wharves. (For more information, call 408-375-3333.)

INSIDERS' INFORMATION FOR THE CENTRAL COAST

Big Sur
(area code 408)
Where to Stay
Ventana Inn ♛ ♛ ♛ ♛ ♛
Highway 1, Big Sur 93920; tel. 624-4812
Single room, double occupancy: $125–$245
Situated 1,200 feet above the Pacific, 8 buildings of weathered cedar offer 40 soothing rooms of various designs and details. Some have hot tubs, most have

fireplaces and ocean views. Japanese hot tubs, saunas, pool, and a clothing-optional sun deck. A true getaway. The restaurant(♛ ♛ ♛ ♛ ♛) serves the best and freshest California cuisine for miles.

Deetjen's Big Sur Inn ♛ ♛ ♛
Highway 1, Big Sur 93920; tel. 667-2377
Single room, double occupancy: $45–$80
Built by Norwegian immigrants, this former stagecoach stop, tucked into the redwoods at the crook in the highway, is simple and appropriately rustic.

Buellton
(area code 805)
Where to Eat
Andersen's Restaurant ♛ ♛
Avenue of the Flags, Buellton; tel. 688-5581
Average dinner: $8–$19
Family-style eatery famous for its pea soup. Sandwiches, salads, hot entrées.

Cambria
(area code 805)
Where to Stay
Moonstone Inn ♛ ♛ ♛
5860 Moonstone Beach, Cambria 93428; tel. 927-4815
Single room, double occupancy: $85–$95
Every room boasts an ocean view. Nicely located with direct access to the beach. Fireplaces, Continental breakfast, wine and cheese.

The Pickford House ♛ ♛ ♛
2555 MacLeod Ave., Cambria 93428; tel. 927-8619
Single room, double occupancy: $70–$90
This 1920s, Victorian house has 8 rooms, pub, and dining room all in one building. Ask about winter rates.

Cambria Pines Lodge ♛ ♛
2905 Burton Dr., Cambria 93428; tel. 927-4200
Single room, double occupancy: $50–$85
Twenty-three acres of flowers, lawns, and trees. Whirlpools, 60-foot, indoor, heated pool, saunas. Some fireplaces. Comfortable.

Where to Eat

Ian's♛♛♛♛

2150 Center St., Cambria; tel. 927-8649

Average dinner: $20–$30

Outstanding menu, changing bi-weekly, features grilled quail and sausage, broiled sea bass, marinated lamb chops. Homemade ice cream.

The Brambles Dinner House♛♛♛

4005 Burton Dr., Cambria; tel. 927-4716

Average dinner: $16–$22

People will travel quite a distance to eat at this romantic and intimate converted home. Great prime rib and Yorkshire pudding, as well as grilled salmon, lobster, prawns, and steaks.

The Chuck Wagon♛♛

Moonstone Dr. on Highway 1, Cambria; tel. 927-4644

Average dinner: $7

Popular smorgasbord. Entrées change daily, but you'll always find homemade soups and breads, and a choice of fish or chicken.

Nightlife

Camozzi's Saloon, 2262 Main St., Cambria; tel. 927-8941. The floor slants, and the pinball game is tilted at this 110-year-old night spot that ranchers frequent after a hard day on the range.

Theater

The Pewter Plough Playhouse, West and Village streets, Cambria; tel. 927-3877. Community theater at its best with a nice blend of dramatic and comedic live theater as well as classic movies.

Shopping

The Cubbyhole Antiques and Small Treasures, 755 N. Main St. Terrific finds in furniture, kitchen gadgets, and pictures.

Ramsgate Gallery, 776 Arlington. Estate-bought antiques, Californian paintings, furniture.

Seekers, 4090 Burton Dr. Cut glass, carved wooden boxes, stained-glass windows, and unusual pottery created by artists countrywide.

Carmel
(area code 408)
Where to Stay
Highlands Inn♛♛♛♛♛

Highway 1, Box 1700, Carmel 93921; tel. 624-3801 or 800-682-3801 in California, 800-538-9525 nationwide

Single rooms, double occupancy: $185–$270

World famous since 1916, this romantic resort is perched atop a pine-covered hillside commanding dramatic coastal views. The turnoff to the property is tricky so keep your eyes open. Once there, enjoy the luxury of spa baths, woodburning fireplaces, and view decks.

Quail Lodge♛♛♛♛♛

8205 Valley Greens Dr., Carmel 93923; tel. 624-1581 or 800-682-9303 in California, 800-538-9516 nationwide

Single rooms, double occupancy: $175–$250

Three miles from downtown Carmel, this peaceful, country setting offers lots of privacy, and 100 low-profile rooms that are both modern and convenient. Pools, hot tubs, lake-view cottages, superb golf and tennis. If you stay in this resort, you'll likely come across many species of wildlife and migratory birds on the adjacent 600 acres known as Quail Meadows.

La Playa Hotel♛♛♛

Camino Real at Eighth, P.O. Box 900, Carmel 93921; tel. 408-624-6476 or 800-582-8900 in California

Single room, double occupancy: $93–$148

Stay in this Mediterranean villa if you're looking for a friendly and helpful staff and a tremendous location only 2 blocks from the beach and 4 blocks from Carmel shopping. Comfortable lobby has hand-loomed rugs, antiques, and a blazing fire. Heated pool. 75 rooms.

The Pine Inn♛♛

Ocean Ave. and Lincoln, Carmel-by-the-Sea 93921; tel. 624-3851

Single room, double occupancy: $65–$85

Located in the center of town, this historic inn has been around for three generations. Authentic period furnishings, fabrics, and art adorn cozy rooms (which tend to be on the small side). Plumbing is probably authentic as well.

Where to Eat

Jimmy's American Place ♕ ♕ ♕ ♕ ♕
26344 Carmel Rancho Lane, Carmel; tel. 625-6666
Average dinner: $13
Dine on American regional cookery at this high-tech restaurant. Six different types of oysters, double-cut pork chop specialty.

Casanova ♕ ♕ ♕ ♕
5th and San Carlos, Carmel; tel. 625-0501
Average dinner: $18–$24
Charming cottage setting, this restaurant in the heart of Carmel has daily specials and excellent pasta, imaginatively prepared.

Creme Carmel ♕ ♕ ♕
San Carlos St. and 7th Ave., Carmel; tel. 624-0444
Average dinner: $16–$22
Seasonal menu, prompt and knowledgeable service. French/California cuisine.

Rio Grill ♕ ♕ ♕
The Crossroads, Carmel; tel. 625-5436
Average dinner: $9–$16
Trendy, in spot, noisy and popular. Blend of Cajun and Southwest cuisine, from rabbit quesadillas to catfish with creole relish and black-eyed peas.

Shopping

The Barnyard, Highway 1 at Carmel Valley Rd., Carmel. Leisurely shopping, dining, browsing. Wander brick walkways among fabulous gardens, 55 shops, and international restaurants.

Finley's Antiques, 220 17th St., Pacific Grove. Antique and estate jewelry, china, mirrors, sterling silver.

Flor de Monterey, 299 W. Franklin St., Monterey. Beautiful arrangements of green and flowering plants, silk flowers, gift items, crystal, brass, pottery, and art objects.

Golf Arts and Imports, Dolores and Sixth Ave., Carmel. Unusual and distinctive gifts for the golfer. Golf pictures, both prints and originals, antique golf clubs, porcelain, crystal, and silver golf memorabilia.

Handworks, Dolores and Sixth Ave., Carmel. Hand-painted, hand-crafted gift items for home or office. Wide price range.

Lillian Johnson Antiques, 405 Third St., San Juan Bautista. Specializing in Haviland China, this store can match fine old French porcelain from its stock of over 4,000 patterns, mainly pre-World War I.

Pebble's Shop For Little Ones, The Lodge at Pebble Beach. A quality selection of clothing and toys for infants and children. Creative, unusual.

R. K. Shugart, Dolores and Seventh Ave., Carmel. A sophisticated women's boutique. Not for the price conscious.

Vintage House, 213 Forest Ave., Pacific Grove. A deli, coffee bar, chocolate shop, shelves of culinary delights, and cooking aids.

The Woodenickel, 529 Central Ave., Pacific Grove. A delightful collection of country knickknacks, candles, linen, and lace.

**Monterey
(area code 408)**
Where to Stay
Spindrift Inn♔♔♔♔♔
652 Cannery Row, Monterey 92940; tel. 646-8900; in California 800-841-1879
Single rooms, double occupancy: $129–$199
Romantic, luxurious, and intimate—only 42 rooms. Hardwood floors, oriental carpets, window seats, draped and canopied beds, wood-burning fireplaces, European down comforters, down featherbeds and pillows, Continental breakfast, afternoon tea and valet parking. Roof garden with spectacular ocean views. Need we say more?
Monterey Plaza♔♔
400 Cannery Row, Monterey 93940; tel. 646-1700, in California 800-334-3999, elsewhere 800-631-1339
Single rooms, double occupancy: $120–$199
Majestic 290-room hotel dominates John Steinbeck's

legendary Monterey Bay on the same site where the Murray Mansion entertained the First Families of America and Europe at the turn-of-the-century. Near Monterey Bay Aquarium.

Where to Eat

Fresh Cream ♛ ♛ ♛ ♛
Heritage Harbor, 100 Pacific St., Monterey; tel. 375-9798
Average dinner: $20
Trendy eatery, expensive but imaginative French/California cuisine. Canard au cassis, rack of lamb, escargots.

The Fishery ♛ ♛ ♛
21 Soledad Dr., Monterey; tel. 373-6200
Average dinner: $12
Off the tourist beat in a small shopping center near downtown, this restaurant has an oriental decor. From fish and chips to blackened Louisiana catfish.

The Old House ♛ ♛ ♛
500 Hartnell, Monterey; tel. 373-3737
Average dinner: $22
A touch of French with a northern California influence dominates the menu. Dishes like calamari, steak, and abalone meunière are served in this elegant old Spanish adobe with turn-of-the-century furnishings and bouquets of flowers.

Neil DeVaughn's ♛ ♛
Cannery Row, Monterey; tel. 372-2141
Average dinner: $30
Adjacent to the Spindrift Inn, seating here is literally on the water. Menu items range from Chateaubriand steak, lamb, and veal to fish. All dinners include cheese fondue with rye bread and mock turtle soup.

Ojai
(area code 805)

Where to Stay

Ojai Manor Hotel ♛ ♛
210 E. Matilija St., Ojai 93023; tel. 646–0961
Rates vary and are negotiable, but about $65–$75 for double. Small B&B, friendly and personable.

Where to Eat
The Ranch House ♛♛♛♛♛
South Lomita St., Ojai; tel. 646-2360
Average dinner: $13
A real find. Dine outdoors in the deliciously aromatic patio surrounded by an enormous herb garden. Natural streams flow swiftly through the garden, irrigating the herbs and creating a peaceful feeling. Award-winning American regional cookery.
L'Auberge ♛♛♛♛
314 Paseo, Ojai; tel. 646-2288
Average dinner: $30
Lovely country inn serves French cuisine in a relaxed family atmosphere. Make reservations!
The Firebird ♛♛♛
960 E. Ojai Ave., Ojai; tel. 646-1566
Average price: $10
American style mixes with Danish. Smorgasbord for lunch, Danish meatballs for dinner.

Shopping
Bird in Paradise, 310 E. Matalija. Way-out, handmade clothes, both casual and dressy.

Fitzgeralds, 238 E. Ojai Ave. Conservative women's sportswear.

Paul's Place, 215 E. Matilija. Large shoe selection and fashions for women.

Pacific Grove
(area code 408)
Where to Stay
The Martine Inn ♛♛♛♛
255 Ocean View Blvd., Pacific Grove 93950; tel. 373-3388
Single room, double occupancy: $95–$175
Oceanfront palace and carriage house, established in the late 1890s and owned for many years by Laura and James Parke (of pharmaceutical fame). Staying here is a step back in time to gracious living, with views overlooking the rocky coastline, elegantly furnished rooms with authentic museum quality antiques, fireplaces, clawfoot tubs.

Centrella Inn♕♕♕
612 Central Ave., Pacific Grove 93950; tel. 372-3372
Single room, double occupancy: $100–$110
Charming bed-and-breakfast inn, private and semi-private baths. Prices include Continental breakfast, evening hors d'oeuvres.

Where to Eat

Fandango♕♕♕
223 17th St. Pacific Grove; tel. 373-0588
Average dinner: $10–$18
Popular peninsula eatery featuring fish, chicken, and beef dishes prepared with a French flair. Tapas bar.

Chili Great Chili♕♕
620 Lighthouse Ave., Pacific Grove; tel. 646-0447
Average dinner: $5–$8
Simple, fun, and cheerful. International award-winning chili, including richly spiced beef chili or the soybean vegetarian alternative. Try the chili combined with pasta, rice, cheese, or beans.

Pebble Beach
(area code 408)

Where to Stay

The Lodge at Pebble Beach♕♕♕♕♕
17-Mile Dr., Pebble Beach 93953; tel. 624-3811
Single rooms, double occupancy: $200–$300
Luxurious accommodations, at the edge of breathtaking landscapes. Preferential golf tee times and rates. Promenade of boutiques, beach and tennis club, 4 restaurants. Club XIX(♕♕♕♕♕) has gourmet fare worth seeking out. Company store offers supplies and baskets for picnics along 17-Mile Drive.

Pismo Beach
(area code 805)

Where to Stay

The Lodge and Inn at Shore Cliff♕♕
2555 Price St., Pismo Beach; tel. 773-4671
Single room, double occupancy: $66–$78
Complete beach resort, all rooms with ocean views. Pool, tennis, clamming, fishing, and even dune buggies.

San Luis Obispo
(area code 805)

Where to Stay

The Madonna Inn ♛ ♛ ♛

100 Madonna Rd., San Luis Obispo 93401; tel. 543-3000

Single room, double occupancy: $70–$130

More than 100 rooms decorated in pure kitsch. Even the public restrooms are a sight.

San Luis Bay Inn ♛ ♛ ♛

P.O. Box 189, Avila Beach 93424; tel. 595-2333

Single room, double occupancy: $95–$125

Classic seaside resort with 18-hole golf course, tennis, pool, bicycles, canoes.

Where to Eat

The Olde Port Inn ♛ ♛ ♛

Port San Luis Pier, Avila Beach; tel. 595-2515

Average dinner: $17

On the pier, the seafood dinners are, of course, a specialty and fresh, fresh, fresh.

Tortilla Flats Restaurant and Cantina ♛ ♛

Higuera and Nipomo sts. (in the Creamery), San Luis Obispo; tel. 544-7575

Average dinner: $7

Live entertainment and hopping bar in a rustic atmosphere.

Shopping

Copelands, 962 Monterey, San Luis Obispo. Large selection of sporting goods and athletic clothing.

Full Circle, 570 Higuera in the Creamery, San Luis Obispo. Ethnic clothing in natural fabrics.

Nightlife

Champions, 1009 Monterey, San Luis Obispo. 541-1161. Good old-fashioned rock 'n roll. Top 40 hits are played by a DJ in this hangout for the college crowd.

The Spirit, 1772 Joaquin Blvd., San Luis Obispo. 549-9466. Rock, calypso, reggae, and even Cajun music.

William Randolf's, 1850 Monterey, San Luis Obispo. 544-8600. Comedy acts, well-known and undiscovered.

Theater

Great American Melodrama, 1827 Pacific, Oceano;

tel. 489-2499. 19th-century melodramas as well as musicals, dramas, and romantic comedies.

Santa Barbara
(area code 805)
Where to Stay
Bayberry Inn ♛ ♛ ♛ ♛
111 West Valerio, Santa Barbara 93103; tel. 682-3199
Single room, double occupancy: $75–$115
Charming B&B. Big quilts.
El Encanto ♛ ♛ ♛ ♛
1900 Lasuen Rd., Santa Barbara 93103; tel. 687-5000
Single room, double occupancy: $100–$300
Enchanting hideaway of 100 secluded cottages in the midst of lush gardens. Swimming and tennis.
Villa Rosa ♛ ♛ ♛ ♛
15 Chapala St., Santa Barbara 93103; tel. 966-0851
Single room, double occupancy: $90–$170
Hidden treasure of 18 rooms tucked away in a Spanish colonial home. Pool, Jacuzzi, close to the beach.
Montecito Inn ♛ ♛ ♛
1295 Coast Village Rd., Montecito 93108; tel. 969-7854
Single room, double occupancy: $85–$130
Although rooms are a bit small, they are finely appointed and pleasant in their country-French style. Sauna, spa.
Four Seasons Biltmore ♛ ♛ ♛
1260 Channel Dr., Santa Barbara 93108; tel. 969-2261 or 800-228-9290
Single room, double occupancy: $170–$210
A tradition for more than 60 years. Spacious guest rooms with ocean, mountain, garden, or pool views. 18-hole putting green, croquet. The LaSala Lounge features one of the city's most romantic sunset views.
Where to Eat
Louie's Restaurant ♛ ♛ ♛
1404 De la Vina St., Santa Barbara; tel. 963-7003
Average dinner: $15
Named for the proprietor's dog, this lovely place is in the historic Upham Hotel. Light, quality dishes with pastas, chicken, or fish. Grazing menu on weekdays.

Casa de Sevilla♛♛
428 Chapala St., Santa Barbara; tel. 966-4370
Average dinner: $10
Locals call this place Pete's, but two things are certain—you'll be sure to get a warm welcome and the best margaritas in town.

Villareal Market♛♛
728 E. Haley St., Santa Barbara; tel. 963-2613
Average dinner: $5
Authentic taco joint. Open kitchen, lively crowd.

The Wine Cask♛♛
813 Anacapa St., Santa Barbara; tel. 966-9463
Average dinner: $15
Wine store tucked in back of a small bistro with changing menu planned around seasonal wines, produce, and local resources.

Shopping

Arabesque, 1114 State St., #18, Santa Barbara. Clothes by California designers.

The Children's Boutique, 1114 State St. Contemporary coverings for newborns to age 10. Books and travel accessories for the little ones.

Nightlife

The Long Bar, 111 State St., Santa Barbara; tel. 564-1215. Noisy place in a Mexican restaurant serving shaken margaritas and poppers, a mixture of tequila, kahlua, and (yuck) ginger ale, the establishment's trademark.

Rocky Galenti's, 35 State St., Santa Barbara; tel. 963-9477. In the California Hotel that the Eagles sang about. Live rock 'n roll. Best burgers in town.

Zacks, 1111 E. Cabrillo, in the Sheraton Hotel, Santa Barbara; tel. 962-2705. Contemporary jazz club.

Zelo, 630 State St., Santa Barbara; tel. 966-5792. Bi-level club with dancing on black-and-white checkered floor. Progressive sounds.

Theater

Arlington Theater, 1317 State St., Santa Barbara; tel. 963-4408. Outdoor feel in a large space that plays host to ballet, top musical concerts, and live theater. Home to Santa Barbara Symphony.

Circle Bar B Dinner Theater, Refugio Rd., Santa Barbara; tel. 968-1113. Nothing glitzy here, just some popular musicals and comedies in a Western atmosphere.

Lobero, 33 E. Canon Perdido St., Santa Barbara; tel. 963-0761. Large, 200-year-old theater is strictly legit with dramas, comedies, dance, and new works.

Solvang
(area code 805)

Where to Eat
Mattei's Tavern in Los Olivos near Solvang; tel. 688-4820
Average dinner: $12
Family menu in a rustic, historical setting. Great salad bar. Oak tables, fireplace.

THE CENTRAL VALLEY

This region, one of the richest farmlands in the world, has taken many hard knocks as a place of no interest to anyone but vegetables. In fact, though it can get unbearably hot in summer, chilling in winter and, along Interstate 5, foggy to the point of depression for drivers, the Central Valley has—dare we say it—a gold mine of historic, cultural, and recreational surprises. Nowhere can you dine better than in the agricultural heartland of California, with fine wines to accompany your meals. Here, too, are rich reminders of the gold rush era—ornate Victorian homes, Old West towns, and museums of mining. The "must sees" are few, but the many possible stops are fun.

SACRAMENTO

State capitals have a way of living in the shadow of larger, more exciting cities in their own states. So does Sacramento, but this city is a surprise. Before the power and money in California shifted south from San Francisco and the gold rush country to Los Angeles, Sacramento was the most important hub of transportation and shipping in the state. All (rail)roads led to Sacramento, and the legacy of history is formidable. Moreover, the city is one of California's prettiest.

Sacramento's wild and woolly past is well captured in several visitor attractions. A good start for a heritage tour is the elegantly renovated California State Capitol ♕ ♕ ♕ ♕ ♕, located downtown at 10th and Capitol Mall. You'll find impressive, turn-of-the-century grandeur in the 210-foot-high rotunda, marble mosaic floors, crystal chandeliers, and elaborate woodwork. A visit to the museum's 7 historic offices takes you back in time to 1906, while tours of the currently used senate and assembly chambers give a glimpse into modern-day politics in progress. Surrounding the capitol is the 40-acre Capitol Park, containing trees and shrubs from around the world.

Just northeast of the capitol on 16th and H streets is the Historic Governor's Mansion♛♛, built in 1877. The 15-room Victorian building is beautifully decorated with chandeliers, oriental rugs, and Italian marble fireplaces. The mansion served as home to 13 California governors until Ronald Reagan took office in 1967. Reagan moved into a more modern home on the north side of town; some say Nancy found the old mansion unsuitable. Then Jerry Brown found the *new* mansion too ostentatious and took a modest apartment next-door to the old mansion.

You can still take a look at Sacramento's earliest settlement, Sutter's Fort♛♛. The restored outpost now contains exhibits depicting daily life of the 19th century. The adjacent State Indian Monument♛ features displays of jewelry, clothing, and art of California's Indian cultures.

We find the most vivid slice of Sacramento's past in the 10-block section of Old Sacramento♛♛♛♛, one mile west of the capitol, along the levee of the Sacramento River. Once Sacramento's commercial district in gold rush days and headquarters of the pony express, this 28-acre park has been redeveloped into an authentic Old West town of cobblestone streets and wooden sidewalks, with museums, saloons, charming restaurants, and specialty shops. (Free walking tours are available on weekends at 10:30 A.M. and 1:30 P.M. from the Passenger Depot.)

A park highlight is the 100,000-square-foot California State Historic Railroad Museum♛♛♛, located at the north end of Old Sacramento. The largest interpretive railroad museum in the U.S., it includes 21 restored locomotives and cars and 46 exhibits, including an extensive toy train collection.

Next to the Railroad Museum is the Sacramento

History Center ♛ ♛ ♛ ♛. This reconstruction of the 1854 City Hall and Waterworks Building houses 4 galleries; one, the Eleanor McClatchy, features a collection of antique printing machines, historical newspapers and publications, and a leaf from the Gutenberg Bible of 1450.

Auto enthusiasts shouldn't pass up the California Towe Ford Museum ♛ ♛ ♛ ♛, located on Front Street in Old Sacramento. The museum exhibits every model and year of Ford from 1903 to 1953, each car lovingly restored.

INSIDERS' TIPS

Be sure to set aside at least 2 hours for Old Sacramento, and wear comfortable, flat shoes. Also bring some credit cards or extra cash; there's great hand-crafted merchandise in the various galleries and specialty shops.

Southeast of Old Sacramento is the oldest public museum in the West, the Crocker Art Museum ♛ ♛ ♛ on O Street. Built in 1873, the handsome Victorian building has been expanded recently to house its expanding collection of European masterpieces, early California paintings, oriental art and sculptures, contemporary art, and photography. The museum is wheelchair accessible, and tours for the hearing- and visually impaired can be scheduled. There's a small admission fee.

A good, post-museum antidote for antsy children is William Land Park ♛ ♛ ♛ ♛, a quarter mile east of the Sacramento River and Highway 5, and 3 miles south of the state capitol. In addition to a public golf course and picnic facilities, this 600-acre park has a small amusement center ♛ ♛, complete with a minitrain ride, merry-go-round, and other rides. Another kids' favorite is Fairytale Town ♛ ♛ ♛ ♛, a theme playground whose name says it all. The whole family should enjoy the modern Sacramento Zoo ♛ ♛ ♛, with its great variety of domestic and exotic animals.

Almond lovers will enjoy the International Visitors Center and Almond Plaza ♛ ♛ ♛, on C Street at the northeast end of downtown. The facility (officially the

Blue Diamond Building) contains a multilingual exhibit on how the almond became California's largest food export, as well as a 230-seat movie theater featuring the roast-to-riches tale of *The Amazing Almond*. Free tours of the processing plant are available during the week, and for souvenirs there's an almond products shop.

For a romantic end to the Sacramento experience, take a cruise down the Sacramento and American rivers ♕♕♕♕. Several companies offer cruise services: two of the best, both departing from Old Sacramento, are the *River City Queen*, a double-decker paddle wheeler with live music and dining, and Capitol City Cruises.

For a wilder ride, try rafting on the American River. American River Recreation ♕♕♕♕ offers guided, white-water tours ranging from rafting small waves to trips through violent rapids. The company also rents rafts for easy-going trips down the "flat water" of the Lower American River ♕♕♕♕. (For more information call 916-635-6400.)

INSIDERS' TIPS

Rafting is a seasonal activity, beginning in April and ending in October. Best conditions are in spring as the snow melt rushes down from the mountains then and it's before summer crowds. For further information on Sacramento, contact the Sacramento Convention and Visitors Bureau, 1421 K Street, Sacramento 95814; tel. 916-442-5542.

FOLSOM

With luck you haven't tired yet of gold rush history, since that's mainly what Folsom (off Highway 50) has to offer. A trip down Sutter Street ♕♕♕♕ takes you back to the golden days of 1849. Many of the structures here have been restored to their original style, including the old Wells Fargo building and the Southern Pacific Depot, both now containing period exhibits.

There are other pleasures not involving history. The

Folsom Lake State Recreation Area♛♛♛♛ is a popular locale for camping, picnicking, fishing, water sports, and horseback riding. Free daily tours of nearby Folsom Dam♛♛ and reservoir are available, too.

INSIDERS' TIPS

Antique collectors will find several fine shops on Sutter Street specializing in American, European, and Asian art, as well as collectibles ranging from old postcards to antique guns. There are also custom craft shops featuring original artwork, quilting supplies, and American Indian art.

If you enjoy wildlife, the Folsom Zoo♛♛♛ displays many animals unable to survive on their own in their original habitats.

INSIDERS' TIPS

We shouldn't forget another site in Folsom frequented by out-of-towners: Folsom Prison. After finishing the Folsom Dam tour, you may want to travel 2 miles north to the famous prison's main gate. There's an art and gift shop with crafts made by inmates; sales go toward trust funds for the artists when they're released.

For more information on Folsom contact the Folsom Chamber of Commerce, 200 Wool Street, Folsom 95630; tel. 916-985-2698.

MARYSVILLE AND YUBA CITY

There's more gold history to be mined in Marysville and Yuba City, located 45 miles north of Sacramento. Because of their prime location, these sister towns became the center of trade for the northern gold mines of the mid-1880s.

Also, in the 19th century, hydraulic mining north of the Yuba River caused the riverbed to rise, threatening Marysville with massive flooding. Levees were constructed, and for good measure, the Chinese community built the Bok Kai Temple♛♛♛ (on the levee at the foot of D Street) in honor of the Chinese water god, Bok

Kai. Bok Kai was apparently impressed (the floods never came), and you should be as well. The temple is the only one of its kind in the Western hemisphere; worship services take place regularly, and virtually the entire city participates in the annual Bok Kai Festival, usually held in March. To visit the temple, call Joe Kim, tel. 916-742-5486 for an appointment.

The Mary Aaron Museum♛, on the corner of Seventh and D streets in Marysville, is a restored home from the mid-1800s that displays mining equipment, historical photographs and documents, and antique furniture. There's no fee.

Yuba City, founded by Samuel Brennan, California's first self-made millionaire, is home to the Community Memorial Museum♛ ♛ ♛, at 1333 Butte House Road. The museum contains exhibits of Native American artifacts, pioneer memorabilia, and early agricultural equipment.

For more information on Marysville and Yuba City call the Greater Yuba City and Marysville Chamber of Commerce; tel. 916-743-6501.

CHICO

A friendly community with its own share of gold rush lore, Chico also boasts a revitalized downtown area, a highly respected college (Chico State University College), and rich agricultural valleys. We would not name it a major tourist attraction but a pleasant one.

Bidwell Mansion♛, constructed by Chico's founder, James Bidwell and located on the university campus, once served as an embassy for Western hospitality to guests like President and Mrs. Hayes, Generals Grant and Sherman, and Susan B. Anthony. Guided tours are daily from 10 A.M. to 5 P.M.; the admission fee is minimal.

Nearby is Bidwell Park♛ ♛, 2,400 acres of varied terrain including an oak and sycamore forest along the banks of Big Chico Creek. The park offers an 18-hole golf course, archery range, running and riding trails, 2 large swimming areas, a rifle range, plus children's playgrounds, and numerous picnic and barbecue facilities.

PERILS & PITFALLS

The forests of Bidwell Park are still in their natural wilderness state; only the hardiest of hikers should venture there. For more information on Bidwell Park, contact the Greater Chico Chamber of Commerce, P.O. Box 3038, 500 Main Street, Chico 95927; tel. 916-891-5556.

STOCKTON

The main claim to fame of this major port city is the Delta, a 1,000-mile inland waterway. Made up of the Sacramento, San Joaquin, and Mokelumne rivers, the Delta provides an abundance of water recreational activities: fishing for bass, sturgeon, catfish, and salmon, and even crawdad trapping. Another popular activity is relaxing on rented houseboats. (For free brochures on all member firms of the Delta Houseboat Rental Association, write: Houseboats, 6333 Pacific Avenue, Suite 152, Stockton 95207; tel. 209-477-1840.)

Although the Delta may seem remote, there are many restaurants, marinas, bistros, and "river-rat hangouts" along the tree-lined banks. One fun stop is the Waterfront Warehouse ♕ ♕ ♕, 445 West Weber Avenue at the head of the Stockton Deepwater Channel. The enormous, airy facility, which has been restored to its original brick-and-wood structure, once stored grain and flour, later to be transported by early, steam-powered paddle wheelers. The warehouse is now filled with restaurants, cafés, boutiques, import shops, and handicrafts. Strolling musicians, festive celebrations, and concerts add to the warm, friendly atmosphere.

There *is* more to Stockton than water. The Haggin Museum ♕ ♕, located in Victory Park, Pershing Avenue at Rose Street in the center of town, pays tribute to local history and international art. Museum highlights include the American Indian Gallery, which has one of the most extensive collections of California Indian basketry; a reconstruction of a turn-of-the-century California town called the Storefronts Gallery; and the Vehicle Gallery, containing historical vehicles like Stockton's own "Old Betsy," the second-oldest steam fire engine in the U.S.

The Haggin Museum's art collection is an impressive one: among the American and French artists represented are Albert Bierstadt, William Bradford, Pierre Auguste Renoir, and Paul Gauguin. Art glass, period lamps, ivory, jade, and porcelain are also on display.

For a look at more contemporary art by nationally known and local artists, visit the Alan Short Gallery♛ at 521 E. Acacia. Gallery hours are 12 to 4 P.M. Monday through Friday; 10 A.M. to 2 P.M. on Saturdays.

For more information on Stockton, contact the Stockton Convention and Visitors Bureau, 46 West Fremont Street, Stockton 95202; tel. 209-943-1987.

INSIDERS' TIPS

We recommend a winery tour through neighboring Lodi. One of California's largest producers of fine wine grapes, Lodi also hosts the Annual Lodi Grape Festival, usually held for a weekend in September. For more information contact the Lodi Chamber of Commerce, 215 W. Oak Street, Lodi 95240; tel. 209-334-4773.

MODESTO

Each year Modesto earns more than $2 billion from its fruits and other agriculture—and it's easy to see why. Throughout Modesto and in nearby communities, growers offer agricultural and tasting tours♛ ♛ ♛ ♛. Most tasting rooms include gift shops, and some facilities let you pick and pay. Treat your tastebuds to delicious fresh fruits and vegetables, enjoy the crunch of almonds and other nuts, and take a sip of the fruit of the vine from some of the local wineries. (Modesto is the home of the family-owned Ernest and Julio Gallo winery.)

Gastronomic adventures don't have to end there. You can sample some of the finest varieties of cheese and observe the cheese-making process in the town of

Riverbank, less than 20 minutes from downtown Modesto. Choc o-holics can sample a bit of paradise at the Hershey Chocolate West Coast Plant ♛ ♛ ♛ ♛ in Oakdale, another community just outside Modesto. (For a listing of growers and tasting facilities see page 210.)

For a taste of Modesto's history, visit the McHenry Museum ♛, a Victorian-style former library located at 1402 I Street downtown. You'll discover an archive of the area's history, full-scale replicas of an 1880s doctor's office, general store, and blacksmith shop, as well as gold-mining equipment, antique guns, and cattle brands. Admission is free.

Also at the same address you'll find the Central California Art League Gallery ♛, featuring works of 100 artists on display for rent or sale.

River rafting trips down the Stanislaus and Tuolumne rivers are available, as are houseboating and waterskiing. Adventure-Sunshine River Trips/Outdoor Center ♛ ♛ in Oakdale (tel. 209-847-8908) provides 1- or 2-day canoe and white-water raft trips, as well as cross-country-ski tours. Great Valley Canoe and Raft Trips ♛ ♛ in Riverbank (tel. 209-869-1235) offer canoe and kayak schools, driftboat fishing, and guided and self-guided river trips.

INSIDERS' TIPS

The Modesto Chamber of Commerce will assist you in planning a trip to the Mother Lode region and with water sports activities. They can be reached at 1114 J Street, P.O. Box 844, Modesto 95353; tel. 209-577-5757.

If you're planning to visit Yosemite National Park, Modesto is within a 2-hour drive of its glacier-carved canyons. Four outstanding scenic routes lead to the national park, each with its own share of history and beauty. For more information contact the Modesto Chamber of Commerce.

MERCED

Merced may be known best as the northern gateway to Yosemite; but if you decide to stop here en route to the great park, you'll find some impressive museums and a terrific spot for outdoor relaxation.

The main attraction of Merced County Courthouse♛♛♛, in Courthouse Park on 21st and N streets, isn't its collection of pioneer artifacts; it's the courthouse itself. Built in 1875 and restored in the early 1980s, the courthouse was designed in the ornate Italian-Renaissance style, resembling the state capitol building.

Aviation and military history buffs shouldn't miss the Castle Air Museum♛♛♛♛, located on Santa Fe Drive and Buhach Road in the nearby town of Atwater. Twenty-four vintage military planes dating back to World War II and up to the present are on display. Museum hours are 10 A.M. to 4 P.M. daily.

The Yosemite Wildlife Museum♛♛♛, 2040 Yosemite Parkway in Merced, allows visitors a close look at (mounted) area wildlife in settings depicting their natural habitat. (The museum also contains a shooting range!) The museum is open daily, and there's a nominal admission charge.

Lake Yosemite♛♛♛♛, just a few miles north of Merced, has something for everyone in outdoor fun: waterskiing, boating, sailing, and canoeing, as well as shaded picnic areas and 2 beaches for those who just enjoy watching the ships go by.

For more information on Merced, contact the Merced County Chamber of Commerce, P.O. Box 1112 Merced 95340; tel. 209-722-3864, or the Merced Convention and Visitors Bureau, P.O. Box 3107, Merced 95344; tel. 209-384-3333.

FRESNO

At the base of the rolling foothills of Sierra Nevada lies Fresno, a city of expanding growth and great beauty. This self-proclaimed "agricultural capital of the world," located 222 miles north of Los Angeles, offers easy access to some of California's most splendid natural wonders.

The grassy and hokey Wonder Valley♛♛♛, 15

miles southeast of Fresno in the Sierra National Forest, was once home to the Yokut Indians and a hideout for those thievin' varmints, the Dalton Brothers. Today (although a bit overdone) visit the rustic Wonder Valley Ranch Resort♕♕♕, California's first dude ranch. Among the old-fashioned activities here are horseback riding, hayrides, goat-milking contests, and chuck-wagon barbecues. Guests usually spend 3 or 4 days at the ranch, but you can decide what's best for you by contacting the resort at Box 71, Star Route, Sanger 93657; tel. 209-787-2551, or 800-821-2801 in California.

The best of the Sierras can be found in Yosemite National Park♕♕♕♕♕, 91 miles north of Fresno on State Highway 41; Kings Canyon National Park♕♕♕♕♕, 56 miles east of Fresno on State Highway 180; and the land of the giant trees, Sequoia National Park♕♕♕♕♕, along State Highway 180 and 84 miles east of Fresno. The recreation possibilities here are almost endless; there's everything from ice-skating and cross-country skiing in the winter to backpacking, swimming, and rock-climbing in the spring and summer.

INSIDERS' TIPS

If you have time, you'll enjoy a tour of Kings Canyon/ Sequoia that departs from Fresno and includes meals and 2 nights' lodging. For more information call 209-565-3373.

Mother Nature wasn't the only architect to work in Fresno: the Forestiere Underground Gardens♕♕♕♕, 5021 West Shaw (near Highway 99), is a unique complex of subterranean rooms, passageways, and gardens with arches and stonework patterned after the Roman catacombs. Its designer, Sicilian immigrant Baldassare Forestiere, hand-sculpted the gardens for almost 40 years. (For information call 209-275-3792.)

In Woodward Park♕♕♕, on the San Joaquin River between Highway 41 and Friant Expressway, you'll find a lake, pond, stream systems, children's play area, fitness course, picnic area, and bird sanctuary.

The park's highlight is the Shin-Zen "Friendship" Garden ♛ ♛ ♛, a Japanese garden with beautiful waterfalls, koi fish, and numerous varieties of trees. The park is open daily from 7 A.M. to dusk, but the garden is open only on weekends, from 10 A.M. to 3 P.M.

You can spend a full day in Roeding Park ♛ ♛ ♛ ♛, 890 W. Belmont Avenue off Highway 90; among its attractions are fishing lakes, 14 tennis courts, an amphitheater, and Story Land ♛ ♛ ♛, a children's playground and amusement park. The Fresno Zoo ♛ ♛ ♛ ♛, also in Roeding Park, is one of the top 3 zoos in California, home to over 700 animals and the site of the world's only computer-controlled habitat, Reptile House. The zoo is especially committed to preserving wildlife and houses one of the few Asian elephant breeding centers in North America. The zoo is open daily; there's a nominal admission fee.

On weekends you can visit Roeding Park's Fort Miller Blockhouse ♛ ♛ ♛, built in 1851 as a refuge for early settlers during the Mariposa Indian War. The blockhouse now features exhibits on life in pre-1900 Fresno, the logging era, and early county history.

Kearney Mansion Museum ♛ ♛ ♛, 7160 Kearney Boulevard in Kearney Park, is a beautifully restored French-Renaissance-style home. The mansion still contains many elegant furnishings and decorations, brought from Western Europe in the early 1900s by its owner, raisin baron M. Theodore Kearney (yes, Fresno is big on raisin' raisins). Tours are available March through December, Wednesday through Sunday from 2 P.M. to 4 P.M. There's a minimal fee.

Another popular mansion is the restored Meux Home Museum ♛ ♛, built in 1889 by Dr. Thomas R. Meux and located at 1007 R Street at Tulare. This lovely Victorian house was probably Fresno's most elaborate residence of its time. In addition to period exhibits, the museum sometimes presents live concerts.

Art has played an important part in Fresno culture, past and present. The Fresno Metropolitan Museum of Art, History, and Science ♛ ♛ ♛, 1555 Van Ness, offers a permanent collection of American and European Old Masters. The museum also features traveling exhibits and Ansel Adams photographs. Hours are 11 A.M. to 5 P.M. Wednesday through Friday; noon to 5 P.M. Saturday and Sunday.

The Fresno Arts Center and Museum♛♛♛, 2233 N. First Street in Radio Park, presents over 22 exhibitions each year focusing on 19th- and 20th-century art. Education programs are offered for adults and children, along with tours, lectures, and concerts. The center is open Tuesday through Sunday, 10 A.M. to 5 P.M. On Saturday and Sunday admission is free to all visitors.

Discover science at the *Discovery Center*♛♛♛, 1944 N. Winery Avenue; you'll find fun family exhibits like the whisper cones, a laser phone, an electronic sound tree, and the Native American Indian Room. The Center is open Tuesday through Sunday.

For more information on Fresno, contact the Fresno Visitors Bureau, P.O. Box 1792, Fresno 93717; tel. 209-486-4636.

INSIDERS' INFORMATION FOR THE CENTRAL VALLEY

Fresno
(area code 209)
Where to Stay
The San Joaquin♛♛♛♛
1309 W. Shaw Ave., Fresno 93711; tel. 225-1309
Single room, double occupancy: $59–$90
All-suite hotel is stylish with pool, whirlpool, nonsmoking rooms, and an attractive environment. 68 units.
Shopping
Collectibles (in Western Boot & Shoe), 1155 Fulton Mall, downtown. More than 4,000 items in stock, from prints to plates.

Fulton's Folly Antique Mall, 920 E. Olive Ave., tower district. More than 80 shops with American and European antiques.
Wineries
Cribari Winery, 3223 East Church Ave., near US 99; tel. 485-3083. Guided tours.

Old Master Winery/Heritage Cellars, 2310 S. Railroad Ave., Fresno; tel. 442-8452. Daily tours.

Theaters

Golden Chain Theater, in Oakhurst (30 miles north of Fresno); tel. 683-7112. Melodrama, audience participation.

Merced
(area code 209)
Where to Stay

Best Western Pine Cone Inn♛♛♛

1213 V St., Merced 95340; tel. 723-3711

Single room, double occupancy: $40

97 rooms overlooking scenic landscape. Pool, gardens.

Where to Eat

Branding Iron♛♛♛♛

642 W. 16th St., Merced; tel. 722-1822

Average dinner: $10

Steak and seafood grilled over oak.

Modesto
(area code 209)
Where to Eat

Cask 'n Cleaver♛♛♛♛♛

3037 Sisk Rd., Modesto; tel. 576-0908

Average dinner: $13

The valley's best bet. Steak and seafood.

Wineries

Delicato Vineyards, 12001 S. Hwy. 99, Monteca, north of Modesto; tel. 239-1215. Tours daily.

Franzia Winery, 17000 Hwy. 120, Ripon, north of Modesto; tel. 599-6511.

Sacramento
(area code 916)
Where to Stay

Briggs House Bed and Breakfast Inn♛♛♛♛

2209 Capitol Ave., Sacramento 95816; tel. 441-3214

Single room, double occupancy: $55 and up

Restored Victorian, cube-type colonial inn, surrounded by stately trees. A few blocks from state capitol. 7

rooms, sauna and spa in shaded backyard. Some shared baths. Bicycles.

The Driver Mansion Inn ♛ ♛ ♛ ♛
2019 21st St., Sacramento 95818; tel. 455-5243
Single room, double occupancy: $55
Elegant Victorian building, near state capitol. Lush gardens with Victorian gazebo. 8 rooms, 6 with private bath.

Sacramento Hilton Inn ♛ ♛ ♛ ♛
2200 Harvard St., Sacramento 95815; tel. 922-4700, or 800-344-4321
Single room, double occupancy: $89
Modern hotel with just about everything: nightclub, health club, hydro-whirlpool, indoor pool, sauna—and even afternoon tea on Sundays.

Sheraton Sunrise Hotel and Towers ♛ ♛ ♛ ♛
11211 Point East Dr., Rancho Cordova 95670; tel. 638-1100, or 800-325-3535
Single room, double occupancy: $75
Modern 11-story, boomerang-shaped building with 265 rooms, off Highway 50 on the way to Lake Tahoe.

Aunt Abigail's Bed and Breakfast Inn ♛ ♛ ♛
2120 G St., Sacramento 95816; tel. 441-5007
Single room, double occupancy: $50–$75
Majestic, colonial-revival mansion on a tree-lined street, 5 rooms, 3 with private bath.

Clarion Hotel Sacramento ♛ ♛ ♛
700 16th St., Sacramento 95814; tel. 444-8000, or 800-CLARION
Single room, double occupancy: $76–$86
Ivy-covered hotel across from the Governor's Mansion. Fountains, lush landscaping. Celebs who appear at the summer Music Circus or the Convention Center stay here. 239 rooms.

Where to Eat

The Firehouse ♛ ♛ ♛ ♛ ♛
1112 Second St., Old Sacramento; tel. 442-4772
Average dinner: $25
Historical landmark, filled with stained glass and antiques, serves Continental cuisine with a flourish. Elegant, extensive wine list.

Harlow's♛♛♛♛
2712 J St., Sacramento; tel. 441-4693
Average dinner: $15
Italian-California cuisine features fresh fish and pasta and a unique ricotta cheesecake.

Crawdad's River Cantina♛♛♛
1375 Garden Highway, Sacramento; tel. 929-2268
Average dinner: $12
Yuppie hangout on the Sacramento River serves Mexican-style dishes, indoors or out.

Fanny Ann's Saloon♛♛
1023 Second St., Old Sacramento; tel. 441-0505
Average dinner: $5
Old West saloon is funky but fun, offering burgers and fries.

Shopping

Artists' Collaboration Gallery, 107 Second St., Old Sacramento. Artists cooperative with eclectic selection of fashions, sculptures, jewelry.

The Emigrants, 1109 Front St., Sacramento. Scandinavian, Russian, and Austrian clothing and crafts.

Gallery of the American West, 121 K St. Authentic Native American art and jewelry. Antique coins, memorabilia of the Old West.

This and That Sales, The Brass Connection, 1019 Second St., Old Sacramento. FCC-approved oak and brass phones, elaborate brass bottle openers, and other various and sundry brass items.

Nightlife

Fox and Goose, 1001 R St., Sacramento; tel. 443-8825. British pub. The local watering hole, but not a meat market. Live jazz or blues.

Laughs Unlimited, 1124 Firehouse Alley, Sacramento; tel. 446-5905. Comedy house with unknowns as well as knowns.

Shire Road Pub, 5525 Auburn, Sacramento; tel. 334-7901. Not what you would call yuppie heaven, more for those stuck in the sixties, with some good old rock and roll.

Stockton
(area code 209)
Where to Stay
Stockton Hilton♛♛♛♛
2323 Grand Canal Blvd., Stockton 95207; tel. 957-9090
Single room, double occupancy: $78 and up
Stockton's most elegant hotel. 198 rooms. Wading pool, pool, health club.
Where to Eat
Le Bistro♛♛♛♛♛
3121 W. Benjamin Halt Dr., Stockton; tel. 951-0885
Average dinner: $20
Fine Continental cuisine, innovative preparations. Expensive wine list.
Shannon's♛♛♛♛
4722 Quail Lakes Dr., Stockton; tel. 952-1637
Average dinner: $15
Seafood specialties, entertainment, cocktail lounge.
Ye Olde Hoosier Inn♛♛♛♛
1537 N. Wilson Way, Stockton; tel. 463-0271
Average dinner: $8
Charming, quaint early American eatery decorated with rare antiques.
Nightlife
Paddle wheeler *Mathew McKinley*, Old Sacramento; tel. 441-6481. Dinner and dancing on the Delta.

Yuba City
(area code 916)
Where to Stay
The Wick's Bed & Breakfast Inn♛♛♛
560 Cooper Ave., Yuba City 95991; tel. 674-7951
Single room, double occupancy: $80
1920s house, modest but comfortable with hand-carved French furnishings. 3 rooms, 2 with private bath.

THE GOLD COUNTRY
NEVADA CITY AND GRASS VALLEY

You can see the gold country in only a day or two, but a 5-day trip gives a much better feel for the area. A good place to begin exploring its northern region is in the Nevada City/Grass Valley area. Here, lots of sites are accessible and the roads easy to navigate. Highway 49, often called the Golden Chain or the Mother Lode Highway, spans the length, crossing gorges, rivers, silent ghost towns, and not-so-silent towns of another era lively with today's tourist trade. Stop at as many landmarks as you have energy for. Most of them are well marked, and signs are placed to give drivers ample warning.

> ### PERILS & PITFALLS
> The Mother Lode, as this area was known, is in full gear for tourists in the summer. In winter, even though the weather is usually temperate, rain frequently makes trails muddy. Many attractions stay open year-round, but others restrict their hours or close altogether. It's smart to call before visiting.

Nevada City ♛♛♛♛, known as the Queen City of the Northern Mines, is probably the most historically realistic of all the Mother Lode cities—not including Columbia, which has been preserved in its gold rush state as a national park. Visitors can still meet wizened, old miners with long gray hair and beards, wearing black-and-red-checked shirts and suspenders. They no longer have mules by their side, so you'll have to use your imagination there.

A good starting point is Firehouse No. 1 ♛♛♛ on Main Street. This Victorian gem with gingerbread trim

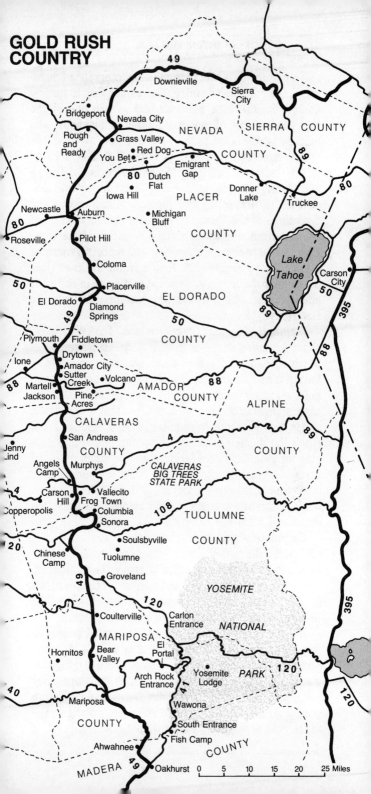

GOLD RUSH COUNTRY

Downieville
Sierra City
SIERRA COUNTY
Bridgeport
Nevada City
NEVADA
Rough and Ready
Grass Valley
You Bet
Red Dog
COUNTY
89
Emigrant Gap
80
Dutch Flat
PLACER
Iowa Hill
Donner Lake
Truckee
80
Newcastle
Auburn
Michigan Bluff
COUNTY
80
Roseville
Pilot Hill
Coloma
Lake Tahoe
Carson City
50
Placerville
EL DORADO
El Dorado
Diamond Springs
50
50
49
Plymouth
Fiddletown
COUNTY
89
Ione
Drytown
Amador City
Sutter Creek
Volcano
88
Martell
Jackson
Pine Acres
AMADOR
88
COUNTY
ALPINE
CALAVERAS
San Andreas
COUNTY
89
Jenny Lind
COUNTY
4
Angels Camp
Murphys
CALAVERAS BIG TREES STATE PARK
Carson Hill
Vallecito
Frog Town
4
Copperopolis
Columbia
108
TUOLUMNE
20
Sonora
Soulsbyville
COUNTY
Chinese Camp
Tuolumne
49
Groveland
YOSEMITE
120
395
Coulterville
Carlon Entrance
NATIONAL
MARIPOSA
El Portal
Hornitos
Bear Valley
Arch Rock Entrance
Yosemite Lodge
PARK
120
40
Mariposa
Wawona
41
COUNTY
South Entrance
Ahwahnee
Fish Camp
49
MADERA
Oakhurst
0 5 10 15 20 25 Miles
395
120

and a bell tower is one of the most photographed buildings in all gold rush country. The Nevada City Historical Society maintains a museum here where one of the finest collections of pioneer clothing, implements, and records is displayed.

The American Victorian Museum♛♛♛♛, located in the Miners Foundry (1865) on the corner of Bridge and Spring streets, is the only museum in the U.S. devoted to presenting the life-style, innovations, and inventions of the Victorian era. The Pelton wheel that sits out front was an important invention of the time. This link between a waterwheel and modern generator was perfected by Lester A. Pelton on the banks of Deer Creek near the foundry. Even today it's one of the most efficient methods of converting the force of water to electricity.

Malakoff Diggins State Historic Park♛♛♛♛, about 11 miles north of Nevada City, off Route 49 at North Bloomfield Road, is a strange, even eerie place. Part of it contains restored buildings from North Bloomfield, a former boomtown. The Diggins reveal the ravages of hydraulic mining, a method that used water, under high pressure from hoses, to flood the land and reach the gold underneath—a method much like panning for gold, only on a larger scale. So much rock and earth was washed into the Yuba River the surrounding land was virtually destroyed. What's left is otherworldly: strange mounds of oddly colored, water-beaten rocks and little vegetation.

Fortunately this hydraulic method was used only briefly, thanks to farmers and ranchers near the "mine." To protect their land, which was always being flooded, they went to court in 1884 and won one of the country's first environmental protection edicts, forcing the Bloomfield Mining Company to stop the practice.

If you're eager to mine some gold yourself, be sure to stop in at Deer Creek Mining♛♛♛♛♛, 426 Broad Street, where the proprietors demonstrate a tried-and-true method of panning for gold right in the store. They use a large tub of rocks and dirt they've taken from a nearby stream and a pan with riffles (or notches). Because gold is 9 times heavier than any other metal, it sinks to the bottom of the pan—provided the miner is lucky *and* uses the proper circular wrist action. Debris drifts off, and whatever gold was hiding in the dirt and rocks becomes trapped by the riffles.

If the demonstration at Deer Creek only whets your appetite for the real thing, you can arrange for a panning expedition led by one, or all, of the characters who run the shop: Curt, an ex-clown; Rusty, a former housewife; Steve; or Dave, a musician.

These people know their streambeds and rivers—especially nearby Deer Creek. They'll also take you to more scenic rivers and not only show you *where* to pan for gold but *how*. The best places are near tree roots, they say, because this is where currents converge. The whole panning lesson out here in the wild progresses from dirt and rocks to black sand, then finally, *hopefully*, pay dirt! Just about everyone can expect to pan at least a bit of gold, if he or she persists.

A few miles south of Nevada City is Grass Valley♛♛♛♛, the largest of the northern mining towns and the site of many of the big mines that operated until the early 1950s. Grass Valley is an ironic name for this town, considering that almost $100 million worth of gold has been unearthed from beneath its streets. Whatever its name, Grass Valley was the home of one of the most colorful figures of the gold rush era, Lola Montez, a dazzling Bavarian performer who presumably came to Grass Valley to retire. Her eccentricities included installing state-of-the-art conveniences like a bathtub—almost unheard of in gold rush boomtowns—and chaining her pet bear to a tree in front of her house. A replica of the Lola Montez House♛♛♛ still stands at 248 Mill Street, where it's now home to the Nevada County Chamber of Commerce as well as a small history museum.

Outside Grass Valley, a tour of the Empire Mine State Park♛♛♛♛♛, 10791 East Empire Street, completes the historical picture of what the gold rush was all about. It shows visitors that alongside panners there were hundreds of men who worked far beneath the land to pull out lots more of the almighty metal.

The Empire Mine was the oldest and richest hard-rock mine in California. Docents who conduct tours here are extremely well versed in the mine's vital statistics. On summer weekends guides dress in period garb as part of a living history program that will soon be expanded to include other costumed "workers" in the refinery and blacksmith shop, too.

Visitors who take the tour can go 40 feet underground to see the working mine itself. The shaft is illuminated for 150 feet; the actual mine descends a total of 11,000 feet. A wire model shows the direction and depth of each vein. There's also a stamp mill—the piece of equipment that flattens the gold—and a compressor house, blacksmith shop, and other mine workshops. Don't miss the mine manager's office, which has been left as it was when the company finally closed its doors, complete with papers on the desk.

The *pièce de résistance*, however, is the Bourn Cottage and grounds. Built by mine-owner William Bourn, Jr. around the turn of the century, the "cottage" is really more of a mansion. In fact, it was one of the first buildings in the area to have electricity. Plants from all over the world grace its beautiful grounds. Most of the roses are early varieties, many pre-1920s.

South of Grass Valley, where Highway 49 meets Interstate 80, is the city of Auburn ♛ ♛ ♛, the dividing line between the mines in the northern gold country and those in the south. Auburn's Old Town is recognized as a state historical site—many of the oldest structures now house antique shops and restaurants. One of the most unique among them is the old firehouse. It's red and white with a steeply pitched tower and dates to 1893. Auburn also has a gold-rush-era Chinese merchants' section.

COLOMA AND PLACERVILLE

Eighteen miles down Route 49 is the town of Coloma ♛ ♛ ♛ ♛, most of which is part of Marshall Discovery State Park. It was here in 1848 that the gold rush began. As the story goes, John Sutter, an agricultural giant in the area, arranged with one of his workmen, James Wilson Marshall, to build a sawmill along the south fork of the American River. Construction of the mill began in late 1847. On the morning of January 24, 1848, when Marshall was inspecting its progress, he spotted shiny flecks in the water, scooped them up, pounded them with a rock, and after testing them with his fingernail, announced, "Boys I believe I have found a gold mine."

The rest is history, of course. Several thousand people flocked to Coloma from all over the world. Today, the town has about 200 residents, but every January hundreds of visitors throng the streets to celebrate the anniversary of the discovery of gold with parades and bands.

There's lots of gold rush memorabilia to see in the park year-round, foremost of which is the working replica of the original mill (now electrically powered), which replaced the original after it had been abandoned and vandalized.

A self-guided tour will take you past exhibits that show various mining methods, tools, and household articles used during gold rush days. One of particular interest is a list of household goods, and how much they cost over a hundred years ago. Many items were actually more expensive than they are today. When you consider the burden and expense of transporting goods across the country—not to mention the spendthrift silliness of those who'd just struck it rich—it's no wonder at all that a canister of tea cost $13, a 50-pound bag of beans was $25, one candle cost $3, and a comb $6!

Other displays at the park include an authentic Chinese store, an ore car, stamp mills, a miner's cabin, gunsmith and blacksmith shops, and a Mormon cabin. The American River is quite accessible from here, and you can hike along it, or swim in it.

PERILS & PITFALLS

While you may be tempted to stop the car for a hike through the hills of the gold country, check first to be sure you're not on private property. Better to keep your hiking and outdoor activities within designated parks and recreation areas.

A 20-minute drive south brings you to Placerville ♛ ♛ ♛, originally known as Dry Diggins and later as Hangtown (it was the site of the first hanging in gold country). Because a fire leveled many of Placerville's oldest buildings, the town is a hodgepodge of old and new. Placerville Hardware, at 441 Main Street, dates to 1856, and there *are* other old buildings in town. Just ask.

Gold Bug Mine ♛ ♛ ♛ on Bedford Avenue, is one of the few neighborhood gold mines open to the public. The shaft is illuminated, the better for visitors to see the gold-bearing quartz vein.

In El Dorado County, outside Placerville, explorers to the area find more than gold rush lore. Agriculture is now top dog, and Apple Hill ♛ ♛ ♛ ♛ is one great way for visitors to experience some of the best firsthand. Off Route 50 outside of Placerville, a group of 45 apple-, pear-, plum-, cherry-, and peach-growers have formed a cooperative. During growing season from June to October, each offers a special treat to visitors who drive from ranch to ranch sampling goodies. During apple season in the fall, for example, treats from the traditional apple turnover to apple donuts and even more exotic apple confections are available depending upon where your nose takes you.

Another attraction that has nothing to do with the gold rush—but remains one we'd visit again and again—is Bennett Sculpture Foundry ♛ ♛ ♛ ♛ ♛, 4504 Greenstone Road. Here, brothers Bob and Tom Bennett create and pour their sleek, whimsical sculptures, so well known among art collectors. There are tours of the foundry which shows visitors how a piece of sculpture is created from start to finish, including the impressive pourings.

SUTTER CREEK AND ANGELS CAMP

Sutter Creek ♛ ♛ ♛, a well-preserved gold rush town and antique-buyer's haven, is about 30 miles from Placerville. You can find everything from old sheriff's badges and early Coca-Cola memorabilia to stately

American antiques at about a dozen shops that line the streets. Sutter Creek is such a peaceful town, full of dainty cottages with white picket fences, that it's hard to believe 13 saloons once lined Main Street. A self-guided walking tour is available at local shops.

INSIDERS' TIPS

Much of gold country is also *wine* country. In Amador, Calaveras, El Dorado, and Tuolumne counties are a number of small, family-run wineries. These include: Granite Springs Winery and Vineyards, and Boeger Winery in El Dorado; Amador Foothill Winery and Shenandoah Vineyards in Amador. Most wineries are open for tours and tasting on the weekends.

Down the road a bit is Jackson♛♛, a town once jumping with gold rush fever. Here the towering tailing wheel from the Kennedy Mine is said to be the most sketched and painted mining item in Mother Lode country. The wheel is on display at the Amador County Museum♛♛♛, along with a working scale model of a head frame, also from the Kennedy Mine.

Continuing south on Route 49 takes you into Angels Camp♛♛♛, in Calaveras County, made famous by Mark Twain in "The Celebrated Jumping Frog of Calaveras County." To this day the city of Angels Camp hosts the Jumping Frog Jubilee. The jubilee is in May, but the frog is a part of the town's image year-round. There are frogs above stores, on signs, and on almost everything that sits on a gift shop shelf.

The Angels Camp Museum♛♛, on Route 49 just before you reach downtown, is small but chock-full of interesting mineral specimens and mining equipment, including a large collection of vehicles used by the railroads. Look for the Pelton waterwheel outside.

At the end of town, take Route 4 toward Murphys for a memorable side trip to Moaning Caverns♛♛♛♛. Follow the signs past Vallecito—even though at first you may seem to be heading nowhere. At the end of the road, you'll find an unassuming little building. That's the entrance to the underground caverns.

The caverns were discovered by miners, who also found the bodies of more than 100 people when they reached the bottom, 165 feet below the surface. Remains of the oldest corpse were tested and found to be about 13,000 years old. Scientists believe they weren't buried here, but that the poor souls fell to their deaths, after which their remains were preserved by the rich mineral deposits.

The name of the caverns—"Moaning"—comes from the sound the water makes when it drips deep inside the caverns. Indians, though, had a different idea. They believed the moaning sound was made by tortured souls.

Farther along on Route 4 you'll reach Murphys ♛ ♛ ♛, another gold rush relic. Murphys is also the name of the city's hotel ♛ ♛ ♛ ♛, built in 1856, making it one of California's oldest. The guest register boasts such familiar names as Ulysses S. Grant, Mark Twain, and Thomas Lipton (of tea fame).

COLUMBIA, SONORA, AND MARIPOSA

About 3 miles off Route 49, just north of Sonora, is Columbia, a town known as the "Gem of the Southern Mines." It's now a state park and a living tribute to the days of the gold rush. The main thoroughfare is closed to traffic daily from 9 A.M. to 5 P.M., which makes a stroll through town that much more pleasant. All storekeepers wear period garb.

Columbia's brick-lined buildings are authentic remnants of the 1850s. Self-activated tape recordings located throughout the park tell tales of some of the boomtown businesses, including the dentist's office, the Chinese market, and drugstore. The Wells Fargo office is complete with a schedule of departing and arriving stages. More fun is a real-life stagecoach ride through town. Columbia even boasts a candy store that sells the kind of homemade confections popular during the gold rush days! If what you're after is something to wet your whistle, not satisfy your sweet tooth, there are several saloons where a weary traveler can rest body and soul—and throw back a few. Those who've still got gold fever can try their luck panning in the nearby stream.

The City Hotel ♕ ♕ ♕ ♕ ♕ is the training center for Columbia Junior College's restaurant management program, and the French food they serve is without rival in these parts. (See Insiders' Information, page 224.) Another main attraction of the town is the repertory season that runs for 8 weeks in summer at the Fallon Theater. Like lots of other things in Columbia, the theater is old-fashioned—complete with an ice-cream parlor. (See under Fallon Hotel, page 225.)

A few miles south is Sonora ♕ ♕ ♕ ♕, the seat of Tuolumne County. Today Sonora is a bustling metropolis. More than 100 years ago, it wasn't only bustling, it was bad. In fact Sonora was reputed to be one of the most wicked towns in all of gold country. Bloody feuds and bandits coexisted with handsome adobe structures, which remain symbols of the city's Mexican heritage. Some of the best shopping in the Mother Lode region is also located here.

Down the road, at the junction of routes 49 and 108, is Jamestown ♕ ♕ ♕ ♕. If you're a movie buff this town may look familiar. *High Noon, Butch Cassidy and the Sundance Kid,* and *The Gambler* were all filmed here. Images of two-storied false-front buildings with intricate wooden railings have made their indelible impression—it's this image that comes most clearly to mind when we think of the gold rush days. Today in Jamestown you'll still find these remnants of the Old West, as well as restored inns, art galleries, and plenty of antique shops.

The biggest attraction is Railtown 1897 Historic Park ♕ ♕ ♕ on Fifth Street, where viewers can climb aboard one of the old steam engines and pretend they're chugging along on the Sierra Railroad (the line built in 1897 to connect the mines of the Mother Lode with freight centers in the San Joaquin Valley). Sierra's "Old Number 3" and other locomotives have been featured in movies and on television shows such as "Petticoat Junction" and "Little House on the Prairie."

About an hour farther south is Mariposa ♕ ♕ ♕. The

County Courthouse♛♛, built in 1854, is a charming New England-style building and the oldest courthouse in continuous use in California. The Mariposa County Museum and History Center♛♛♛ houses a unique collection of gold rush mementos.

If you're not exhausted by now, you'll soon reach the southernmost area of the Mother Lode. Madera County links gold country with Yosemite National Park. Recreational activities abound. There's skiing, boating, swimming, and hiking. Oakhurst♛♛♛♛ is Madera's largest city. It's full of turn-of-the-century architecture and sponsors lots of popular festivals throughout the year. For instance, in March there's Cowchilla's Stampede, a world famous rodeo; in September, Oakhurst's Mountaineer Days, and Madera's Olde Timers Day, which honors 50-year residents with a parade, barbecues, and other events.

The 7 historic buildings of the Fresno Flats Historical Park♛♛♛, 427 School Road, are an attempt by volunteers of the Sierra Historical Sites Association to capture the flavor of life as it was in the central California foothills and mountains a century ago. And they do it well. Among the offerings are Madera County's second oldest schoolhouse/museum; a collection of wagons from the gold rush era; two 19th-century jails; and a log house built in 1867.

INSIDERS' INFORMATION FOR THE GOLD COUNTRY

Angels Camp
(area code 209)
Where to Eat
The Pickle Barrel♛
1225 South Main St., Angels Camp; tel. 736-4704
Average dinner: $7–$9
Surprisingly good Italian fare in a deli-like atmosphere.

Coloma
(area code 916)
Where to Stay
The Vineyard House ♛ ♛ ♛ ♛
Cold Springs Rd., P.O. Box 176, Coloma 95613; tel. 622-2217
Single room, double occupancy: $54–$64
Tiny, 7-room Victorian inn, circa 1878, on the South Fork of the American River. The closest place to the Gold Discovery Park. Idyllic setting. Country cooking at the in-house restaurant(♛ ♛ ♛ ♛ ♛), with favorites like chicken and dumplings, and bread pudding for an average price of $10.

Columbia
(area code 209)
Where to Stay
The City Hotel ♛ ♛ ♛ ♛ ♛
Main St. (P.O. Box 1870), Columbia 95310; tel. 532-1479
Single room, double occupancy: $65
In the middle of Columbia State Park, this link to the turn of the century looks the same as it did to the gold miners who stayed there; lace curtains, brass beds, heavy wood furniture. 9 rooms (shower room down the hall). You get robes, slippers, and a complimentary Continental breakfast. The City Hotel Restaurant(♛ ♛ ♛ ♛ ♛) is the best French restaurant for miles. For an average of $25 per person, you'll dine on delicious meals like lobster in puffed pastry with whiskey sauce.
Fallon Hotel ♛
Main St. (P.O. Box 1870), Columbia 95310; tel. 532-1470
Single room, double occupancy: $60
This 14-room, brick Victorian hostelry is in Columbia State Park. Established in 1857, it has such convenient amenities as an ice-cream parlor and a theater (for current production, call 532-4644.)

Grass Valley
(area code 916)
Where to Stay
Murphy's Inn ♛ ♛ ♛ ♛

318 Neal St., Grass Valley 95945; tel. 273-6873

Single room, double occupancy: $70

8-room Victorian B&B in city's historic district. Mark Murphy is known for the best breakfasts in town. Quaint touches like antique grooming kits in the bedrooms.

Holbrooke Hotel ♛

212 W. Main St., Grass Valley 95945; tel. 273-1353

Single room, double occupancy: $60

Historic landmark, established 1851 has 27 guest rooms that are meticulously restored with brass beds and antiques. Rooms are named after famous people who have spent the night. We liked the one named for Mark Twain. André's restaurant (♛) serves a diverse Continental menu amid lots of plants and flowers. (Average meal, $14.)

Jamestown
(area code 209)
Where to Stay
Royal Hotel ♛

Main St., Jamestown 95327; tel. 984-5271

Single room, double occupancy: $49

A dainty B&B with 16 secluded cottages and rooms decorated with chenille bedspreads, brass beds, and other period touches. Library, television in the lounge.

Where to Eat
James Hotel Restaurant ♛ ♛ ♛

Main St., Jamestown; tel. 984-3902

Average dinner: $10.50

Period garb hangs from hooks on the calico walls, renowned for its unusual fish dishes.

Murphys
(area code 209)
Where to Stay
Murphys Hotel ♛ ♛ ♛

457 Main St., Murphys 95247; tel. 728-3444

Single room, double occupancy: $45
One of the longest operating hotels in California, this
quaint hotel, circa 1856, has named several rooms for
famous guests, like John Jacob Astor, J. Pierpont Mor-
gan, Ulysses S. Grant. Book one of the 9 rooms in the
historic section of the hotel, not in the new motor court.
Murphys Hotel Restaurant(♛♛♛) has stone walls
dressed up with lace and is known for excellent prime
rib at an average of $10 per dinner.

Nevada City
(area code 916)
Where to Eat
The Country Rose Café♛♛♛
300 Commercial St., Nevada City; tel. 265-6248
Average dinner: $12
Casual country dining with a changing blackboard
menu featuring French food, fresh meats, and vegetari-
an dishes.
Friar Tuck♛♛
111 N. Pine St., Nevada City; tel. 265-9093
Average dinner: $14.95
Popular for fondue dinners as well as specialties like
Coquille St. Tuck—scallops with mushrooms and
Gruyere cheese.
Theater
Nevada Theater, 701 Broad St., Nevada City; tel.
265-6161. Film animation festival, stage plays, film
lectures, concerts.
Shopping
Little Crystal Rock Shop, 310 Commercial St. Spec-
tacular selection of rock and mineral specimens.

Placerville
(area code 916)

Where to Stay
The Rupley House♛♛
25000 Highway 50, Placerville 95667; tel. 626-0630
Single room, double occupancy: $65
This Pennsylvania-Dutch farmhouse is run by the

Cormiers who treat you as if you are their personal guests. Gardens and pastures surround the place, and you can even pan for gold in the tranquil backyard creek. Only 4 rooms.

Shopping

Friday House Gallery, 2936 Mosquito Rd., Placerville. Prints and lithos of the historic West by well-known artist George Mathis.

Smith Flat
(area code 916)
Where to Eat
Smith Flat House ♛
2021 Smith Flat Rd., Smith Flat; tel. 626-9003
Average dinner: $10.95
Original mile house, a stopping place for miners and coaches during the gold rush.

Sonora
(area code 209)
Where to Stay
Sonora Inn ♛ ♛
160 S. Washington St., Sonora 95370; tel. 532-7468
Single room, double occupancy: $45
Old West, Spanish-style hostelry in the heart of the Mother Lode. Elegant, brightly tiled lobby, red tile roof, and plenty of places to sun. Pool. 66 rooms.

Where to Eat
Good Heavens ♛ ♛ ♛ ♛ ♛
49 N. Washington St., Sonora; tel. 532-FOOD
Lunch only, average: $7
Eclectic and unusual nouvelle cuisine in a European atmosphere; exposed-brick building built in 1856.

Sutter Creek
(area code 209)
Shopping
Early Attic Antiques, 74 Main St. Wide selection of

antiques: Limoges china, signed cut glass, sterling silver.

Sutter Creek Antiques, Central Shops, 28 Main St. Refinished furniture and a variety of country household items from lamps to folk art.

THE HIGH SIERRA

The image of California may be all beaches and surf-boards, but just as many Californians love to take to the hills as to the sandy shore. Hiking boots, backpacks, and 4-wheel-drive Jeeps (and Suzuki Samurais of late) are every bit as common as bikinis. Ski racks are as much an auto accessory as pine-tree deodorizers. And the place most people head for is the High Sierra. For here we find California's raw natural beauty at its lofti-est, most pristine, and awe-inspiring. This is a place where waterfalls cascade over towering, glacier-carved, granite cliffs to stark inland seas and crystal-clear mountain lakes and streams. It's a region where super-latives do not exaggerate: the world's oldest trees, the world's largest trees, the highest peak and lowest point in the mainland U.S., and so much more.

This huge region, almost 400 miles long, in-corporates about two thirds of California's territory, including some of its most enviable natural assets: Yosemite, Kings Canyon, and Sequoia national parks, 8 national forests, 5 national wilderness areas, hundreds of ski lifts, and thousands of lakes, including Mono Lake and Lake Tahoe.

LAKE TAHOE

Tahoe ♛ ♛ ♛ ♛, the largest alpine lake in North Amer-ica, is a sapphire jewel set at 6,228 feet above sea level. Four-thousand-foot granite mountains frame her beauty, 72 miles of scenic shoreline contain it. The area's first inhabitants, the Washoe Indians, named the lake *Tahoe* or "Big Water," and in fact, Tahoe holds

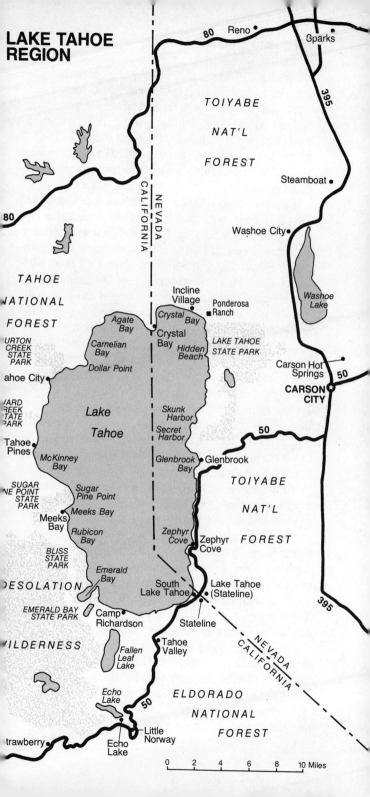

waters 1,645 feet deep . . . enough to cover the entire state to a depth of 14 inches. Over 20 ski resorts offer more than 126,000 vertical feet of scenic ski terrain. Sailing, waterskiing, fishing, boating, rafting, ballooning, camping, and hiking draw vacationers in all 4 seasons. The resort offers more than 10,000 rooms and over 100 restaurants, some featuring extraordinary gourmet fare.

Because Lake Tahoe straddles the California/Nevada border, with one third of the lake and all of nearby Reno actually in Nevada, legalized gambling adds another dimension to a Tahoe vacation. Luxurious casino-hotels, like the 546-room Harrah's Tahoe, winner of Mobil Five Star and AAA Five Diamond awards, provide posh accommodations, plenty of amenities and fine dining, in addition to 24-hour gambling and big-name entertainment. Caesar's Tahoe Resort, another splashy casino-hotel, draws the most contemporary headliners, from the Pointer Sisters to George Carlin and Kenny Loggins. These South Lake Tahoe, high-rise gaming palaces, along with newly expanded Harvey's, are the heart of the neon action on South Shore. Hyatt Lake Tahoe offers gambling in a quieter, elegant setting at North Shore's Incline Village, and the historic Cal Neva Lodge gives you gaming lakeside at North Shore's Crystal Bay.

To get acquainted with the scenic beauty and historic attractions of Lake Tahoe, as well as the different character of the towns and resorts that surround it, we suggest you circle the lake if you have the time. The North Shore, with a moratorium on high-rise development and neon, appeals to families and those willing to trade an active nightlife for easy access to wilderness areas, hidden beaches, and solitude. The South Shore has more of everything—lodgings, restaurants, bars, and clubs—hence more traffic and crowds.

Driving from San Francisco, via Route 50, takes you into South Shore; coming over Interstate 80 you reach the North Shore first, after crossing the infamous Donner Pass. Here at Donner Memorial State Park, a massive monument pays tribute to 41 pioneers of the Donner party, who died trying to cross the Sierra during heavy early snows in 1846. The snow level reached 22 feet that winter, commemorated by the height of the monument's base. We must confess our morbid fascination. The Emigrant Trail Museum♛♛ recounts the story of the tragic event, the natural history of the Sierra Nevada, and the construction of the Central Pacific Railroad. Camping, fishing, boating, and hiking are all available at lovely Donner Lake.

PERILS & PITFALLS

Avoid driving into Lake Tahoe from California at night. The road is a very difficult one, poorly lit.

Head next to the Western town of Truckee, where the history of this once bustling lumber town is preserved with false-front buildings, wooden walkways, and a historic hotel. As in its heyday, Truckee's saloons are still popular watering holes. Modern times are evident in some fine gourmet eateries and shops.

INSIDERS' TIPS

Leave the driving to Amtrak and try the California Zephyr between Oakland and Truckee for spectacular views of the Sierra. The train leaves Oakland just before noon daily, arriving in Truckee, via Sacramento, just past 5 P.M. Round-trip fare is $77.

The nearby town of Tahoe City is, surprisingly, a "gourmet ghetto." Its scenic, lakeside setting has enticed top chefs from Europe and the San Francisco Bay Area to give up big-city life for the pleasures of a more pristine mountain setting. Exquisite dining, fine shops, and charming accommodations make Tahoe City the focus of North Shore. Visit the Gatekeepers Log Cabin Museum♛, Fanny Bridge♛, and Truckee River Outlet while there. The museum, open May through October, displays Indian baskets, clothing, tools, pictures, and early logging and railroad equipment. At Fanny Bridge watch the giant trout in the Truckee River, Tahoe's only outlet. And think about booking a leisurely 2-hour raft trip from Tahoe City down a 4-mile stretch of this gentle river.

Skirting the lake south along Highway 89 we love Emerald Bay State Park, perhaps the lake's most picturesque and photographed corner, which typifies the Sierra with its granite peaks and deep emerald color. There are trails, boat docking, and camping, as well as Tahoe's sole island, tiny Fanette Island with its stone teahouse.

INSIDERS' TIPS

An interesting calendar of events is highlighted by the North Lake Tahoe-Truckee Snowfest in February, a week-long celebration with spectacular torchlight skiing, and Summer Music and Shakespeare Festivals in July and August at Sand Harbor in Lake Tahoe State Park.

At the head of the bay near cascading Eagle Falls is Vikingsholm Castle♛♛♛, a striking 38-room reproduction of a 9th-century Norse fortress, with a series of towers and a sod roof, covered with grasses and flowers. Guided tours are offered June through September. The castle is reached by a steep one-mile hike or by boat.

INSIDERS' TIPS

Northstar at Tahoe is great for family skiing and for beginners. The resort limits the number of lift tickets sold, so crowds aren't irksome and lines not too long. Squaw Valley, site of the 1960 Winter Olympics, offers fine expert skiing in a breathtaking setting. Heavenly Valley, the largest ski area, has long lines but dramatic views. Kirkwood, located 30 miles south of Lake Tahoe, is a high-elevation resort with excellent cross-country skiing. Alpine Meadows' ski season generally extends for 7 months.

The Tallac Historical Site♛♛ at Pope Beach includes the Pope, Baldwin, and Valhalla estates, 3 opulent 19th-century mansions. Along with the Ehrman Mansion in D. L. Bliss State Park, where many scenes of *The Godfather, II* were filmed, these estates recall an era when Tahoe was a summer sanctuary for the wealthy. The Tallac Historic Site also features art exhibits, children's activities, literary readings, artists in action and entertainment. Sunday chamber music concerts begin at 3 P.M. and Thursday evening jazz at 7 P.M. at Valhalla. (Call 916-573-2600 or 916-542-ARTS.)

By now you are well into South Lake Tahoe and should stop at the Lake Tahoe Visitors Center♛♛♛. This U.S. Forest Service center offers interpretive trail information. A nearby Stream Profile Chamber provides viewing of the giant Kokanee salmon on their October run. The Lake Tahoe Historical Society Museum♛ displays historical photos, pioneer artifacts, and Indian relics.

The Heavenly Valley Tram♛♛♛ will take you, winter or summer, to 8,200 feet, where there is an unforgettable panorama of the mountain-ringed lake. We like to eat lunch or dinner at the top and watch daring skiers tackle the steep slopes in winter. We've even seen a couple make their wedding vows before this stunning backdrop.

INSIDERS' TIPS

Rates go up about 20 percent around Lake Tahoe during peak summer and Christmas seasons, weekends, and holidays. So do occupancies. If you must come with the crowds, book well in advance. Three months is a good lead time for summer for your first choices, especially for the casino-hotels which go fast. However, with South Lake Tahoe's huge room inventory, from rustic cabins to luxurious suites, you can almost always get a last-minute accommodation.

Both North and South Lake Tahoe offer toll-free, lodging information numbers to call for advice and reservations. For North Shore call 800-822-5959 in California; from the rest of the U.S., call 800-824-8557. For South Lake Tahoe lodgings call 800-822-5922. Both services will also fill you in on dining and other tips.

For example, in the South Lake Tahoe area there are private homes for rent (over 1,000 rooms) starting at $100 a night. For several families traveling together, renting a 5-bedroom home for $200 per night, for instance, could prove more economical and flexible than renting several hotel or condominium units.

Another perspective on Lake Tahoe can be seen from an afternoon sight-seeing cruise on a paddle-wheel steamer around Emerald Bay April through November. Also the 350-passenger M. S. *Dixie* also serves up an interesting Historic Glenbrook Breakfast Cruise ♛♛ north along the Nevada shoreline in summer. The 500-passenger *Tahoe Queen* runs a ski shuttle in winter to the North Shore. Both companies offer dinner cruises too.

Our favorite rejuvenation spot is at Grover Hot Springs State Park, off Route 89 near Markleeville. Soak in an outdoor hot tub surrounded by the beauty of Toiyabe National Forest. The park has hiking, fishing, camping, and a swimming pool in addition to the hot mineral bath.

YOSEMITE

Pardon our Valley Girl description, but Yosemite Valley is the most awesome, whatever season one visits. Scottish naturalist John Muir put it most eloquently when he called it "the grandest of all the special temples of Nature I was ever permitted to enter . . . the sanctum sanctorum of the Sierra." Abraham Lincoln was impressed enough by Yosemite's natural wonders to set the valley aside as the nation's first state park in 1864. Muir's efforts led to the creation of Yosemite National Park 26 years later.

The sculptors of Yosemite's granite peaks, domes, and ridges were ice-age glaciers, shaping massive monoliths that challenge expert rock climbers, not to mention camera buffs trying to capture their scale in 3-by-5 snapshots. Each formation—El Capitan, Half Dome, Cathedral Rocks, Three Brothers, Sentinel Rock—becomes familiar as it is observed from different angles and in different light, towering over and adding grandeur to Yosemite Valley.

The valley itself, also carved by glacial action, is the focal point of the park, though it occupies but 7 of Yosemite's 1,200 square miles. A walk along the flat, mile-wide valley floor leads readily to wonders like

YOSEMITE AREA

Yosemite Falls, the highest in North America at 2,425 feet; Bridalveil Falls, Mirror Lake, and much more, all contained within steep walls of vertical granite. Here, too are campgrounds, cabins, and lodges, the world-class Ahwahnee hotel, along with shops, restaurants, and galleries.

PERILS & PITFALLS

The Visitor Center, this hub of Yosemite, is, alas, the most crowded part of the park, especially in summer, holidays, and weekends when traffic jams plague would-be wilderness seekers. Of the nearly 3 million people who visit Yosemite National Park each year, 70 percent arrive during summer, and most *never* venture beyond the 7 square miles of the valley. If you're heading to the valley, park your car at your campsite, at your hotel, or in a day-use parking lot, and avail yourself of the free shuttle service to explore the valley. There are also guided tours for a fee, or try hiking, bicycling, horseback riding, or rafting down the Merced River.

Make your first stop the Visitor Center ♛ ♛ ♛ ♛, for detailed information about Yosemite and help in getting the most out of your visit. Pick up the weekly *Yosemite Guide* for a schedule of activities that range from sunset, full-moon, or astronomy walks to snowshoe outings, Snowcat rides, camera tours, slide presentations, evening programs, and many more creative options.

INSIDERS' TIPS

Even when you can't venture up into the High Country, you can find awesome panoramas from the overlook just before Wawona Tunnel and from Glacier Point, 3,200 feet along the valley's rim. Wawona is a gracious settlement near the park's southwest entrance, where herds of deer graze and the verandah-framed Wawona Hotel awaits visitors seeking a tranquil and refined getaway. There's also the excellent Pioneer Yosemite History Center ♛ ♛ ♛, which preserves a blacksmith shop, Wells Fargo office, jail, some old log cabins, and other relics of the last century.

Behind the center is the Indian Cultural Museum ♔ ♔ with displays on the Miwok and Paiute Indians, former inhabitants of the area. Visit also the Ansel Adams Gallery ♔ ♔ for a look at the photographer's timeless images of the majestic park.

INSIDERS' TIPS

Some marvelous special events take place each winter, beginning in January with the Yosemite Chefs' Holidays showcasing the best in American regional cooking with classes, seminars, and fabulous banquets. There are Musicians Holidays, complete with opera and musical theater, and Vintners Holidays with seminars, tastings, and fine dining. All take place at the Ahwahnee Hotel. Photographic Holidays, centered at Yosemite Lodge, offer an opportunity to learn from the masters in seminars and on field trips in this idyllic setting. For information on any of these programs, call 209-252-2828.

Don't confine yourself to the valley. The High Country gives you access to hundreds of peaks over 11,000 feet, lakes dazzling blue beneath the white granite cliffs, and the alpine meadows brilliant with lupines, azaleas, asters, and other wildflowers. Route 120, or Tioga Road, the highest Sierra crossing (open May through October), leads to Tuolumne Meadows, at 8,600 feet, the Sierra's largest subalpine meadow. This is the heart of the High Country and the start of hundreds of miles of trails, from simple loops to strenuous ascents. Here you'll find an information center, campground, lodge, stables, store, and restaurant—and no crowds.

PERILS & PITFALLS

If you go in winter, carry chains for access to the higher elevations. Call Yosemite's 24-hour hotline for information on weather: 209-372-4605. For downhill ski conditions contact Badger Pass at 209-372-1338.

Closer to the park's south entrance, you'll meet the "Grizzly Giant," along with some 200 other giant sequoias. These are the verdant pillars of Mariposa

Grove, one of nature's truly impressive cathedrals, whose up to 3,500-year-old trees have attained awesome stature, measuring more than 30 feet around and reaching up to 200 feet.

INSIDERS' TIPS

The Yosemite Stables operates 4- and 6-day saddle trips to the park's famous High Sierra camps in summer. While similar hiking trips sell out early, quotas for these saddle trips are available into February. For information call the High Sierra Reservations Desk at 209-252-3010, or write to Yosemite Reservations, 5410 East Home Ave., Fresno, CA 93727.

Yosemite changes like nature herself with the seasons. Winter, mild in the valley with temperatures between 20 and 60 degrees, brings the opportunity to ski at Badger Pass Ski Area, the oldest ski area in California. Open Thanksgiving through mid-April, Badger Pass offers beginning, intermediate, and family skiing. Cross-country skiing along more than 90 miles of well-marked trails and snowshoeing are other ways to venture into Yosemite's backcountry. In Curry Village, try skating at the newly modernized ice rink while viewing the ice forests towered over by snow-capped Half Dome.

INSIDERS' TIPS

Reservations are required for campsites and cabins on the valley floor from May through September and can be made up to 8 weeks in advance at any Ticketron outlet or in person at the National Park Service Campgrounds Reservations Center in Curry Village. Call 209-372-4485 for campground information.

Spring brings waterfalls, thunderous with energy, and meadows, exploding with a myriad of wildflower colors. In summer, the High Country is most accessible and swimming in mountain lakes and streams is a refreshing reward. Autumn is another season of flaming colors. California black oak, big leaf maple, dogwood, and cottonwood blaze with vibrance. Each of these seasons' delights can be enjoyed by biking, hiking, or horseback riding. Rent bikes at Yosemite Lodge and Curry Village to enjoy a good network of bike trails around the valley. Most are flat and separate from auto traffic. Yosemite has one of the largest horse rental facilities in the U.S. with stables at Curry Village, Wawona, Tuolumne Meadows, and White Wolf.

In one of the world's premiere rock climbing areas, the prestigious Yosemite Mountaineering School provides expert instruction for all levels of skill.

Some of the newest and most popular summer activities are rafting and kayaking on the Merced River. It's a leisurely 3½-mile glide down calm waters with incredible scenery May through June. Those coming to fish in the area have a choice of 131 trout-stocked lakes.

PERILS & PITFALLS

Accommodations at The Ahwahnee, Yosemite Lodge, and High Sierra camps are often reserved months in advance, especially mid-May through mid-September and holidays. Yet there are cancellations every night, so keep in touch. Curry Village and Housekeeping Camp is a bit easier to book, yet it's still advisable to reserve in advance. Call Yosemite Park and Curry Company at 209-252-4848.

EASTERN SIERRA

After following Tioga Road through the thrilling High Country of Yosemite, continue along to the crest, Tioga Pass, whence you look down at the winding road into Lee Vining Canyon, and get your first vision of the hauntingly beautiful Mono Lake. This striking blue inland sea stretches for miles in the Great Basin desert, with eerie tufa towers, once underwater, emerging from the lake's shrinking surface like prehistoric sculptures. The lake is a nesting place for most of California's gulls, lured from the Pacific Coast each summer, along with many other species, by the brine shrimp which thrive in the saline water.

This unique ecosystem can be explored on a guided

walk offered by the U.S. Forest Service at South Tufa Grove daily in summer. Stop first at the Mono Lake Visitor Center♛♛♛ in Lee Vining to get oriented and browse through the excellent collection of photos, books, posters, and displays on the lake. Watch the free slide show on the lake and its continuing struggle for survival as its water sources from Sierra streams are diverted to supply Los Angeles' needs.

Lee Vining also has gas stations, restaurants, food markets, and 5 motels including a Best Western. Campers and trout fishermen would enjoy Lundy Lake Resort, 6 miles west of Mono Lake's north shore, for rustic campgrounds set among pines and aspens. A bit farther north and even more secluded is Virginia Lakes with 2 emerald bodies of water surrounded by evergreens. Camping and cabins are available.

Thirty miles north of Tioga Pass, off Highway 395, you come to Bodie State Historic Park♛♛♛, a ghost town infamous in gold rush days. The last 3 miles of road are unpaved, and there's no food, drink, or gas along the way once you've left the north shores of Mono Lake. Go forewarned—and not in winter. Allow time to immerse yourself in the legends generated by Bodie when it had 12,000 inhabitants in 1879, mining more than $90 million worth of gold from its hills. With 65 saloons and a murder a day, Bodie attracted the "wickedest men in the West." One young girl heading there was said to have prayed, "Goodbye, God. We're going to Bodie." We can never resist a peek inside the 150 weathered wood structures, maintained in a state of "arrested decay," for glimpses of the way the settlers lived. Don't miss the fascinating museum in the legendary Western Federation of Miners Union Hall♛♛.

INSIDERS' TIPS

Both Bodie and Mono Lake can be blazing hot, so bring a hat, suntan lotion, and water. The saloons offer no California Coolers.

Seven miles north, Bridgeport rents boats and guide services to hunters and fishermen heading to Twin Lakes Recreation Area. Mono County Courthouse♛ is an imposing Victorian beauty, built in 1880 to bring some law and order to the area.

Head south from Mono Lake to reach the June Lake Loop, a road winding 14 miles past lakes and streams and culminating in the alpine June Lake Resort. This year-round resort, looking like a slice of Switzerland, draws skiers in winter, families and fishermen in summer.

Further south along Route 395 you'll see a sign to Hot Creek at the Mammoth Lakes Airport exit. Follow signs past the state fish hatchery on a partially paved road. The U.S. Forest Service warns bathers of the sudden temperature changes in this active volcanic area. Yet if you are bold enough to get past the signs, you will experience one of the eastern Sierra's special treats, a cold mountain trout stream with large pools heated by geothermal activity.

Mammoth Lakes ♛ ♛, one of the largest downhill ski resorts in the United States, is L.A.'s favorite ski area. More than 29 lifts service 150 trails and 3,100 vertical feet of skiing diversity. The ski season is one of the longest, with spring skiing lasting until the Fourth of July. Winter is a wonderland of cross-country trails, helicopter skiing, snowmobiling, snowshoeing, old-fashioned sleigh rides, sledding, tobogganing, and ice-skating on nearby June Lake, Convict Lake, Twin Lakes, and Mammoth's alkali ponds. (Call the 24-hour Snowline at 619-934-6166.) In spring and summer, there's fishing, biking, hiking into the John Muir Wilderness, backpacking and mountain climbing, golf, tennis, hayrides, canoeing, catamaran rides, sailboarding, and waterskiing.

Scenic attractions are everywhere you turn in the area. In summer, take the 30-minute drive west of Mammoth Lakes to Devils Postpile National Monument ♛ ♛. The 60-foot-high basalt columns were created 100,000 years ago by molten lava flowing from Mammoth Pass. Visit, too, Rainbow Falls ♛, where the San Joaquin River drops 140 feet over lava ledges. Mammoth itself offers a full range of shopping, dining, and lodging options.

Bishop is the next town south on Highway 395, a

quiet friendly base from which to enjoy more fishing, swimming, backpacking, camping, hang gliding, and hiking. Pack trips by horse or mule through the Sierra can also be arranged.

Four miles north, off Highway 6, stop at the Laws Railroad Museum and Historical Site♛ to see exhibits on the town's early mining history. There's a gold rush post office, Wells Fargo Bank, and the Slim Princess, one of the last narrow-gauge trains to be used in those days.

Continue exploring history of the area one hour south in Independence. The Eastern California Museum♛ ♛, open year-round, displays Native American and pioneer artifacts, photos and documentation on local history, and an exhibit on Manzanar, the first camp where Americans of Japanese descent were interned during World War II. Visit the 11-room Victorian Commander's House♛, Sunday afternoons March through October, to view furniture and clothing dating back to the 1820s in this well-preserved building.

INSIDERS' TIPS

Relive the Old West during Mule Days Celebration, 4 days of rodeos, parades, and down-home cooking each Memorial Day Weekend. Call the Bishop Chamber of Commerce at 619-873-8405.

North of Independence and 15 miles south of Bishop, in Inyo National Forest, stand fond favorites of ours, the world's oldest living trees: the Bristlecone Pines. Methuselah, the Elder is 4,700 years old, while many of the fallen trees are nearly double that age. These survivors have thrived in a most barren and inhospitable landscape. For your own survival and comfort, bring plenty of drinking water, a picnic, warm clothes, and good walking shoes. Also a full tank of gas. And don't be embarrassed to talk to the trees. Many do.

At Lone Pine, a turn-of-the-century Old West town farther south along Highway 395, are unforgettable views of Mt. Whitney's carved canyons and Death Valley's sand dunes.

This truly diverse and frequently surreal landscape

extends to the strangely eroded formation of rocks and pinnacles known as the Alabama Hills. It not only looks like the perfect set for a Western, it actually is a spot chosen by filmmakers. Rock climbers and sightseers also enjoy this 30,000-acre area, a former site of Indian battles. The area is located between Mt. Whitney and Lone Pine, along the Whitney Portal Road, which leads to a campground by that name. This is a good starting point for climbers challenging Mt. Whitney's 14,496-foot peak. The trail to the top takes about 2 days up, one down and draws thousands of climbers each summer. In fact, you should reserve a year in advance through Inyo National Forest, Mount Whitney Ranger District, Lone Pine, CA 93545. This majestic granite mass is the highest mountain in the contiguous 48 states.

In contrast, Bad Water in Death Valley, only 90 miles southeast of Lone Pine, is one of the lowest points in the U.S. at 282 feet below sea level.

KINGS AND SEQUOIA CANYONS

The soaring summit of Mt. Whitney serves as the eastern boundary of Sequoia and Kings Canyon national parks. We favor these magnificent parks for the lack of crowds and traffic that plague Yosemite in peak summer season. They are home to the giant sequoia, the world's largest living trees, which flourished with the dinosaurs (we don't know if the reptiles could lift a leg high enough to use them as we've seen modern dogs do). While most of the ancient forests were destroyed during the Ice Age, a few sheltered groves along a 200-mile narrow stretch of the western Sierra survived.

The trees were named by an Australian botanist to honor Chief Sequoyah, the story goes, a Cherokee Indian whom he respected as a giant among men. Among other accomplishments, Sequoyah had created an 85-character phonetic alphabet for his people.

Connecting Kings Canyon and Sequoia national parks is the Generals Highway, a 46-mile drive lined with scenic pleasures. From the north, the highway leads to Grant Grove, home of 4 of the world's 5 largest sequoias and site of the General Grant Tree, second largest of these giants. The tree, 107 feet around and 267 feet high, was declared by Congress as "the Nation's Christmas Tree," a memorial to the war dead. On the Sunday before Christmas every year a carol service is held at the base.

Continuing south, stop at Lodgepole Visitors Center for information, then head to Giant Forest. Here we feel small and insignificant beside the General Sherman Tree, whose more than 3,000 years of age are as impressive as its 114.6-foot girth and 274.9 feet of height. (This compares to a 27-story building, for us urbanites who can visualize a skyscraper easier than a giant tree.) Wander along the 2-mile Congress Trail loop to experience the presence of more of these aged giants.

Back on the drive south, you'll pass more interesting spots: Tunnel Log, a redwood doorway built from a fallen tree; Beadle Rock, a premier vista to catch the sunset on the San Joaquin Valley; Moro Rock which rewards climbers with a 360-degree panorama of the Sierra and surrounding valley; Crystal Cave, with alien looking geological formations; and Hospital Rock to see petroglyphs of the Mono Indians, early inhabitants of the region.

While this leisurely, 2-hour drive incorporates some of the parks' key sites, those who leave cars behind can hike along more than 1,000 miles of self-guided paths in the High Country, horseback ride from Wolverton Pack Station, or take a walk with a ranger through spring wildflowers or along glacial paths. Fishermen will find brook, brown, rainbow, and golden trout in the Kings River, Park Lake, or any of the parks' well-stocked lakes and streams. June to September draws backpackers. Many overnight treks into the High Country depart from Cedar Grove in Kings Canyon. Wilderness permits are required for overnight trips into the backcountry and are available from any California Ticketron outlet. (Call 209-565-3307 for information on outdoor activities; 209-565-3351 for weather and road conditions.)

In winter, choose a snowshoe walk, moonlight skiing at Wolverton Ski Bowl, cross-country skiing along 75 miles of marked trails through the redwoods, or snow camping at Big Meadows.

Year-round camping in the parks' 130 campsites is supplemented by overnight accommodations in deluxe motels and cabins or rustic cottages. (Call 209-565-3373, or write to Sequoia National Park Guest Services, Inc., Sequoia National Park, CA 93262.)

INSIDERS' INFORMATION FOR THE HIGH SIERRA

Mammoth Lakes
(area code 619)

Where to Stay

Snowcreek ♛ ♛ ♛
P.O. Box 48, Mammoth Lakes 93546; tel. 934-3333
Single room, double occupancy: $60–$210
150 low-density, spacious, creekside condominiums on 355 acres of alpine meadows that harmonize with the surroundings. Great mountain views, 9 tennis courts, 8 racquetball courts, 3 hot pools, 2 steam rooms, indoor-outdoor pool, daily aerobic classes, Nautilus gym, courtesy shuttle to ski resorts.

Mammoth Mountain Inn ♛ ♛
P.O. Box 48, Mammoth Lakes 93546; tel. 934-2581
Single room, double occupancy: $53–$103; condo units $48–$175
Mammoth's traditional ski lodge and only full-service hotel located right across from the ski lifts. 118 rooms, 99 condos, 3 indoor Jacuzzis, game room, gift shop, sports shop, lounge with fireplace, conference room, child care.

Snow Goose Inn ♛ ♛
P.O. Box 946, Mammoth Lakes 93546; tel. 934-2660
Single room, double occupancy: $65
Quaint B&B in the heart of the village; elegant lounge

and deluxe rooms are full of antiques. Sauna, Jacuzzi, wine and cheese served every evening. 21 rooms.

South Lake Tahoe
(area code 916)
Where to Stay
Inn by the Lake ♛ ♛ ♛
3300 Lake Tahoe Blvd., South Lake Tahoe 95705; tel. 542-0330
Single room, double occupancy: From $65 and up in off season; $85 and up in high season
3-story luxury property with appealing designer rooms (ask for one with a lake view). Setting is attractively landscaped beneath towering ponderosas. 100 rooms. Pool, hot tub, Jacuzzi, sauna, Continental breakfast, free shuttle to casinos.

Lakeland Village Beach & Ski Resort ♛ ♛ ♛
3535 Highway 50, South Lake Tahoe 95705; tel. 541-7711
Single room, double occupancy: $80
In a wooded setting, this attractive place offers 215 rooms in 2-story townhouses and a main lodge along the lake with 1,000 feet of private beach. Pool, tennis courts, saunas, spas.

Camp Richardson Resort ♛ ♛
Highway 89 at Jameson Beach Rd., P.O. Box 9028, South Lake Tahoe 95705; tel. 541-1801
Single rooms, double occupancy: Cabins $85–$95; lodge, $54–$69
Historic 1920s lodge offers Continental breakfast and a large fireplace to set a perfect ambience; the cabins, winterized and refurbished, have kitchens and fireplaces. There's also a tiny (7-room) beach motel, campgrounds, lakeside restaurant, corrals, marina, general store. Totally self-contained.

Where to Eat
Cantina Los Tres Hombres ♛ ♛
765 Highway 89, South Lake Tahoe; tel. 544-1233
Average dinner: $10
A Mexican cantina with that south-of-the-border feel.

Cozy bar, stone fireplace, and good food; popular Tahoe hangout. (There's one at North Shore too.)

Tahoe City
(area code 916)
Where to Stay
Cottage Inn♛♛♛

P.O. Box 66, Tahoe City 95730; tel. 581-4073

Single room, double occupancy: $65–$115

Knotty-pine cottages (with modern amenities) are run by friendly folks so outgoing they create an atmosphere conducive to mixing and meeting. Beach. 14 rooms.

Where to Eat
River Ranch♛♛

Highway 89 at Alpine Meadows Rd., Tahoe City; tel. 583-4264

Average dinner: $20

Savor seafood, ribs, or chicken from a hickory-wood-burning oven. Overlooks the Truckee River and wooded ridges beyond. Patio diners in the summer sip strawberry Margaritas while watching unsuspecting river rafters hit or miss the riverbend below.

Tahoe Vista
(area code 916)
Where to Eat
Captain John's♛♛♛♛

7220 N. Lake Blvd., Tahoe Vista; tel. 546-4819

Average dinner: $30

Great menu: Roast duck with blueberry or oyster sauce, fresh eastern scallops with shitake mushrooms and snowpeas . . . and the daily special created by a fine European chef. Romantic, cozy, elegant, and a great wine list.

Le Petit Pier♛♛♛♛

7252 N. Lake Blvd., Tahoe Vista; tel. 546-4464

Average dinner: $25

Chef John du Fau brings more than 2 decades of experience in Europe's finest hotels (like Paris's Georges V) to this intimate French-country find.

Truckee
(area code 916)
Where to Stay
Northstar-at-Tahoe ♛ ♛ ♛

P.O. Box 129, Truckee 95734; tel. 562-1113

Single room, double occupancy: $52–$61; 4-bedroom house $131–$154

Choose from a hotel room, condo, or house built into the heavily forested mountainside. This place is noted for its quiet, friendly, family feeling; off the beaten track, yet full of amenities and activities, 200 rooms, 5 restaurants.

Restaurant
Schaffer's Mill ♛ ♛

P.O. Box 129, Truckee; tel. 587-0250

Average dinner: $25

Fashioned after a lumber mill of the same name, decor is homey yet elegant. Try the cajun shrimp. Mmmm-mmmm.

Yosemite National Park
(area code 209)
Where to Stay
The Ahwahnee ♛ ♛ ♛ ♛ ♛

5410 E. Home Ave., Yosemite 93727; tel. 252-4848

Single room, double occupancy: $150

An architectural wonder, this American wood-and-stone castle was built in 1927 at the base of a massive granite peak; listed in the National Register of Historic Places. Huge cathedral ceilings, stone hearths, chandeliers. American Indian art and breathtaking views. Not-to-be-missed landmark. Be sure to reserve a table in the elegant dining room(♛ ♛ ♛ ♛ ♛), which reflects the grandeur of the hotel with its massive beamed ceilings and stone-and-glass interior (average dinner $27). Entertainment nightly, nonguests also invited.

Wawona Hotel ♛ ♛ ♛ ♛

5410 E. Home Ave., Yosemite 93727; tel. 252-4848

Single room, double occupancy: $64.50 ($51.50 without bath)

Gracious, Victorian, white-pillared hotel overlooking

rich, green lawns in the park's southwest corner. One of California's oldest mountain retreats, built in 1876. Open mid-spring to early fall. Victorian-era furnishings. Expect a slow pace and herds of mule deer sharing your space. 9-hole golf course, tennis, swimming pool, stables nearby. Dining room(♛ ♛ ♛ ♛) serves up fine Southern cooking—corn fritters, fried chicken, and the like. Arrive before sunset (it's a 45-minute drive from the valley) for cocktails on the verandah. Open May-October.

Curry Village ♛ ♛ ♛
5410 East Home Ave., Fresno 93727; tel. 252-4848
Single room, double occupancy: Hotel rooms $59; cabins $46; tent cabins $22.50
Beneath Glacier Point, with views of Half Dome and Royal Arches, you can have that rustic flavor without the inconvenience. Ice rink, ice-cream stand, river rafting office, Yosemite Mountaineering School, bikes, near trailheads to Tenaya and Mered Canyons.

Yosemite Lodge ♛ ♛ ♛
5410 E. Home Ave., Fresno 93727; tel. 252-4848
Single rooms, double occupancy: Lodge rooms $75; cottage rooms $61; cabins $46—less without private bath
The wood-and-glass, National Park architecture incorporates open space and landscaping in a setting near the base of Yosemite Falls. Cozy and comfortable to bring you in touch with nature. Swimming pool, tour desk, evening nature lectures, shuttle bus stop, 3 restaurants, including Mountain Room Broiler(♛ ♛ ♛) for patio dining and plenty of broiled fish and steaks (call 372-1281). Average dinner $19.

Camping
White Wolf Lodge, Tuolumne Meadows Lodge and 5 High Sierra trail camps
5410 E. Home Ave., Fresno 93727; tel. 252-4848
Canvas tents come with beds, linens, and blankets. The network of 5 High Sierra camps are situated within a half-day's walk from each other. Showers; breakfast and dinner in central dining tent (restaurants at lodges).

SHASTA-CASCADE

California's Shasta-Cascade region, stretching north of the Sacramento Valley all the way to the Oregon border, and east from the Coast Range to Nevada, is a wonderland of enormous proportions. Picture wilderness areas and wildlife refuges, towering peaks and pristine lakes, volcanic hotbeds and caves, limestone caverns and restored mining towns—not to mention great examples of Victorian architecture. This California is ideal for hiking or backpacking on foot, horse, or llama; fishing, swimming, river rafting, houseboating, and skiing. Unlike other parts of the state, in this uncrowded northeastern corner of California, scenic beauty often goes hand in hand with solitude, an asset ever more valuable in these travelin' times.

INSIDERS' TIPS

Try packing with Shasta Llamas for a spectacular experience. $300 for a 3-day trip, $500 for 6 days. Call 916-926-3959. Box 1137, Mt. Shasta, CA 96067.

REDDING

A fast 4-hour freeway drive from San Francisco takes you to the heart of the region and its largest town, Redding, population 51,000. It's a lucky populace since an hour's drive in any direction leads to areas of scenic, geologic, and historic import, with excellent recreational opportunities at every turn. We found a range of dining and lodging options in Redding, including a strip of budget-priced motels in addition to dependable names like Red Lion, Best Western, and Holiday Inn, and fast-food restaurants not operating elsewhere in the vicinity.

PERILS & PITFALLS

Located in the valley, Redding has summer temperatures often reaching into the 100s. The heat is dry, so it's not as bad as it sounds, but be prepared.

Stop at the Redding Museum and Art Center♛♛, in Caldwell Park, to view a fine collection of Native American artifacts, exhibits on local pioneer life, and contemporary works by local and national artists. Caldwell Park also has a 9-hole golf course, a public swimming pool, and waterfalls on the Sacramento River that are lit at night. In fall you can view the salmon run.

INSIDERS' TIPS

A stop at the Shasta-Cascade Wonderland Association on Market Street and Parkview Avenue will provide you with fishing, hunting, and other visitor information, while the Redding Convention and Visitors Bureau, 777 Auditorium Drive, will give you all the brochures, maps, and advice you need to fine-tune your visit.

From Redding, Highway 200 winds west past many points of scenic and historic interest. Three miles out is Shasta State Historic Park♛♛♛. This is a ghost town—old brick buildings are all that remain of the former queen of northern California's gold mining region in the 1850s. Things came to a halt here in the 1880s when hydraulic mining was stopped by law. Visit the museum in the old county courthouse, the Litsch general store, and the jail with leg irons and gallows.

Five miles west is Whiskeytown Lake, part of the Whiskeytown-Shasta-Trinity National Recreation Area. These 100,000 acres of national park and forest lands resulted from a federal project of dams built on the Sacramento and Trinity rivers to divert northern waters to California's thirsty Central Valley. The project, completed only recently, led to the creation of Shasta,

Whiskeytown, Clair Engle (popularly known as Trinity), and Lewiston Lakes.

Whiskeytown Lake makes for a beautiful stop to swim on a hot summer day. Its 5 square miles of open blue water are also great for sailing, boating, waterskiing, and fishing for trout, bass, kokanee salmon, bluegill, crappie, and catfish. Along the 36 miles of shoreline, we found tiny, wooded isles and coves. You can pan for gold at several streams entering the lake and camp at Brandy Creek or Oak Bottom camping areas.

Past the lake turn off to the tiny hamlet of French Gulch ♥, named for the French Canadians who mined gold in the region in the late 1840s. Once the largest gold-producer among the northern California mines, French Gulch today offers a picturesque slice of history with its French Gulch Hotel (now closed), a former brothel, and the pretty, woodframe St. Rose's Church.

Next stop along this ever more scenic winding road is another historic town, Weaverville. Here you learn the Chinese side of the gold rush story, a tale of hardship, heavy taxes and second-rate lodging for the 2,500-plus Chinese miners who came to the "Land of the Golden Mountains." The centerpiece of the town's Chinese community was the Joss House ♥ ♥ ♥, a fine Taoist temple that still serves a small community of Chinese elders. Incense still burns and worshippers leave offerings of fruit, whiskey, and money. The temple, now a state park, contains priceless tapestries, gilded wooden scrollwork, and an ornately carved altar.

More gold rush history is on display at the J. J. (Jake) Jackson Memorial Museum and Trinity County Historical Park ♥ ♥ in the form of an old miner's cabin, a blacksmith's shop, and a steam-powered paymaster mine stampmill, which crushes gold-bearing ore. A detour at Weaverville along Highway 3 leads to the Hayfork Natural Bridge ♥, a natural limestone arch spanning a narrow ravine. Early pioneers who picnicked on the natural bridge engraved their names with dates into the limestone rock.

Continuing north on Route 3, the old California-Oregon Wagon Road, leads into the heart of the Trinity

Alps Wilderness Area, a scenic refuge of deep glacial canyons and rugged peaks topping 7,000 feet. Headwaters of large streams, including the Salmon and Trinity rivers, Stuart's Fork, Coffee, Swift, and Canyon creeks are starting points for the main trails into the Trinity Alps. More than 300 trails lead into this area, and all-inclusive outings can be planned by a licensed packer. A free wilderness permit is required to enter the area, and the U.S. Forest Service publishes a brochure *Trinity Alps Wilderness* listing trailheads and charting the area's numerous lakes and mileage between destinations. A left turn on Coffee Creek Road, 8 miles past Trinity Center, leads into the Trinity Alps Primitive Area.

INSIDERS' TIPS

River rafting on the Klamath River is suited to every skill level at Turtle River Rafting, 507 McCloud Ave., Mt. Shasta, CA 96067; call 916-926-3223 for excellent trips, priced at $213 for 2 days, including storytelling and all food.

The Trinity Alps rise up strikingly behind Trinity Lake, whose 157 miles of shoreline and 16,000 surface acres are remarkably uncrowded—despite 4 marinas and recreational opportunities that include houseboating, swimming, hiking, camping, hunting, gold-panning, and fishing for small- and large-mouth bass. Trinity Lake's deepest waters form Lewiston Lake, whose icy temperatures make it ideal for trout fishing.

LASSEN VOLCANIC NATIONAL PARK

Forty-seven miles east of Redding along Highway 44 is Lassen Volcanic National Park ♛ ♛ ♛ ♛, a magnificent recreation area that hisses, bubbles, and steams with volcanic activity. Lassen Peak dominates the park. This 10,457-foot, plug-dome volcano forms the southern end of the Cascades. The mountain range, which stretches north into Canada, has gained notoriety with the recent eruptions of Mount St. Helen's. Lassen last erupted between 1914 and 1921, and the park offers an ever-evolving testimonial as to how landscapes recover from volcanic episodes. For example, the Devastated Area of Lassen is undergoing a process of revegetation with herbs, grasses, shrubs, and finally trees reclaiming the land. Hat Lake, rapidly filling with debris from higher elevations, will soon disappear, leaving a meadow that will some day give way to forests.

Geothermal activity can be studied along Spatter-cone Crest Trail, Sulphur Works, or Bumpass Hell Basin, the park's largest area, with boiling pools, rumbling steam vents, and lava fields. After witnessing the rumblings of the earth's crust, you can immerse yourself in silent wilderness corners where it feels the entire earth is at peace. Fortunately this 106,000-acre park, with 50 lakes, numerous streams, and 7 camp-grounds doesn't draw Yosemite-size hordes. It can be surprisingly uncrowded even in summertime.

Thirty miles of the park's key attractions are acces-sible from Route 89, the Lassen Peak Road. If you buy *The Road Guide to Lassen National Park* at any informa-tion center, you'll find it keyed to these roadside mark-ers to enhance your explorations. The road offers dramatic views as it rises to an elevation of 8,512 feet and skirts three sides of Lassen Peak.

Activities and programs, including naturalist and Indian lore, abound in summer, centered at Manzanita Lake campground. Winter offers downhill and cross-country skiing, snowmobiling and snowshoeing atop Lassen Peak. Prices are reasonable. Note that the northern entrance to Lassen, Route 44, is usually closed in winter.

North of Lassen on Highway 89 you'll reach McAr-thur-Burney Falls Memorial State Park♛ ♛. This love-ly spot has towering ponderosa pines and twin falls that drop precipitously over a 129-foot cliff into an emerald pool below. A trail winds past the falls and over the creek.

The falls lie near the midpoint of the road between Lassen and Mount Shasta, the 14,162-foot peak that you see towering above the landscape for 100 miles. Its appearance is often surreal, almost a mirage when it suddenly materializes beyond a freeway or in some other unexpected and incongruous place. Sacred to local Indian tribes and respected by climbers and skiers alike, Shasta is majestic with 5 glaciers straddling her flanks, 2 volcanic cones composing her peaks, and white-bark pine forests, alpine lakes, and flowering meadows beautifying her face. You can cross-country ski, snowmobile, and ice-skate in winter, and camp, hike, boat, and white-water raft in summer.

INSIDERS' TIPS

If you're in good shape, you can hike to the summit from the 7,800-foot elevation where the road ends. Get information and equipment in the tiny town of Mt. Shasta, where you must register before attempting the ascent.

In the northeastern part of Siskiyou County near the Oregon border is Lava Beds National Monument♛, another fascinating example of volcanic activity. This 46,000-acre preserve calls for some rugged exploring over jagged lava fields. With park-provided lantern and hardhat and your own sweater, you can nose around in some 19 caves open to the public. These cylindrical caves, of which there are more than 300, are tubes formed by *pahoehoe* or smooth-lava flows. They're actually the hardened shells of flows that cooled first on the outside, allowing the lava inside to remain hot and continue flowing through. Some of the caves contain perpetually frozen rivers of ice, one has a garden of ferns and moss, still others have Indian pictographs and petroglyphs. They have foreboding names like Labyrinth, Catacombs, and Skull caves.

Surrounding these lava beds are several wildlife refuges. An incredible sight in spring and fall is to see the sky darkening with more than a million waterfowl drawn to Tule Lake, Lower Klamath, and other neighboring areas. In winter, more than 500 bald eagles, the largest concentration in the continental U.S., come to the Klamath Basin.

If you're heading north from Mount Shasta on I-5, stop in Yreka♛ ♛ to see some of the town's 75 turn-of-the-century Victorian homes. Visit, also, the former commercial center, Miner Street, and the Siskiyou County Museum ♛ ♛ at 910 South Main Street to see relics of 7 periods including Indian, Trapper, and Gold Rush. Displays include musical instruments, dolls, dishes, and a vintage 1850s cabin. At the Siskiyou County Court House ♛, 311 Fourth Street, see gold rush history come alive with displays of gold nuggets and panned gold.

PERILS & PITFALLS

Rattlesnakes like living in the mountains, and they don't like people crowding them. Watch your step when walking and do not use bare hands to reach into any holes, recesses, or rotten logs. As their name suggests, upset rattlers will shake their tail rattles producing a sound like maracas. They are more likely to slither away on hearing you before you would ever hear them, but it is a wise precaution to carry along a snake-bite kit.

From Yreka, Highway 3 winds south into the pastoral Scott Valley, past tiny towns like Etna and Callahan. You'll see the glistening rock formations that named the 280,000-acre Marble Mountains Wilderness Area, surrounded by the Klamath River on the north and west and the Salmon River to the south.

If you take I-5 south from Yreka, stop at Dunsmuir to see steam-train-era relics at Railroad Park Resort ♛ ♛. Then continue to Castle Crags State Park ♛ ♛ in Castella. Formed over 200 million years ago, these granite crags soar over 6,000 feet in the heart of a wilderness area with fishing, swimming, and canoeing in the Sacramento River.

Five miles west of I-5 is the second highest dam in the U.S. Take the free, guided tour through the interior of Shasta Dam ♛ ♛. It's 3 times higher than Niagara Falls, and took 8 years of labor and 6 million cubic yards of concrete to build between 1938 and 1945.

The enormous blue waters of Shasta Lake, California's largest man-made lake, were created by the dam. With 365 miles of shoreline and 30,000 surface acres, the lake offers tremendously popular recreational opportunities. There are 23 species of fish, miles of hiking trails, campgrounds and lakeside resorts around the shores, some accessible only by boat. Shasta Lake is heaven for boaters, who can find their own seclusion even on the most crowded summer days. Arms of the lake reach into 4 other waterways, the Sacramento, McCloud, and Pit rivers, and Squaw Creek.

INSIDERS' TIPS

If you don't have your own boat, try renting a houseboat. It's not prohibitive if you divide the cost with friends or several families. High season summer prices average about $1,500 a week for a boat that sleeps 12. Holiday Harbor, P.O. Box 112W, O'Brien, CA 96070 is one of many good companies to rent from; tel. 916-238-2383.

Take time out to visit Lake Shasta Caverns ♛ ♛. Bring a sweater before entering these limestone wonders with 20-foot-high stalactite and stalagmite formations studded with crystals. The caverns are reached by boat from O'Brien. The 2-hour excursion includes a ride across the McCloud area of the lake, then a bus tour up to the entrance 800 feet above. Open 9 A.M. to 4 P.M. daily, $9 adults, $4 ages 4–12. Tel. 916-238-2341.

South of Redding on I-5, visit either the Coleman National Fish Hatchery ♛, or further south in Red Bluff the Tehama-Colusa Fish Facilities ♛, one of the most technically advanced spawning channels in the world. In fall you can watch the king salmon climbing the ladders to get back to their original spawning grounds.

INSIDERS' TIPS

For a taste of local color, visit the area in early April to catch the Shasta Dixieland Jazz Festival in Redding, mid-April for the Red Bluff Rodeo, or mid-May for Redding's colorful night rodeo. You can tie in the Shasta Art Faire and Fiddle Jamboree in the town of Shasta with the rodeo. Redding also has a big air show in mid-June. Check with Redding Convention and Visitors Bureau (916-255-4100) or Shasta-Cascade Wonderland Association (916-243-2643) for specifics.

While in Red Bluff, visit the Kelly Griggs House Museum♛ at 311 Washington Street, an 1880s Victorian house, and the William B. Ide State Historic Park♛ ♛. The one-room, historic adobe dwelling of the only president of the short-lived California Republic is filled with period furnishings and offers demonstrations of pioneer crafts using old-fashioned woodworking tools. A smokehouse and a carriage house with covered wagons are open to the public.

INSIDERS' INFORMATION FOR SHASTA-CASCADE

Chester
(area code 916)
Where to Stay
Drakesbad Guest Ranch♛ ♛
Chester 96020, call operator and ask for Drakesbad #2 or write California Guest Services, 2150 N. Main #7, Red Bluff 96080.
Single room, double occupancy: $51–$63 (includes 3 meals)
These modest accommodations are the only lodgings inside Lassen Volcanic National Park. Open mid-July to end of September, this resort is so rustic most of it is without electricity, but you'll forget about the inconvenience because the setting—in a mountain valley by a trout stream—is so breathtaking. Hot-spring pools and baths, fishing, horseback riding.

Dunsmuir
(area code 916)
Where to Eat
Railroad Park Restaurant and Lounge♛ ♛
100 Railroad Park Rd., Dunsmuir; tel. 235-9976
Average dinner: $18–$20
3 restored dining cars provide a unique setting with a gorgeous view of the 6,000-foot granite Castle Crags.

Klamath River
(area code 916)
Where to Stay
Big Foot Recreation♛
30841 Walker Rd., Horse Creek 96045; tel. 496-3313
Single room, double occupancy: $20
Family inn has glass doors looking out on Klamath
River where visitors can canoe, fish, raft, and kayak.
Almost 40 acres connect endless national forest
acreage in Scott Mountains. Inside, a living room beck-
ons with fireplace, card room, and pool table.

Lakehead
(area code 916)
Where to Stay
Cascade Cove♛♛♛
902 Gregory Creek Rd., Lakehead 96051; tel. 238-
2701
Room rate: $375–$500 per week, for 4-bedroom chalets
that sleep 6–7
A luxury hideaway. 3 chalets. Private swimming dock.
Tsadi Resort♛♛♛
801 Lakeshore Dr., Lakehead 96051; tel. 238-2575
Room rate: $610–$750 per week, for cabins that sleep
7–9
Overlooking Shasta Lake, the 10 cabins have knotty-
pine interiors, kitchens, decks, barbecues, and picnic
tables. This is a delightful scenic getaway. Swimming
pool, dock, recreation room, grocery store.

Lewiston
(area code 916)
Where to Stay
Trinity Alps Resort♛♛
Star Route, Box 490, Lewiston 96052; tel. 286-2205
in-season April–September; 246-3077 off-season, October–March
Room rate: $275 for cabins that sleep 4 up to $395 for
large cabins sleeping 10. Weekly rate in season, Memorial Day to Labor Day

40 rustic cabins overlooking Stuart Fork River. Every activity imaginable in this scenic spot within 2 miles of the trailheads to the Trinity Alps Wilderness Area and Trinity Lake. General store, horseback riding, pack trips, gold panning, tennis, swimming, fishing, deer, hunting, tubing.

McCloud
(area code 916)
Where to Stay
McCloud Guest House ♛ ♛ ♛
606 West Colombero Dr., McCloud 96057; tel. 964–3160
Single room, double occupancy: $65
Country B&B set amid stately oaks and pines, a former logging baron's abode with large parlor, pool table from the Hearst collection. 5 rooms each with fireplace, 2 have clawfoot tubs. Very romantic place to stay or dine in their restaurant (♛ ♛ ♛) that serves up Continental cuisine. Average dinner $15.

Redding
(area code 916)
Where to Eat
Jack's ♛ ♛ ♛ ♛
1743 California St., Redding; tel. 241-9705
Average dinner: $9
The long lines at this popular local hangout are not for the decor but for the "best steaks in town." Local beef grilled to perfection. Good salads, too.

Nello's Place ♛ ♛ ♛ ♛
3055 Bechelli Lane, Redding; tel. 223-1636
Average dinner: $18
Veal dishes are outstanding at this Italian sidewalk café. A flower to each lady is one example of the personalized service.

El Papagayo ♛ ♛ ♛ ♛
460 Market St., Redding; tel. 243-2493
Average dinner: $10
Colorful hacienda-style Mexican restaurant. Fun place to eat and the chimichangas are outstanding.

J. D. Bennett's ♛ ♛ ♛
1800 Churn Creek, Redding; tel. 221-6177
Average dinner: $20
Sophisticated brass and mahogany decor and a varied
menu from steaks to Mexican and Chinese cuisine
make this a place for a group with eclectic tastes.

Shasta
(area code 916)
Where to Stay
Spring Creek Inn ♛ ♛ ♛
15201 Highway 299 West, Shasta 96087; tel. 243-0914
Single room, double occupancy: $45–$50
B&B with country charm in a historic town. Sun porch,
fruit orchards, breakfast included. Only 2 rooms.

Susanville
(area code 916)
Where to Stay
Hotel Mt. Lassen ♛
28 S. Lassen St., Susanville 96130; tel. 257-6609
Single room, double occupancy: $18–$30
Historic 70-room hotel with a wonderful bar and restaurant that are popular with the locals. Recreation room
has pool table. The restaurant (♛ ♛) boasts beef dishes
as part of the Western flavor. Average dinner: $12.

Weaverville
(area code 916)
Where to Eat
The Mustard Seed ♛ ♛ ♛
252 S. Main St., Weaverville; tel. 623-2922
Average dinner: $5
Great breakfast or lunch stop in historic town.

THE NORTH COAST

If San Francisco is for many the epitome of a pleasurable city, a seductress of all the senses, nearby Marin County and the wine country allow for the ultimate hedonism. The hot tub became a national symbol of sensual indulgence, based on its use among the former-hippie yuppies of Marin, and the growing reputation of California wines owes most to the vintners of the Napa and Sonoma valleys, who produce the state's finest reds and whites. Both areas blend beautiful scenery with fine food experiences; both make city life a distant unreality. A car is essential to the footloose enjoyment of these clusters of tiny towns and stretches of unspoiled nature.

PERILS & PITFALLS

Do not drink and drive, or drink and use the hot tub. Each activity on its own is a delight; together, they can curtail a good trip.

More northerly yet, stretching 400 miles up the coast to the Oregon border, forests, including the mighty redwood range, are dotted with lake and river resorts, luxurious and rustic, as well as New England-like coastal villages, former logging ports, and fishing harbors. Mendocino adds more wine land to the Napa and Sonoma bounty, and the renowned Skunk trains chug through some of the most spectacular woods in the world. Whether you prefer redwoods or red wines—or both—the north coast of California will not disappoint.

MARIN COUNTY

Just head over the Golden Gate Bridge north from San Francisco, and you'll suddenly be surrounded by magical Marin. In less than a mile, you'll know you're there when you spot the Waldo Tunnel, painted to look like a rainbow—shades of the 1960s. Though often the butt of satire for its self-indulgent, hot-tub-centered life-style, Marin is a place where the unwinding is easy.

You might want to begin Marin at some of the bars or cafés of Sausalito♛♛♛, a picturesque village with waterfront shops and restaurants, gorgeous homes winding into the hillside above, and a slew of funky-to-fancy houseboats moored along the docks at the edge of town. It's the French Riviera with a touch of Greenwich Village, where the artsy and the commercial mix.

Though the crowds and consequent traffic and parking hassles detract, Sausalito nonetheless has a real charm. If you doubt it, climb the hillside and sip a drink on the patio of the Alta Mara Hotel overlooking the dazzling blue bay below. You'll see sailboats and ocean-going liners passing Belvedere and Angel Islands.

Sausalito's wealthy neighbor Tiberon♛♛ is equally quaint with a much smaller waterfront. This is Marin's enclave for the moneyed set. If you want to rub elbows with them, drop into a popular bar or restaurant like Sam's Anchor Café.

Nearby, the Tiberon Uplands Nature Preserve♛♛ offers a loop hiking trail and the 900-acre Richardson Bay Wildlife Sanctuary. Another neighbor, Angel Island State Park, is a must if you like to picnic, hike, or sit and stare at the view.

INSIDERS' TIPS

The most pleasurable way to visit Sausalito, Tiberon, or Angel Island from San Francisco is by ferry.

The high point of Marin, both in literal and figurative terms, is Mount Tamalpais State Park♛♛♛♛, whose summit at nearly 2,600 feet provides a striking panorama. On a clear day you can see forever . . . well, you can at least see as far as the snow-capped Sierra Nevada peaks over 200 miles away. Mount Tam, as it is affectionately called, with 50 miles of hiking trails, 10 rustic, overnight cabins, picnicking, and a hillside amphitheater is an incomparable place to get lost for the day with your favorite companion. (A historical note: Back in the sixties, this mountain retreat also served as a dropping point for many Bay Area hallucinogenic experiments.)

Mount Tam is best known for Muir Woods National Monument ♛ ♛ ♛ ♛ ♛. Some 500 acres of majestic coastal redwoods inspire awe and offer refuge for neighboring urban dwellers among the more than one million annual visitors. This enchanting forest has self-guided, marked paths for hikes and a Miwok Braille Trail for the blind.

Winding around the base of Mount Tam along scenic Highway 1 you'll reach the coast at lovely Muir Beach ♛ ♛ ♛. Though some brave the cold waters to swim, there are tidepools to explore and an adjacent bird sanctuary to discover. If you climb over the rocks to the right as you face the ocean, you'll find a secluded beach where some people bathe au naturel.

Up the coast another 7 miles is Stinson Beach ♛ ♛ ♛. Its broad, white expanse of sand makes a popular venue for al fresco dining and for warming up after a quick swim. (No one stays in these numbing waters very long.) The tiny town of Stinson Beach has become somewhat of an artists' colony, although not on the grand scale of Venice, for example, in the Los Angeles area.

PERILS & PITFALLS

You may be taken by surprise when you decide to escape inland heat in the summer for a swim at the beach, only to discover that the coast is socked in with fog. Bring along pants and a heavy sweater just in case.

North of Stinson Beach, at the tidal inlet of Bolinas Lagoon, you'll find Audubon Canyon Ranch ♛ ♛ ♛, a 1,000-acre bird sanctuary where great blue herons and

American egrets come to nest from March to July. Some of these exotic birds choose the giant redwoods as a place to usher their young into the world.

Point Reyes National Seashore♛♛♛♛♛ is Marin's northernmost coastal treasure. This magnificent 73,000-acre recreational area has a dramatic coastline with rugged windswept beaches, forests, and a network of hiking trails extending some 150 miles to secluded lakes, promontories, and even along an earthquake fault. Stop at the Bear Valley Visitor's Center for information on camping and backpacking sights, hiking and horseback riding trails, and swimming, then go off to find your own private piece of paradise. If you have time, visit the replica of a Miwok Indian Village♛ near the center.

If you head out to the historic Point Reyes Lighthouse♛♛, stop on the way at Drakes Beach♛♛, sheltered by great white cliffs, and at Johnson's Oyster Farm♛♛ to buy fresh oysters in their shells or a deliciously fresh oyster cocktail served unceremoniously in a paper cup. If you go between December and April, the deck of the lighthouse is a prime vantage point from which to watch the whales on their southward migration.

Tomales Bay separates Point Reyes from the mainland. The town of Inverness♛♛, on the bay's western shore, has some charming hideaway lodgings and restaurants. Farther north, the town of Marshall sports several seafood houses serving oysters fresh from the bay.

WINE COUNTRY

When you say the words *wine country* in California, you're almost always talking about the two north coast counties of Napa and Sonoma. This area, bordered on the west by the Pacific Ocean, on the south by Marin County and the San Pablo Bay, on the east by Solano and Yolo counties, and on the north by Mendocino and Lake counties, is home to over 260 wineries. But being a wine lover is certainly no prerequisite for enjoying

CALIFORNIA WINE COUNTRY

Sonoma Valley Wineries
(Not to Scale)

Napa Valley Wineries
(Not to Scale)

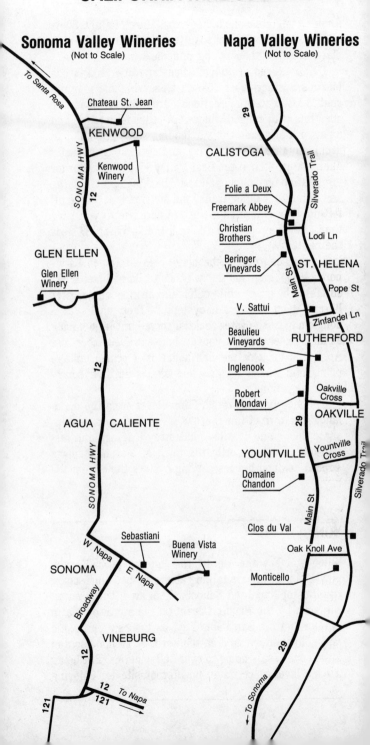

this area's spectacular coastline, its rolling, grassy hills and oak-covered mountains, or its charming, turn-of-the-century towns with outstanding restaurants, intimate B&Bs, and lavish resorts. For the energetic there are golf, tennis, cycling, hiking, swimming, and rafting. For those who don't view sloth as a deadly sin, there are more sedentary pursuits: ballooning, soaring, picnicking, and mud bathing. But it is a love of the grape, or at least a desire to learn its secrets, that makes a visit to the wine country so special.

NAPA . . . THE CITY

Heading north toward Napa Valley, the first city you'll encounter is Napa♛. It's the business center for the area and is really too big and modernized to be called charming. Nonetheless, wonderful examples of late 19th-century, Victorian architecture can be found among the squat new bank buildings with their cash machines and drive-up teller windows.

INSIDERS' TIPS

Visit the big name wineries along Highway 29 either before noon or after 4 P.M. Otherwise, head east out of Yountville on Yountville Cross Road to the Silverado Trail and go north. This route parallels Highway 29, gets you out of the heavy traffic, and takes you past some of Napa's best small wineries.

YOUNTVILLE

Continue north on Highway 29 to Yountville♛♛♛, the unofficial gateway to Napa Valley wine country. Stop at Vintage 1870♛♛♛, a beautifully restored stone winery that has become a collection of upscale boutiques. Browse through the terrific selection of local wines at Groezinger Wine Co.♛♛♛ and take the time to see a surprisingly well-produced slide show called *The Napa Valley Show*♛♛♛. Three dollars pays for this excellent primer for a first-time visitor to these parts. The Yountville Market♛♛♛ can send you picnicking in style. Don't let its Mayberry exterior fool you. Inside, this place has enough pâté, French cheese, and exotic fruit to satisfy the most ravenous yuppies. Don't miss visiting Domaine Chandon♛♛♛♛, on the west side of Highway 29. Its beautifully designed buildings suggest the champagne barrels this French-owned winery is famous for filling. There's a champagne museum, a tasting salon, and a top-notch, classic French restaurant for those who find picnicking too earthy.

PERILS & PITFALLS

North of Yountville, Highway 29 becomes a simple two-lane road along which lie nearly 40 wineries, among them, Napa's most popular: Robert Mondavi (known for its modern sculptures), Inglenook, Beaulieu, Beringer (modeled after its founder's original home in Germany), Christian Brothers, and Charles Krug. Consequently, the traffic on weekends during high season (May–October) is enough to drive you to drink. But even that's difficult, as you will likely find the tasting rooms just as crowded. See Insiders' Information for Crown ratings and opening hours, pages 295–296.)

ST. HELENA

Located midway between Yountville and Calistoga in the heart of Napa wine country is St. Helena ♛♛♛♛♛, a town of over 5,000 people that retains all its 19th-century charm despite its emergence as the capital of one of the world's great wine-producing areas. While tourists will discover much of interest in St. Helena, like the Wine Library♛♛ and the Silverado Museum♛♛ with its Robert Louis Stevenson memorabilia, they will also discover that St. Helena does not exist primarily to attract and amuse tourists. It's a real, working example of small-town America. And that, perhaps, is its greatest charm. Because of its central location in the relatively flat Napa Valley, St. Helena is a good place to rent a bicycle. St. Helena Cyclery downtown, at 1156 Main St. (707-963-7736) will get you rolling by the hour, day, or week.

Six hot-air balloon companies operate in the Napa Valley, 4 between St. Helena and Yountville, one in Napa to the south, and the other in Calistoga at the northern end of the valley. Let's deal with the bad news first: It's going to cost you about $145, and you'll have to get up at 5 A.M. Those are the *only* drawbacks. There is no more pleasurable experience to be found anywhere, for any price, that isn't fattening or illegal. As early-morning sun floods the valley, you'll drift over manicured vineyards, glistening lakes and ponds, and an occasional apple or cherry orchard. You'll discover an unreal quiet, broken only by the sound of barking dogs hundreds of feet below and random blasts from the balloon's propane burner. Most companies feature a champagne breakfast or picnic brunch after the one-hour flight. (See Balloon Companies, page 292.)

CALISTOGA

Eight miles north of St. Helena is Calistoga ♛♛♛♛♛, another small town that defines the words *quaint* and *charming*. To a wine lover, it also defines *sacrilege*, being more popular for its water than its wine. But it wasn't water that millionaire developer Sam Brannan was drinking back in 1859 when, wishing to recreate the famed Saratoga, N.Y., resort in California, he said, "We'll make this the Calistoga of Sarafornia!"

PERILS & PITFALLS

Two miles north of town is the Old Faithful geyser, billed as one of the few regularly erupting geysers in the world. It costs $2 and blows every 40 minutes or so. If you've ever lost the head of a lawn sprinkler while the water was on, you've approximated the drama of this unimpressive "natural wonder."

Calistoga is justifiably famous for its mud baths ♛♛♛, made from white volcanic ash mixed with naturally heated mineral water, as well as its sparkling water that is bottled and distributed in town. Both are the natural residue of the area's relatively recent volcanic past.

It is also becoming famous for a handful of great restaurants and specialty shops within easy walking distance on Calistoga's main street. Stop at the All Seasons Market♕♕♕♕♕ and put together a picnic lunch from its selection of delicious cold cuts, pâté, homemade bread, and cheese from around the world. Try some homemade ice cream while you wait. It's also the best place in all of Napa Valley to buy wine, with over 1,500 different selections in stock.

For another bird's-eye view of the valley, with a bit more speed and drama, try a trip in a glider♕♕♕♕. Cheaper than ballooning ($40–$100), if you decide to glide you don't have to get up with the sun. Call the Calistoga Soaring Center (707-942-5592) for information about flights lasting from 15 to 40 minutes.

INSIDERS' TIPS

With the money your group has saved by missing the Old Faithful geyser, drive another half mile down Tubbs Lane and buy a bottle of wine at Chateau Montelena. This is one of the prettiest wineries in the valley, built in the style of a French chateau. Its beautiful lake and Chinese water garden are adorned with lacquered pavilions and arched footbridges—a perfect place for a picnic but you must reserve in advance. Call the winery at 707-942-5105.

About 4 miles south of Calistoga is Bothe-Napa Valley State Park♕♕♕. Its 1,800 acres include redwood forests, fishing streams, marked hiking trails, a swimming pool, and camping facilities.

Six miles to the north of town is the Robert Louis Stevenson State Park♕♕, where you can either drive or take a beautiful 5-mile hike to the top of Mt. St. Helena (not to be confused with Mt. St. Helens). At 4,343 feet, this highest point in the area affords commanding views of the Bay Area, Pacific Ocean, and Napa and Sonoma valleys. If you hike, you'll pass the spot where Stevenson honeymooned and was inspired to write *The Silverado Squatters*.

Five miles west of Calistoga at 4100 Petrified Forest Road is the Petrified Forest♛♛♛, a wonderful example of what nature can do when it decides to blow off a little steam. This private park contains fossilized remains of fallen redwoods covered millions of years ago with volcanic ash.

SONOMA COUNTY

West of Napa Valley, just over the Mayacamus Mountains, lies Sonoma County, California's oldest wine-producing area and today a close second to Napa Valley as the finest wine-producing area in the country. Sonoma County is, however, far more diverse than Napa both agriculturally and recreationally. Thus, it is infinitely more appealing to those who don't know their cabernets from their chardonnays.

The area is most easily approached via Route 101 north from San Francisco or by following Route 12/121-West out of Napa Valley.

No other town captures the spirit and flavor of Sonoma County better than historic Sonoma♛♛♛♛♛ perhaps that's why nearly a million people a year pay it a visit. We're also betting that its world-famous wine, cheese, sausages, and chocolate attract their share of tourists as well.

Sonoma was founded in 1823 by the Franciscan Fathers as the northernmost mission in their Camino Real chain. The mission chapel♛♛ is on the north side of the town plaza and is open to the public for a small fee ($1.00 for adults, 50¢ for children). In fact, most of the structures surrounding the plaza date back to the 19th century, but today they are filled with gourmet food stores, hotels, boutiques, and bars.

Stop into the old Carnegie Library at 453 First Street, which is now the Sonoma Valley Visitors Bureau, and pick a guidebook for the Sonoma Walking Tour♛♛♛♛. Don't miss the Sonoma Cheese

Factory♛ ♛ ♛ ♛, 2 W. Spain Street, home of the world-famous Sonoma Jack cheese, for terrific deli sandwiches and picnic supplies. If you like sausage, or ever thought you might, do yourself a favor and check out the Sonoma Sausage Co.♛ ♛ ♛ ♛ at 453 First Street. The only other "must" is to indulge your sweet tooth at the Sonoma French Bakery♛ ♛ ♛ ♛ at 470 E. First Street. This tiny shop, run by Gratien and Lilli Guerras serves up some of the best Basque cakes, pastries, and sourdough bread to be found anywhere.

Head north out of Sonoma on Route 12♛ ♛ ♛ ♛, a state-designated scenic highway that definitely earns its stripes, or at least its dotted white lines. After about 4 miles, turn left on Arnold Road toward the tiny town of Glen Ellen and follow the signs to Jack London State Historic Park♛ ♛ ♛ ♛. This was home to the famous author for nearly 13 years. Visitors can tour his widow's "House of Happy Walls," which has an excellent collection of London memorabilia, and view the remains of London's dream home "Wolf House," which was destroyed by fire before completion.

SANTA ROSA

Routes 12 and 101 come together in Santa Rosa♛ ♛, Sonoma County's largest city (pop. 100,000). Here, turn-of-the-century buildings stand, not always comfortably, alongside brand-new office buildings, thanks to the combined forces of the 1906 earthquake and urban renewal. Good examples of how all this works (or doesn't, depending on how you feel about such things) is Fourth Street Mall♛ ♛ ♛ and Santa Rosa Plaza♛ ♛. Here many of Santa Rosa's finest, old, retail outlets along Fourth Street are joined to a huge, new shopping center by a grand arched walkway. Combined, these centers offer shop-a-holics nearly 150 department stores, gift shops, specialty stores, and restaurants.

Across Route 101 from the Santa Rosa Plaza is Old Railroad Square♛ ♛ ♛ ♛, a great example of what urbanologists like to call "adaptive reuse." Some of

Santa Rosa's best restaurants, quirkiest retail outlets, biggest antique shops, and most hell-raisin' bars can be found among these great, old buildings that could have been reduced to rubble by the wrecking balls developers swing so freely these days.

For 53 years, the "plant wizard," Luther Burbank, called Santa Rosa his home. His pioneering botanical experiments resulted in more than 800 new plant species, including 275 new varieties of fruits and vegetables. Burbank's home and gardens♛♛ are now a national historic landmark and are open to the public free of charge every day but Monday. (Call 707-576-5115 for more information.)

EXCURSIONS FROM SANTA ROSA

If you take Route 12 out of Santa Rosa through Sebastopol♛♛♛ to Bodega Bay♛♛♛, you will not only begin one of the loveliest drives to be found in the state of California, you'll also experience firsthand what Luther Burbank meant about Sonoma County when he said, "This is the chosen spot of all the earth as far as nature is concerned." You will be traveling through the heart of an enormously fertile and diverse agricultural region. The small farms in this area produce countless varieties of fruit, vegetables, cheeses, flowers, wine, and livestock.

INSIDERS' TIPS

Over 160 small farms are in the Sonoma County Farm Trails Association, whose members sell their products directly to the consumer, often at greatly reduced wholesale prices. Special maps listing all the Farm Trail members are available free by sending a self-addressed, stamped envelope to: Sonoma County Farm Trails, P.O. Box 6674, Santa Rosa, CA 95406. Or you can pick one up at the Chamber of Commerce office in just about any town in Sonoma County.

On inland Highway 101, Petaluma is the place to sample the local dairy production characteristic of this rolling-hilled country. The Marin French Cheese Company♕♕♕, on Petaluma–Point Reyes Road just west of Novato Boulevard (707-762-6001), or The Creamery♕♕♕, 711 Western Avenue at Baker Street (707-778-1234), are your best bet. Tour, taste, then head off on a self-guided walking tour♕♕♕ (707-762-2785) of historic downtown buildings with wrought-iron facades. Petaluma Adobe State Historic Park♕♕♕♕ (707-762-2785) is a fine example of an early California ranchero.

Nature and the California Highway department have cooperated in your introduction to the North Coast—the best way to maximize your time here is to follow Highway 1 north to its terminus in Leggett, then proceed along Highway 101 to the Oregon border. Take your time. Take plenty of film. Any number of detours will, no doubt, demand their due, depending on your mood.

Fewer than a dozen towns with 600 or more residents speckle the region, and most of them are found on Highway 101, which runs parallel to the coastal Route 1. Stick to the coast, and Bodega Bay♕♕♕, 30 minutes north of Marin, may look familiar as the setting for Alfred Hitchcock's *The Birds;* it's really a tame, little fishing village where you may camp and picnic.

From there take Route 1 north along the coast♕♕♕♕ to Jenner—one of the most beautiful stretches of northern California's craggy shoreline you'll find. The 12 miles of steep, rocky cliffs and secluded beaches comprise the Sonoma Coast State Beach and are ideal for fishing, whale watching (in season), hiking, and camping.

PERILS & PITFALLS

While North Coast beaches promise spectacular vistas, winters are rainy and summers (especially mornings) are foggy. Few beaches are hospitable for swimming because of cold water and unpredictable ocean currents.

At Jenner, head inland on Route 116 along the banks of the Russian River♕♕♕, named by the Russian fur traders who settled the area in the early 1800s. This beautiful river valley is populated by small farmers and ranchers, expensive summer cottages and weekend get-aways, and vacationers taking advantage of the abundant rental units and water-sport activities in the area. Many of the lodges and resorts in and around Guerneville ♔ ♔ ♔ have become particularly popular with the gay community. (For more information write or call the Russian River Chamber of Commerce, 14034 Armstrong Woods Rd., Guerneville, CA 95446; tel. 707-869-3357.)

Two miles north of Guerneville is the Armstrong Redwood State Reserve ♔ ♔ ♔, where you can enjoy horseback riding, bicycling, and picnicking, or simply transcending your troubles in one of the most serene stands of redwoods anywhere.

HEALDSBURG

About 15 miles northeast of Guerneville is Healdsburg ♔ ♔ ♔ ♔, ideal for exploring the wineries of northern Sonoma County or for taking canoe trips down the Russian River. Healdsburg's central plaza is a great spot for a picnic. It's also a great spot to rent a bike for exploring the Russian River Wine Road ♔ ♔ ♔. Wine Road maps, as well as Farm Trail maps, are available from the Healdsburg Chamber of Commerce at 217 Healdsburg Avenue. One of the newest recreational facilities in the area, Lake Sonoma ♔ ♔, is easily accessible from Healdsburg. This artificially created lake has 53 miles of shoreline and offers boating, waterskiing, fishing, and horseback riding.

Linguists and those interested in the peculiarities of rural life should call on Boonville ♔ ♔ ♔, halfway between Highways 1 and 101, on Highway 253. This town of 900 has, over 100 years of existence, developed "Boontling," a language at once charming and bizarre. Still spoken by town elders, its genesis was a method of gossiping among adults without fear of comprehension by the children. Smile for the *Charlie Walker*, but don't let the local *broadies japin'* across the road get in the way.

You are well into the Redwood Empire ♛ ♛ ♛ ♛ ♛, so named for the unbelievable majesty of the world's tallest trees. It's as if they suffer from an arboreal pituitary problem—some are higher than a football field is long. The coastal redwoods differ somewhat from those found in the Sierra, but despite a slightly smaller size and shorter lifespan, they still dominate their landscape.

INSIDERS' TIP

For maps and information about trails and amenities throughout the Redwood Empire, send $1 to the Redwood Empire Association, One Market Plaza, Spear Street Tower, #1001, San Francisco, CA 94105. Another excellent map and sourcebook covering the area in greater depth is the *Recreation Guide & Touring Maps of Humboldt County, the Redwoods and Eureka,* $1.50 from Don Hunt Advertising, 537 G Street, Eureka, CA 95501.

MENDOCINO

An increasingly recognized wine-producing region, Mendocino ♛ ♛ ♛ ♛ is fecund, routinely yielding first-rate Zinfandel and Chardonnay wines, known for their intense character. Small, specialty wineries freckle the hillsides around a series of valleys, and vineyards spread across the valley floors. Probably three fourths of Mendocino's wine is produced from local grapes, and much of it is unavailable outside the immediate area.

The town of Mendocino is an arty enclave of galleries, shops, and inns, infused with a distinctly New England air. Russian Gulch State Park ♛ ♛ ♛ ♛ is filled with redwoods, wave-etched bluffs, tunnels, and trails for the adventuresome (tel. 707-937-5804). But don't limit yourself to civilized pursuits. Nature asserts itself powerfully here, from the dramatic Pacific shores, hemmed by wildflowers, to the inland hiking, biking, and horseback-riding trails. Contact the County Department of Parks and Beaches in Ukiah (tel. 707-463-4267) for a guide to the bountiful recreation possibilities.

INSIDERS' TIPS

Fetzer Vineyards has long been a family-owned-and-operated concern where 9 brothers and sisters work alongside the family matriarch. The Tasting Room is open daily from 9 A.M. to 5 P.M. on Highway 101 in downtown Hopland. Picnic grounds supply the appropriately beautiful setting in which to enjoy a meal and the local elixir. Check the local newspaper, *Ukiah Lifestyles,* for other vineyards with scenic picnic areas.

Just beyond lies Fort Bragg, another harbor-hugging hamlet noted for deep-sea fishing and, in season, whale watching (tel. 707-964-3153). Here, also, is where to catch the California Western Railway "Skunk" train♔ ♔ ♔ ♔. Originally a logging railroad, in 1925 it was converted to gas engines, prompting locals to remark, "You can smell 'em before you can see 'em." The 40-mile line now runs for the pleasure of visitors along narrow-gauge tracks. For schedules, call 707-964-6371.

PERILS & PITFALLS

Considered a challenge by some drivers, the tortuously curvaceous route between the Mendocino coast and Highway 101 on Highway 128 may seem a bit tough to others. It's scenic, but the "highway to the sea" demands all your driving attention.

If you've opted for inland Highway 101, Ukiah, population 15,000 (a *big* town for this part of the world), brings Native American culture to the masses in Grace Hudson's "Sun House" Museum♔ ♔ ♔ (tel. 707-462-4705). The turn-of-the-century painter and her husband dedicated themselves to memorializing the Pomo Indians.

Off of Highway 101, several lakes serve the sporting

pleasures of savvy sailors, anglers, swimmers, skiers, and those who simply like being wet. Lake Mendocino♛♛♛, on Highway 20, is open for camping from April through September, a venue from which you can venture further on a number of hiking trails. For details, call 707-462-7581. But Clear Lake♛♛♛♛♛, another 30 minutes inland in Lake County, is the main attraction here. It was the home of the Pomo Indians, whose lore includes a rock-throwing skirmish between two chiefs that resulted in the formation of Mt. Konocti looming above the shore. The largest, natural freshwater lake in the state, it is frequently a landmark for pilots on a Seattle–Los Angeles run because of the predictably clear air.

Clear Lake is rightfully called the "Bass Capital of the West," and all manner of pan fish populate its generous waters. Its warmth keeps swimmers as happy as anglers. Bask in the sun and water, and enjoy your choice of cuisine and accommodation—a hot dog roasting on a stick over a campfire, and a sleeping bag, or a 5-course Continental meal in the elegant confines of a luxury resort.

Blue Lakes♛♛♛, further up Highway 20, restricts boat speeds, rendering these waters ideal for the quieter pursuits of canoeing, sailing, and swimming. Lake Pillsbury♛♛♛, encompassed by the Mendocino National Forest, is also filled with campgrounds and resorts. The nearby Eel River and its tributaries is the place to be when the steelhead are in season. For information concerning activities and amenities in Lake County, call 707-263-6131.

Lake County rightfully boasts its share of wineries♛♛♛, most of which specialize in Zinfandel and Chardonnay, although the vineyards are more likely to be interspersed with fruit orchards. For information on winery tours, call 707-263-6131.

After the confluence of the coastal and inland highways at Leggett, head for Redway and take the 23-mile-long Shelter Cove Road♛♛♛♛ (4-wheel drive vehicles only) which offers a breathtaking trip to the ocean, where private campgrounds, stores, a small airport, and boat-launching facilities are available. To the north, you will find a black sand beach and abalone diving for the stout of heart. For information, call 707-923-3936. Another detour worthy of consideration runs between South Fork and Fernbridge, circuitously venturing to the westernmost point of the contiguous United States at Cape Mendocino. This route includes passage through Ferndale, an authentically restored, New England-style, Victorian village.

Running parallel to Highway 101, the redwoods flourish in astonishing profusion along Avenue of the Giants ♛ ♛ ♛ ♛. It meanders 33 miles along the Eel River beginning in Phillipsville. Don't plan to race through, however; too many diversions wrest one's attention away from the yellow center line. Sunbathe along the banks of the Eel; stream fish for trout, salmon, or steelhead in Mattole River; rockhound for jade and jasper formations. Redwoods State Park headquarters can answer any questions, tel. 707-946-2311.

PERILS & PITFALLS

All of the outstanding features within the Redwood Empire are well marked—some to an extreme. Ignore the cheesy signage if you can, for the natural attraction more than speaks for itself.

Thirty miles south of Eureka, the town of Scotia ♛ ♛ ♛ aptly reflects its environment—it's built entirely of redwood lumber. The world's largest redwood lumber mill, the Pacific Lumber Company, offers free, self-guided tours when in operation. Call 707-923-3936 for details.

The largest city on the northern California coast, Eureka is a major commercial fishing center. Its Greek moniker means "I have found it," despite the fact that the seafarers who founded it in 1850 were Yankee to the bone. Old Town ♛ ♛ ♛ is restored to circa 1880 status, replete with horse-drawn stages rolling along brick-paved streets. Victorian architecture and a lively mix of culinary options (focusing on the local seafood) are Eureka trademarks.

Guides for Victorian Architectural Tours are available from the Eureka Chamber of Commerce, 2112

Broadway; tel. 707-442-3738. The Indian Art Gallery ♛ ♛ ♛ on F Street is a must for those interested in Native American art and artifacts. The Coast Oyster Company ♛ ♛ ♛, at the foot of A Street, invites visitors to tour its processing plant, but hours are irregular; call 707-442-2947.

INSIDERS' TIPS

For the most breathtaking hike on the north coast, try Trinidad Head Trail ♛ ♛ ♛ ♛ ♛, right off Highway 101 about 10 miles north of Arcata. Park near the beach and walk up the road until you reach the gate with the opening in the middle. Keep to the trail lest you veer off into private property *and* poison oak.

If the desire to ride the waves runs strong, hop aboard the *Madaket* ♛ ♛ ♛ ♛ on Humboldt Bay and explore the area of the ancient Wiyot Indians. Although the ship was named for the Nantucket Island Indians, she has never left this bay. The 75-minute tour, several daily from May through September, will clue you into the flora, fauna, and gossip of the region.

INSIDERS' TIPS

Within Prairie Creek Redwoods State Park lies the Revelation Trail, specially marked for the blind.

Some 40 miles beyond lies Redwood National Park—more than 100,000 acres astride Humboldt and Del Norte counties. It umbrellas Prairie Creek Redwoods State Park ♛ ♛ ♛ (tel. 707-488-2171), 6 miles north of Orick off Highway 101, where meadows and Roosevelt elk vie for space with the trees; Del Norte Coast Redwoods State Park ♛ ♛ ♛ ♛ (tel. 707-464-9533), with a more developed system of hiking trails and a biking camp 7 miles south of Crescent City; and Jedediah Smith Redwoods State Park ♛ ♛ ♛ ♛ (tel. 707-458-3310), east of Crescent City, where the narrow Howland Hill road leads to the world's largest tree—20 feet in diameter, 340 feet tall.

With children in tow, a visit to the Trees of Mystery♛♛♛ in Klamath is in order. March through November, this "shrine of the redwoods" explains the physical development of the great trees and their significance in California legend (tel. 707-482-5613).

Crescent City♛♛♛♛ is blessed with pristine beaches and abundant good fishing. Watch the fleets unload their catches of salmon, Dungeness crab, and shrimp, when in season. Launch a boat or charter one. Check out the Battery Point Lighthouse Museum♛♛, but only at low tide when it is accessible. Drop in to the Del Norte County Historical Society Museum♛♛ for Indian exhibits and general Californiana. And don't forget Undersea Gardens♛♛♛♛, where wolf eels, sharks, and their friends are viewed in their natural habitat. Call 707-464-3174 for details.

By all means, salmon fishermen should toss a line into the Klamath River♛♛♛♛♛, renowned as far as Europe for steelhead salmon. Eight miles north of Crescent City, Earl and Talawa lakes♛♛♛ open onto a 6-mile coastal beach, dotted with ponds and dunes called home by hundreds of species of birds. Now under development, parking, picnic- and campsites are available, with more to come. For additional information, call 707-443-4588.

INSIDERS' INFORMATION FOR THE NORTH COAST

Bodega Bay
(area code 707)
Where to Stay
Inn at the Tides♛♛♛♛
800 Coast Highway 1, Bodega Bay 94923; tel. 875-2751, or 800-541-7788
Single room, double occupancy: $100
Classic, cedar-shake guest lodges overlooking Bodega Bay. Comfortable rooms. Pool, massage, sauna, whirlpool spa, laundromat, refrigerators. 88 rooms.

Calistoga
(area code 707)
Where to Stay
Mount View Hotel♛♛♛♛
1457 Lincoln Ave., Calistoga 94515; tel. 942-6877
Single room, double occupancy: $80
An art-deco dream in the heart of Calistoga. Becoming *the* place to stay in northern Napa Valley. Pool, Jacuzzi, complimentary breakfast. 34 rooms. Restaurant (♛♛♛♛) has a changing menu, with seasonal offerings, great California cuisine.

Brannan Cottage♛♛♛
109 Wapoo, Calistoga 94515; tel. 942-4200
Single room, double occupancy: $65
Gingerbread Victorian building in middle of beautiful gardens. National Historic Landmark. Walking distance to spas. 6 rooms, all air-conditioned and with private baths.

Where to Eat
Silverado Restaurant♛♛♛♛
1374 Lincoln Ave., Calistoga; tel. 942-6725
Average dinner: $30
Casual and elegant with changing menu and one of the best wine lists in the world.

Crescent City
(area code 707)
Where to Eat
View Grotto♛♛♛
Citizen's Dock Rd., Crescent City; tel. 464-3815
Average dinner: $10
Panoramic ocean view makes dining here a delight. Seafood, steaks, and prime rib.

Eureka
(area code 707)
Where to Stay
Eagle House Bed & Breakfast♛♛♛♛
Second and C streets, Eureka 95501; tel. 442-2334
Single room, double occupancy: $70
Victorian landmark building in Old Town; you'll fall in

love with the exquisitely decorated rooms. Not to worry—the furnishings are available for purchase.

Eureka Inn♛♛♛♛

Seventh and F streets, Eureka 95501; tel. 442-6441

Single room, double occupancy: $80

National historic landmark of redwood construction, but in Tudor style. Some fireplaces, sauna, Jacuzzi, hot tub, airport transportation. 110 rooms.

Where to Eat

Eaglecrest♛♛♛♛♛

139 Second St., Eureka; tel. 444-8051

Average dinner: $22

Located above the more informal Buon Gusto (♛♛♛), this is Eureka's most elegant dining room. Continental menu offers fresh Maine lobster and local sea fare.

Art's Gallery♛♛♛

1917 Fifth St., Eureka; tel. 442-5278

Average dinner: $15

Prime rib reigns supreme, but try the local seafood too.

Enrico's Wine Shop, Tasting Bar & Delicatessen♛♛♛

1595 Myrtle Ave., Eureka; tel. 442-1771

Average dinner: $9

Specialty food store featuring European imported beer with distinctly non-Californian merchandise. Take-outs for picnics.

Samoa Cookhouse♛♛♛

On Humboldt Bay, Eureka; tel. 442-1659

Average dinner: $10

Last surviving cookhouse in the West. Copious meals served in lumber-camp style. Dining room is a veritable museum with early culinary items and lodging industry wares as decor.

Ferndale

(area code 707)

Where to Stay

Gingerbread Mansion Bed & Breakfast Inn♛♛♛♛♛

400 Berding St., Ferndale 95536; tel. 786-4000

Single room, double occupancy: $65

Restored, gabled, Victorian house with turrets and English gardens. Individually appointed rooms, intimate setting, the ultimate in period pampering. 5 rooms. Bicycles for touring, library, robes.

Fort Bragg
(area code 707)
Where to Stay
Glass Beach Bed & Breakfast Inn ♛ ♛ ♛ ♛
726 N. Main St., Fort Bragg 95437; tel. 964-6774
Single room, double occupancy: $60
1920s house, fully renovated, each room individually decorated, exuding charm. Wine and snacks served in the evening. 9 rooms.
Pudding Creek Inn ♛ ♛ ♛
700 N. Main St., Fort Bragg 95437; tel. 964-9529
Single room, double occupancy: $60
2 Victorian buildings joined by a garden. Country store, Continental breakfast. 10 rooms.
Where to Eat
Lost Coast Restaurant ♛ ♛ ♛ ♛ ♛
647 N. Main St., Fort Bragg; tel. 964-7689
Average dinner: $15
Mediterranean specialties in a restored Edwardian house. Homemade bread, local wines complete the repast. Closed in December.

Garberville
(area code 707)
Where to Stay
Benbow Inn ♛ ♛ ♛ ♛ ♛ ♛
445 Lake Benbow Dr., Garberville 95440; tel. 923-2124
Single room, double occupancy: $80 and up
Tudor-style inn on the lake. English gardens. A bit of the old country in the midst of overwhelmingly New England influences. In-room Jacuzzis, antiques, teas and scones. Golf, tennis. 55 rooms. Open April through December.

Healdsburg
(area code 707)
Where to Stay
Haydon House ♛ ♛ ♛ ♛
321 Haydon St., Healdsburg 95448; tel. 433-5228
Single room, double occupancy: $60
Lovingly maintained Victorian house on quiet residential street. The quintessential B&B. Laura Ashley prints, handmade dhurrie rugs, French and American antiques. Perfect location for northern Sonoma exploring and excursions on the Russian River. 5 rooms.
Madrona Manor ♛ ♛ ♛ ♛
1001 Westwide Rd., Healdsburg 95448; tel. 433-4231
Single room, double occupancy: $90
Majestic 3-story mansion on 8 wooded, landscaped acres. Opulent. Innkeepers John and Carol Muir are the perfect hosts. 20 rooms. Dining room (♛ ♛ ♛ ♛ ♛) is one of the finest in the area. California cuisine (average dinner $25). The Petrale sole is to die for. Vintage wines for big bucks.

Inverness
(area code 415)
Where to Stay
Blackthorne Inn ♛ ♛
226 Vallejo Ave., Inverness 94937; tel. 663-8621
Single room, double occupancy: $85–$145
Fantasy treehouse set in wooded, fragrant bay-filled canyon. Stained-glass windows, skylights, and a spiral staircase that leads to an eagle's-nest room high in the treetops. The ultimate California-style hideaway with scads of outdoor deck space, hot tub, and a comfortable laid-back feel. 5 rooms.
Manka's Inverness Lodge ♛
30 Calendar Way, Inverness 94937; tel. 669-1034
Single room, double occupancy: $36.50–$45
Rustic, brown-shingled country inn nestled among laurel and oaks. Rooms are plain but special because of the wonderful Czech family who runs the 9-room place.

Restaurant (♛♛♛) serves marvelous Czechoslovakian cuisine, especially veal and roast duckling with caraway sauce. Save room for Manka's own pastries; we like the lemon meringue torte.

Kelseyville
(area code 707)
Where to Stay
Konocti Harbor Inn♛♛♛♛♛
8727 Soda Bay Rd., Kelseyville 95451; tel. 707-279-4281, or 800-862-4930
Single room, double occupancy: $110
Hotel/resort/convention center on the shores of busy Clear Lake. Recreational opportunities abound, with the largest marina in Lake County. 2 Olympic pools, 8 lighted tennis courts, 5 golf courses, nightly entertainment. 250 rooms, cottage- or motel-style.

Little River
(area code 707)
Where to Stay
Heritage House♛♛♛♛♛
5200 N. Highway 1, Little River 95437; tel. 937-5885
Single room, double occupancy: $150
A country inn perched on cliffs overlooking the ocean; 67 rooms, some with fireplaces. Full Continental menu in the restaurant (♛♛♛).
Little River Inn♛♛♛
North Highway 1, P.O. Drawer B, Little River 95482; tel. 937-5942
Single room, double occupancy: $56
1853 Victorian inn by the sea, all 50 rooms with ocean views of the crashing surf. Landscaped 9-hole golf course.

Mendocino
(area code 707)
Where to Stay
Mendocino Hotel & Garden Cottages♛♛♛♛
45080 Main St., P.O. Box 587, Mendocino 95460; tel. 937-0511, or 800-421-6662

Single room, double occupancy: $95
On the bluffs overlooking the Pacific. Authentically restored from its turn-of-the-century construction. Four-poster beds, wrought-iron and brass appointments. Surrounded by forests, rivers, coastal mountains. Art classes, plays, and concerts occasionally available. Room service. 50 rooms.

Where to Eat
Café Beaujolais ♛ ♛ ♛ ♛
961 Ukiah St., Mendocino; tel. 937-5614
Average dinner: $15
Homemade pastries are the perfect compliment to the tasty omelettes, salads, and espresso served up in warmly intimate surroundings.

Elk Cove Inn ♛ ♛ ♛
6300 S. Highway 1, Elk; tel. 877-3321
Average dinner: $12
Heavy German-French cuisine served in one seating only.

Mill Valley
(area code 415)
Where to Eat
Butler's ♛ ♛ ♛ ♛
625 Redwood Hwy., Mill Valley; tel. 383-1900
Average dinner: $25
Fresh and innovative international cuisine in a bright and open setting. Views of Mount Tam and Richardson Bay. Grilled salmon cured with juniper and orange is great. In-spot for Bay Area diners.

Muir Beach
(area code 415)
Where to Stay
Pelican Inn ♛ ♛
10 Pacific Way, Muir Beach 94965; tel. 383-6000
Single room, double occupancy: $110
Authentic reproduction of an English country inn, just off Muir Beach at the base of Mount Tam. Cozy and romantic, furnished in velvets and damasks. Rural setting. Popular pub serves fine ales and restaurant

(♛ ♛ ♛) features hearty British fare. Try the Beef Wellington.

Napa
(area code 707)
Where to Stay
Silverado Country Club ♛ ♛ ♛ ♛
1600 Atlas Peak Rd., Napa 94558; tel. 257-0200
Single room, double occupancy: $100
There is no other place in all of Napa Valley quite like this for the serious sports enthusiast. Beautiful location off the Silverado trail. 350 rooms. A couple of 18-hole golf courses, 20 tennis courts, 5 pools.

Rutherford
(area code 707)
Where to Stay
Auberge Du Soleil ♛ ♛ ♛ ♛ ♛
180 Rutherford Hill Rd., Rutherford 94573; tel. 963-1211
Single room, double occupancy: $210
Elegant south-of-France maisons with commanding view of the valley and mountains. This place is expensive, but worth every penny. Suites are sumptuous and romantic. Tennis, pool, Jacuzzi. Fireplaces in every room. An outstanding classic and nouvelle French restaurant (♛ ♛ ♛ ♛ ♛) is one of Napa's loveliest, with views forever. Average dinner $40.
Rancho Caymus Inn ♛ ♛ ♛
P.O. Box 78, 170 Rutherford Rd., Rutherford 94573; tel. 963-1777
Single room, double occupancy: $115
The Spanish theme is played out beautifully here, from the building itself to the furnishings. Good central valley location. Fireplaces, wet bars, balconies. 26 rooms.

St. Helena
(area code 707)
Where to Stay
Meadowwood Resort ♛ ♛ ♛ ♛
900 Meadowwood Lane, St. Helena 94574; tel. 963-3646

Single room, double occupancy: $140
Beautiful, clapboard buildings dispersed throughout 256 quiet, wooded acres. A great place to get away and to learn about Napa's bounty at the on-premises wine school. Golf, tennis, hiking, and even croquet. 58 rooms.

Hotel St. Helena ♛ ♛ ♛
1309 Main St., St. Helena 94574; tel. 963-4388
Single room, double occupancy: $70
Century-old hotel restored to former grandeur. Within walking distance of all of St. Helena's finest shops and restaurants. 18 rooms.

Where to Eat
Miramonte ♛ ♛ ♛ ♛
1327 Railroad Ave., St. Helena; tel. 963-3970
Average dinner: $30
Legendary Napa chef Udo Nechutny made this place one of the best spots in the valley for classic French cuisine.

Doidges ♛ ♛ ♛
1313 Main St., St. Helena; tel. 963-1788
Average dinner: $12
Terrific little café featuring fresh pastries and wines by the glass.

Shopping
Freemark Abbey Complex, 3020 N. Caza. In old winery building. Huge candle factory and great regional bookstore.

Napa Valley Olive Oil Manufacturing Co., 835 McCorkle Ave. Fine olive oil, great cheese and sausage selection.

Santa Rosa
(area code 707)
Where to Stay
Vintners Inn ♛ ♛ ♛ ♛
4350 Barnes Rd., Santa Rosa 95401; tel. 575-7350
Single room, double occupancy: $78
Beautiful country-French inn situated in middle of vineyards. Oversized rooms, with antiques and balconies or patios overlooking vineyards or courtyard. Sauna. Complimentary breakfast. 45 rooms.

Sheraton Round Barn Inn ♛ ♛ ♛
Highway 101 and Mendocino Ave., Santa Rosa 95401,
tel. 523-7555
Single room, double occupancy: $80
Large hotel with country-inn feel. Overlooks Santa
Rosa from historic Fountain Grove Ranch. Award win-
ning dining room (♛ ♛ ♛ ♛). Pool, jogging path, 18-
hole golf course, spa.
Where to Eat
Restaurant Matisse ♛ ♛ ♛
620 5th St., Santa Rosa; tel. 527-9797
Average dinner: $20
Wonderful French-influenced cuisine featuring mes-
quite-grilled meats and fish, and locally grown produce.
W. H. Frazier's Seafood and Grill ♛ ♛ ♛
3785 Cleveland Ave.; tel. 579-9550
Average dinner: $12
Daily fresh fish selections. Mesquite broiling, private
booths.
Shopping
Whistle Stop Antiques, 130 4th St. Largest antique
collection in the wine country.

Sausalito
(area code 415)
Where to Stay
Casa Madrona ♛ ♛ ♛
801 Bridgeway, Sausalito 94965; tel. 332-0502
Single room, double occupancy: $75–$175
1885 Victorian mansion with cottages and contemporary suites, nestled in wooded hillside overlooking
Sausalito harbor and San Francisco Bay. Decor ranges
from Paris bohemian to oriental. 32 rooms. Restaurant
(♛ ♛ ♛) features fresh, contemporary American
cuisine created by Stephen Simmons, former sous-chef
at Campton Place in San Francisco. Impressive wine
list, good brunch.
Where to Eat
Alta Mira Hotel ♛
125 Bulkley Ave., Sausalito; tel. 332-1350
Average dinner: $20–$25
The food is fair, but the view's the thing here. People

come for brunch on the outdoor deck overlooking the city skyline and the bay.

Bars

No Name, 757 Bridgeway, tel. 332-1392. One of Sausalito's oldest bars, the No Name has a lot of history including notorious locals like Sterling Hayden who used to frequent the place. It's still a local hangout. Comfortable with stained glass and original wood. Outdoor patio, chess games, and steam beer on tap.

Sonoma
(area code 707)
Where to Stay
Sonoma Mission Inn & Spa♛♛♛♛♛

P.O. Box 1447, Sonoma 95476; tel. 938-9000

Single room, double occupancy: $120 and up

Opulent Spanish-style inn on 7 landscaped acres in the heart of the wine country. Once a retreat for Hollywood stars, the refurbished inn is perfect for the healthy hedonist. Tennis, Olympic pool, ultramodern spa. 171 rooms. The Grille (♛♛♛♛) prepares spa cuisine, low in fat, salt, and calories—high in flavor. Average dinner $30.

Sonoma Hotel♛♛♛

110 West Spain St., Sonoma 95476; tel. 996-2996

Single room, double occupancy: $65

1870s restored meeting hall on Sonoma's historic plaza. Entirely furnished with antiques of the era. 29 rooms. Fine restaurant (♛♛♛♛) with outstanding wine list; favored by the locals.

Where to Eat
Les Arcades♛♛♛

133 E. Napa St., Sonoma; tel. 938-3723

Average dinner: $20

Old-world country-French at its best with outstanding art-nouveau bar. Outstanding!

Shopping

Arts Guild of Sonoma, 460 1st St., E. Wonderful selection of works from area artists and crafts people.

Déjà Vu Antiques, 107 W. Napa St. Great values in 19th-century, French, country furniture and accessories.

Tiberon
(area code 415)
Where to Eat
Sam's Anchor Café ♛ ♛
27 Main St., Tiberon; tel. 435-4527
Average dinner: $16–$23
In-spot for casual outdoor dining on the water. Seafood, hamburgers, and Ramos fizzes, or Sam's Smoothies, a famous local drink—a real tradition.

Yountville
(area code 707)
Where to Stay
Burgundy House ♛ ♛ ♛ ♛
6711 Washington St., Yountville 94599; tel. 944-2855
Single room, double occupancy: $90
Old brandy distillery converted into B&B. Charming, downtown location. 8 rooms.
Where to Eat
The French Laundry ♛ ♛ ♛ ♛ ♛
6640 Washington St., Yountville 94599; tel. 944-2380
Average dinner: $30
Don and Sally Schmitt transformed this old laundry into a legend of country-French, California cuisine. Fixed price menu changes daily, and there's just one seating. A must.
Mustards Grill ♛ ♛ ♛ ♛ ♛
7399 St. Helena Hwy., Yountville 94599; tel. 944-2424
Average dinner: $20
Not just a great Napa restaurant, probably one of the best grills in California. A favorite of local winery owners. Don't miss this place.
The Diner ♛ ♛ ♛ ♛
6476 Washington St., Yountville 94599; tel. 944-2626
Average dinner: $10
No better classic American breakfast or lunch in Napa. Small roadside diner with a hint of Mexican savvy.

Upper Lake
(area code 707)
Where to Stay
The Narrows Lodge ♛ ♛ ♛ ♛ ♛
5690 Bluelakes Rd., Upper Lake 95485; tel. 275-2718
Average dinner: $18
Amid redwoods and oaks, dine next to the blue lakes and under the stars, weather permitting.

Wineries

(**Note:** Ratings are for tours and facilities, *not* the quality of the wines!)

Napa Valley (area code 707)

Beaulieu Vineyard ♛ ♛, 1960 St. Helena Hwy., Rutherford; 963-2411. One of Napa's oldest and best. Offers free tours daily 10 A.M.–3:15 P.M. Tasting and sales available to 4 P.M.

Beringer Vineyards ♛ ♛ ♛, 2000 Main St., St. Helena; 963-7115. This winery founded in 1876 has an outstanding example of German architecture in its office building. Open daily 10 A.M.–5 P.M. with tours, tasting, and sales.

Christian Brothers ♛ ♛ ♛, 2555 St. Helena Hwy., St. Helena; 963-4480. A wide variety of wines, some surprisingly good. Tours by appointment only. Tastings and sales, 10:30 A.M.–2:30 P.M., Mon.–Fri.

Clos du Val ♛, 5330 Silverado Trail, Napa; 252-6711. Great picnic area. Tours are by appointment, but there are tastings and sales from 10 A.M. to 4 P.M.

Domaine Chandon ♛ ♛, California Dr., Yountville; 944-2280. Tours, Wed.–Sun. 11 A.M.–5 P.M. Tastings and sales daily, 11 A.M.–6 P.M.

Folie à Deux Winery ♛ ♛ ♛, 3070 St. Helena Hwy., St. Helena; 963-1160. This is a terrific example of one of Napa's small wineries turning out excellent wines. Tasting and sales available, 11 A.M.–5 P.M. daily. No tours.

Freemark Abbey Winery ♛ ♛, 3022 St. Helena Hwy., St. Helena; 963-9694. One tour per day at 2 P.M. Nice gift shop, tasting and sales daily, 10 A.M.–4:30 P.M.

Inglenook Napa Valley♕♕♕, 1991 St. Helena Hwy., Rutherford; 963-2616. One of Napa's oldest and best. Great museum and wine library, tours, tasting, and sales.

Robert Mondavi Winery♕♕♕♕, 7801 St. Helena Hwy., Oakville; 963-9611. Probably the most popular winery in Napa. Reservations advised on weekends. Tours, tasting, sales daily, Apr.–Oct., 9 A.M.–5 P.M.; Nov.–Mar., 10 A.M.–4 P.M.

Monticello Cellars♕♕♕, 4242 Big Ranch Rd., Napa; 253-2187. This is one of Napa's newest wineries turning out terrific vintages. Tasting and sales daily. Tours at 10:30 A.M., and 12:30 and 2:30 P.M.

V. Sattui Winery♕♕, St. Helena Hwy. at White Lane, St. Helena; 963-7774. These wines can only be bought at the winery. There's a nice picnic area and deli on the grounds. Tasting and sales daily, 9 A.M.–5 P.M. No tours.

Sonoma Valley

Buena Vista Winery♕♕♕, 18000 Old Winery Rd., Sonoma; 938-1266. The oldest commercial winery in the valley. Impressive wine caves dug into the hillside. Nice picnic area. Self-guided tour, tasting, and sales daily, 9 A.M.–5 P.M.

Chateau St. Jean♕♕♕, 8555 Route 12, Kenwood; 833-4134. Large producer of outstanding white wines. Beautiful grounds with picnic area. Tasting, tours, and sales daily 10 A.M.– 4:30 P.M.

Glen Ellen Winery♕♕, 1883 London Ranch Rd., Glen Ellen; 996-1066. This historic winery offers some spectacular wine available only at the winery. Beautiful picnic grounds. Tours by appointment. Tasting and sales daily.

Kenwood Vineyards♕♕♕, 9592 Route 12, Kenwood; 833-5891. This notable winery drips with rustic charm. Generous tasting and sales available daily, 10 A.M.–4:30 P.M. Tours by appointment only.

Sebastiani Vineyards♕♕♕, 389 Fourth St., Sonoma; 938-5532. The largest winery operation in the valley. Great collection of carved casks. Tours, tasting, and sales.

Balloon Companies

Adventures Aloft, P.O. Box 2500, Yountville, CA 94599; tel. 707-255-8688.

Balloon Aviation, 2299 Third St., Napa, CA 94558; tel. 707-252-7067.

Bonaventure Balloon Company, P.O. Box 5176, Napa, CA 94581; tel. 707-944-2822.

Napa's Great Balloon Escape, P.O. Box 4197, Napa, CA. 94558; tel. 707-253-0860.

Napa Valley Balloons Inc., P.O. Box 2860, Yountville, CA 94599; tel. 707-253-2224.

Once in a Lifetime Balloon Co., 1458 Lincoln Ave. #12, P.O. Box 795, Calistoga, CA 94515; tel. 707-942-6541.

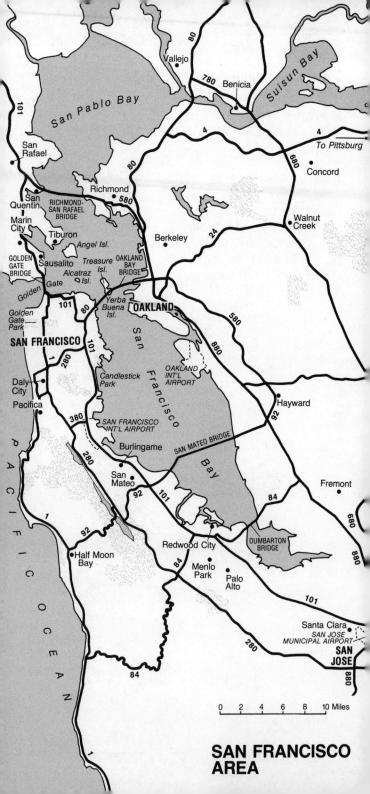

SAN FRANCISCO AREA

SAN FRANCISCO

SAN FRANCISCO IN A HURRY

Compressed as it is onto a peninsula separating San Francisco Bay from the Pacific Ocean, this city is a cinch to do in a hurry—except for its 40-odd hills, which compel you to take it easier. San Francisco lives up to its romantic reputation: Victorian houses lining hill after hill; majestic bridges spanning the bay; and graceful skyscrapers everyone hopes will defy the next earthquake, fondly called The Big One. When you see it up close, San Francisco changes character around every corner: Chinatown, Italian North Beach, old-money Pacific Heights, New-Age pioneer neighborhoods, elegant department stores, funky shops, and enough street peddlers and musicians to bring back the sixties.

ITINERARIES IN SAN FRANCISCO

First Day

Scenic 49-Mile Drive, Union Square, cable car ride, Nob Hill, Chinatown, Golden Gate Bridge, evening in North Beach.

Second Day

Alcatraz, Fisherman's Wharf and Pier 39, Lombard Street, sunset from Coit Tower on Telegraph Hill, the symphony, opera, or theater.

Third Day

Downtown and Embarcadero Center (shopping), the Cannery and Ghirardelli Square, Golden Gate Park (gardens, museums), Japantown.

Transportation is easy, so forget a car. In fact, unlike in Los Angeles, get ready to walk—and climb. You won't believe how much territory you'll have covered by the time we're through.

Scenic 49-Mile Drive

Okay, we lied. You *could* use a car for this introductory circumnavigation of San Francisco. Well-marked by blue, white, and orange seagull-symbol signs, this route around the city👑 👑 👑 👑 👑 will take you past things you would stop to see if you had more time.

Start at Civic Center with its splendid plaza and stately domed City Hall (it looks like a state capitol building). You will pass the Museum of Modern Art, the modern Louise Davies Symphony Hall, and the venerable Opera House and Civic Auditorium.

INSIDERS' TIPS

A visitors' map of the scenic 49-Mile Drive is published and distributed free by the San Francisco Convention & Visitors Bureau. (Commercial versions are sold at news stands.) Ask for it at the San Francisco Visitor Information Center, Hallidie Plaza (lower level) at Powell and Market streets (cable car stop) from 9 A.M.–5:30 P.M. Monday–Friday; 9 A.M.–3 P.M. Saturday; and 10 A.M.–2 P.M. Sunday.

If you don't have a car, Gray Line Limousine Service (415-885-8500) can chauffeur you at a surprisingly reasonable rate, or take Gray Line's Tour No. 1, a motorcoach city-circuit from the company terminal at First and Mission streets (771-4000).

You will need a map to keep your bearings in the "City by the Bay" because your sense of north and south will dissolve, not necessarily in a fog. But to tell you the highlights, you will see Japantown, Union Square, Chinatown, Nob Hill, North Beach, Telegraph Hill, the fairly new Pier 39 and the classic Fisherman's Wharf, the Cannery and Ghirardelli Square, the monumental Palace of Fine Arts, the Golden Gate Bridge and Golden Gate Park, Lands End with its Palace of the Legion of

Honor, the San Francisco Zoo, towering Twin Peaks, and the Spanish colonial Mission Dolores. Not bad for a half day's drive.

As you can see, this one excursion could convey you to every sight on our 3-day list except Alcatraz (boat required). But you will *see* Alcatraz, "The Rock," standing solid amid the swirling currents where the Pacific tides rush in and out of the Bay beneath the Golden Gate Bridge.

Union Square

Let's assume that, like most tourists, you have opted to discover San Francisco by foot and public transportation. Union Square ♛ ♛ ♛ ♛ ♛ is the heart of the city, a living testament to its tenacity. Named to honor the northern states after demonstrators here supported the Union cause in Civil War days, this grassy, hedge-lined square is surrounded by a renaissance of fine stores (Macy's, Saks Fifth Avenue, Neiman-Marcus, and the grande dame of native San Francisco department stores, I. Magnin). The granite victory column, flanked by palm trees which seem out of place in San Francisco, salutes Admiral George Dewey's Spanish-American War victory at Manila Bay in 1898.

Here the grand old St. Francis Hotel ♛ ♛ ♛ ♛, opulently refurbished by Westin Hotels, stands where it stood through the Great Earthquake of 1906. Kings and queens, the Emperor of Japan, many U.S. presidents, and mighty military officers have unofficially made this the official hotel of San Francisco. To meet by its lobby clock is a local tradition and a convenient tourist tip. Afternoon tea or evening cocktails at the art-deco Compass Rose lounge is to return to the salon era of gracious languor. Other hotels making their mark on Union Square are the newly remade Sir Francis Drake, popular for nightly dancing at its Starlite Roof, and the Hyatt Union Square, known for a bounteous Sunday brunch spread in its skylit atrium lobby.

Cable Car Ride

America's only mobile National Historic Landmark, the cable cars ♛ ♛ ♛ ♛ ♛, began in 1873, invented by Andrew Hallidie (for whom Hallidie Plaza, site of the Visitor Information Center, is named). The 9 miles of track cover 3 routes: Powell/Hyde, Powell/Mason, and California streets. A $60-million overhaul of the system left it shut down and the streets dug up for 20 months prior to the cable cars' comeback in mid-1984. Today, they are ready to run for another 100 years. On summer days when tourists abound, it can feel as though it may take that long to get aboard one.

As if the historic cars weren't enough to enjoy, their drivers or "gripmen" are a show in themselves. Their title refers to how they control a lever which causes a grip on the car's underside to grab the constantly moving cable running in a slot between the tracks; if they release the grip, the car stops (with the help of 3 backup braking systems). But it is their bell-clanging, wisecracking style that is the real thrill—in addition to the sharp turns and steep drops the cars take. San Franciscans ride the cable cars to work; they are not just a tourist attraction.

PERILS & PITFALLS

Be sure to buy your $1.50 ticket before getting aboard. The line most used by tourists is the Powell/Mason line, which leads to Fisherman's Wharf; most spectacular, though, is the dramatic Powell/Hyde line to the Cannery and Ghirardelli Square. Steepest drop (a 21 percent grade) is on the Powell/Hyde line between Chestnut and Francisco streets. The plunge from Nob Hill down California Street toward Chinatown and Embarcadero Center is a 17 percent thriller. When the conductor hollers "Heeeeere we go!" or, on a curve, "Hold on!" listen to him. The cable cars operate from 6 A.M. to 1 A.M.

If you catch a cable car on Powell Street in front of the St. Francis Hotel, it will take you "halfway to the stars" to the top of Nob Hill. Get off at California Street to catch the downhill cable car to Chinatown. But before leaving Nob Hill, take time to discover this summit of San Francisco society.

Nob Hill

Merchants who made a fortune in the Far East became known as *nabobs,* a derivative of the Hindu word *naw-wab* for a very wealthy person. The contracted term *nob* came to be used for San Franciscans who made their millions from gold, silver, and railroads in the mid-1800s. When the Big Four railroad barons all built their mansions atop this hill♕ ♕ ♕ ♕ ♕, the name was a natural. Their wooden palaces burned down in the 1906 earthquake fire, but monuments to their grandeur remain.

The Stanford Court, possibly the most luxurious hotel in town, stands on the site of Leland Stanford's mansion. The Mark Hopkins–Intercontinental Hotel rises on the ashes of Mark Hopkins's panoramic estate (a sunset or evening cocktail in its rooftop lounge is a local tradition and visitor must). The Fairmont Hotel is built on Comstock Lode gold baron James Fair's former lot. And one still-standing mansion, gold king James Flood's brownstone, is now home to the stuffy Pacific-Union Club (known as "the P-U" locally) of modern-day kings of commerce; it's in the center of the hilltop square.

The Fairmont♕ ♕ ♕ holds the greatest curiosity for visitors due to its prominence as the hotel of television's "Hotel" series. The building then under construction survived the 1906 quake, but the ensuing fire gutted its interiors. The marble floors and columns were restored in time to open a year later. Its massive halls for socialites' promenades come to life with formally dressed guests at the hotel's posh supper club, the Venetian Room. To walk or drive into the front carriageway is an experience in grand entrances. A glass elevator ride to the top of the hotel's Tower annex (1961) is a breathtaking thrill (fun for lunch at the Fairmont Crown dining room).

Chinatown

Lunch is also a good time to come to Chinatown♛♛♛♛♛. Be warned: It will be as hectic as Hong Kong, with old women shopping for fish and glazed Peking duck, delivery boys darting through the crowds with hot food and shop parcels—and tourists, tourists everywhere. But that is Chinatown, the largest Chinese settlement (at least 150,000 residents) outside of Asia and a commercial stronghold of San Francisco.

INSIDERS' TIPS

Chinese New Year comes in with a bang of firecrackers sometime between mid-January and mid-February, depending on the moon. The most exuberant and colorful nighttime parade in America climaxes the week-long festivities, and hundreds of thousands of people jam the narrow streets of Chinatown for it.

Stepping off the California Street cable car at Grant Street, you will see the oriental gateway to Chinatown 2 blocks to the right at Bush Street and Grant. The bricks of old St. Mary's Church (California Street and Grant) were shipped here from China, and the church withstood the 1906 earthquake. As for quality shops, Tai Chong (506 Grant) and the Canton Bazaar (616 Grant) offer everything from trinkets to treasures—cheap porcelains, precious silks, lacquered lamps, and intricate wood carvings.

But the aromas assaulting your nose may turn your mind to lunch, in which case you need to know one term: dim sum. It means heart's delight in Chinese, though stomach's delight may be more accurate. Dim sum is a series of cooked snacks brought to your table—meat-filled dumplings, egg rolls, spareribs, and some more mysterious—from which you choose what you want.

At Pacific Avenue turn left. The Asia Garden and the Hong Kong are temples of dim sum. Adventurous eating, yes; but expensive, no. Then again, if you would prefer a regular Chinese meal, some of the most authentic are served in the simplest storefront eateries. Stroll Stockton Street for the most Chinese ambience in Chinatown; when the souvenir shops took more and more of Grant Street, Chinese foods and wares moved onto Stockton.

The Golden Gate Bridge is a fair distance from Chinatown (Fisherman's Wharf or Embarcadero Center are much closer if you would prefer those in your one day to sightsee), but it is worth the effort. Either walk back to California Street or take a Powell Street car back to it, ride back up over Nob Hill to the end of the California Street line at Van Ness Avenue. There the Golden Gate Transit buses (green and white) stop at green-and-white-signed bus stops (Clay Street, 2 blocks to the right, is the closest) and take you to the View Area at the toll plaza, or across the bridge itself if you wish.

The Golden Gate Bridge

The U.S. Travel Service has called it the greatest man-made sight in the country. Certainly it is the most beautiful bridge in the world ♛ ♛ ♛ ♛ ♛, as much for its spectacular setting as for its own grace. Some visitors are surprised the bridge is not golden but a sunset orange-red. It is the juncture of land and sea—the Pacific surging through a narrow land break in and out of San Francisco Bay—that is the Golden Gate. The bridge is the bridge over the watergate, you might say.

The 2 towers of the bridge soar to about 65 stories high, and painting them with protective lead paint is a never-ending task. The bridge celebrated its 50th birthday in 1987. Today more than 100,000 cars per day cross over it. Hundreds more stop at the View Area ♛ ♛ ♛ to take dramatic photographs. We say drive across it if you can. Even if it's foggy, you will have a thrill at being suspended in midair amid the echoes of foghorns.

On the other side of the Golden Gate Bridge is Sausalito, a colorful waterfront town popular with tourists for its galleries and beautiful views of San Francisco (see Marin County, page 265).

PERILS & PITFALLS

Walking across the Golden Gate Bridge is popular and spectacular. You can see why Alcatraz cons preferred prison to the cold, shark-infested waters that swirl around the huge pylons. No matter how sunny the day, wear warm clothes to walk the 2-mile bridge; it's chilly in the windswept middle. Avid walkers could hike from the end of the Powell/Hyde cable-car line along Golden Gate Promenade to the bridge—over 3 miles but beautiful.

A sunset return ride through the Presidio(♛ ♛ ♛), the 18th-century, Spanish, colonial fort made over into a U.S. army base, gives some sense of the northern California forests. Covering the San Francisco side of the Golden Gate land mass, the Presidio has a museum of army activities in San Francisco, open Tuesday–Sunday, 10 A.M.–4 P.M.

Evening in North Beach

Don't say we didn't tell you it was tawdry. This neighborhood lining Broadway next to Chinatown is Times Square West with its bright lights, loud music, and leering doormen at the "totally nude" revues—and this is side by side with piously Catholic Little Italy and its espresso cafés, pasta shops, and bocce ball games. But North Beach♛ ♛ ♛ ♛ is still this city's most lively night scene, short of more conventional cultural centers across town.

Unconventional is the word for North Beach, home of a 1940s (and still running) naughtily clean, boys-will-be-girls, drag show at Finocchios♛ ♛, 1950s Beat poet Lawrence Ferlinghetti's City Lights bookstore♛ on Columbus Street (the poet still presides), 1960s topless dancer Carol Doda's Condor Club (she still appears nightly with her silicone marvels), and other notable night spots now long gone—the original Hungry i of Kingston Trio fame, and the Purple Onion, which spawned Phyllis Diller.

Cheapest seat in the house is a sidewalk-café table at Enrico's♛ ♛, run by North Beach veteran and friend of the famous Enrico Banducci, him with the black beret. Celebrities, major and minor, drop by here nightly, and the people watching in general is an entertainment. Luckily, the food is tasty and, of course, Italian (Enrico prides himself on the fresh fish dishes).

For fine Italian dining experiences, Tommaso's is a treat and there are always lines at Vanessi's, Mama's, Little Joe's, Caffe Sport, and the North Beach Restaurant. The ultimate nightcap is a cappuccino at the Tosca Café (on Columbus near City Lights bookstore)—where else would you find a jukebox of opera records?

SAN FRANCISCO THE SECOND DAY

Alcatraz

Escape, always part of the fascination with this fabled federal penitentiary, is what you want to do by visiting first thing in the day: Escape the lines of people that form to fill the tour boats. The wisest move is to phone ahead for reservations, especially in peak summer season, *weeks* ahead if possible (tel. 546-2805). With luck you may get right aboard.

INSIDERS' TIPS

Mist and stiff winds often chill Alcatraz (it's right in the path of the Golden Gate currents), so take along a sweater and/or light jacket. Indeed for San Francisco in general, it is wise to "dress in layers," as temperatures can change radically from one block to the next. A sweater at hand is always a good idea—especially in summer.

Named by the Spanish for the pelicans *(alcatraces)* that would gather on the island, Alcatraz 👑 👑 👑 👑 served as America's most notorious prison from 1933 to 1963. Previously it had held a Civil War brig, but its greatest fame came with the arrivals of Al Capone and Machine Gun Kelly to the pastel prison built in the 1930s. You will feel the ghost of Jimmy Cagney and Burt "Birdman" Lancaster on the one-hour tour of the cell blocks given by the National Park Service rangers who now patrol the crumbling buildings. (High maintenance costs in the face of the constantly corrosive weather caused the U.S. government to discontinue use of Alcatraz as a prison; so far they have just let it rot.)

INSIDERS' TIPS

Boats leave Pier 41 daily every 45 minutes from 9 A.M. to 5:15 P.M. But for a bird's-eye view of Alcatraz and the Golden Gate Bridge, Commodore Helicopters at nearby Pier 43 at Fisherman's Wharf whirl off regularly from 9:30 A.M. to sunset for 15-minute city-bay tour flights (332-4482). Pricey ($60 per person) but unforgettable.

The thought of a bleak prison tour may sound grim to some, but the Alcatraz tour is a surprisingly fascinating experience—from the wildflowers that grow on "The Rock" to the incredible views of the city, even if you don't care to experience a quick lockup in the pitch-black, solitary-confinement cell. To learn that Al Capone wore silk pajamas makes it all more civilized.

Fisherman's Wharf and Pier 39

These 2 attractions lie on either side of the Pier 41 Alcatraz boat dock (and Pier 43 from which bay sightseeing boats depart). Both are quintessential tourist traps but charming nonetheless.

Fisherman's Wharf♕♕♕♕ became charming when Italian fishermen made it their wharf in the 1880s. They used to take tourists out for rides (and some still do) on their boats docked between Jones and Leavenworth streets (small fee). But most visitors today come here for the Italian seafood restaurants, the sidewalk stands serving Dungeness crab and crusty sourdough bread, and the blatantly touristic attractions—the Wax Museum (on the wharf), Ripley's Believe It or Not Museum (175 Jefferson Street), or the Enchanted World of San Francisco (Jefferson and Mason), each open from 9 A.M. till at least 10 P.M.

A stroll along the waterfront Embarcadero past more sourdough shops, T-shirt boutiques, and the *Balclutha* clipper ship brings you to Pier 39 ♛ ♛ (981-PIER). Built in 1978 from the timbers of other old piers and designed to emulate a New England whaling village, this 1,000-foot pier holds over 100 shops (open 10:30 A.M.–8:30 P.M.) and nearly 25 restaurants (open 11:30 A.M.–2 A.M.), only one of which is authentic San Francisco: the Eagle Café, a historic hangout for fishermen and dockworkers.

PERILS & PITFALLS

Pier 39 can be fun, but it really is pure commercialism with not an ounce of historically redeeming value. If authentic San Francisco is your interest, head from Fisherman's Wharf to the nearby Cannery and Ghirardelli Square instead (see "A Third Day in San Francisco," page 311) and possibly on to Aquatic Park with its National Maritime Museum.

Lombard Street

The "crookedest street in San Francisco" ♛ ♛ ♛ is more than a hairpin-curved hill street or the theme of an old Bill Cosby routine. Take the No. 60 cable car from behind the Cannery (not the line ending at Fisherman's Wharf itself—3 blocks farther west) and get off at Hyde and Lombard. You will be at the top of this flower-bedded street, which cars crawl down in an endless stream. Its one block length holds 10 Z-turns, easier for pedestrians using its steps than for cars using their brakes.

Before heading downhill, pause for one of the city's finest panoramas: the silver Oakland-Bay Bridge to the right, the Golden Gate Bridge to the left, Alcatraz straight ahead between them, and Coit Tower atop Telegraph Hill off to the east. That is our next destination.

Sunset from Telegraph Hill

If no one told you that Coit Tower ♛ ♛ ♛ was designed to look like a fire-hose nozzle you might never think of it. This graceful art deco monument was built in 1934 with money from Lillie Coit, an honorary firefighter, to salute San Francisco's fire brigades. Its 16 WPA-era murals of California industry inside and its awesome view of the city outside make it a visitor must.

Telegraph Hill got its name from a semaphore station in gold rush days that would signal businessmen in the financial quarter of the coming of clipper ships, thus enabling them to be dockside for transacting commerce as soon as the ships tied up. Today, the hill is a residential enclave of artists' studios and upper-middle-class villas—just one social step below the wealthier warrens of Lombard Street's Russian Hill, home of the Randolph Hearsts among others. There is no telegraph transmitter anymore.

Symphony, Opera, or Theater

Unlike any other California city, San Francisco supports culture. The performing arts are enshrined in a variety of grand halls, and street musicians, playing everything from Bach to bluegrass, earn enough money to make the city musical all over. A formality pervades the night-on-the-town scene, also unlike elsewhere in California. Your dressiest clothes will look well here.

Under the umbrella title of the Performing Arts Center♛♛♛♛, the modern Louise M. Davies Symphony Hall, (1980) and the classic War Memorial Opera House (1932), with its newer Herbst Theater and Zellerbach Rehearsal Hall, offer endless events: orchestral concerts, ballet, touring companies, and a nearly year-round bounty of San Francisco Opera Company productions with world-class stars. The San Francisco Symphony's official season is September to May with a Pops series in July.

INSIDERS' TIPS

Summer weekend visitors can enjoy free symphony, ballet, and opera on Sunday afternoons at Sigmund Stern Memorial Grove, south of Golden Gate Park, and organ recitals on Saturday and Sunday afternoons at the Palace of the Legion of Honor. Tel. 415-221-4811.

Theater lovers will revel in San Francisco's 6 downtown theaters, at least one or 2 of which will be hosting a Broadway or Broadway-bound play or musical at any given time. From October to May, the Geary Theater ♛ ♛ ♛, 415 Geary Street near Union Square (tel. 673-6440), presents the American Conservatory Theater, one of the country's finest regional repertory companies doing 10 different plays per season. Smaller "Off Broadway" theaters are plentiful, and cinemas cater to the sophisticated taste of San Franciscans with numerous foreign and art films in addition to the current hit features.

INSIDERS' TIPS

For half-price tickets to all types of performing arts events, sold on a day-of-performance basis, bring cash to STBS (San Francisco Ticket Box-Office Service) on the Stockton Street side of Union Square from noon till evening showtimes. In-person sales only. Tel. 433-STBS for general information.

For full-price, advance-purchase tickets, the most efficient outlet is Ticketron (392-SHOW) located in all Tower and Rainbow Record Stores, as well as in the Emporium department store (an architectural wonder of its own) on Market Street.

If you exit from the curtain calls still wanting something to do, you could dance at Oz, the rooftop club of the St. Francis Hotel's tower annex, or catch the late show at the Fairmont Hotel's Venetian Room atop Nob Hill. Bars are open till 2 A.M.

A THIRD DAY IN SAN FRANCISCO

Downtown and Embarcadero Center

A breakfast of Swedish pancakes and sausage at Sears' ♛ ♛ (439 Powell Street near Post) will fortify you for the wonder that awaits you in shopping San Francisco. (Sears' is closed Mondays and Tuesdays, but it's a renowned local day-starter otherwise.) We find some of the world's most fun, tempting, and pleasurable shopping here. You will find San Franciscans dress as well to shop as to go to work or the theater, so polyester pantsuits are a tourist giveaway.

INSIDERS' TIPS

Montgomery Street is the spine of the financial district, and the histories of Bank of America and Wells Fargo are enshrined in two interesting museums at their respective headquarters here.

Between Union Square and Embarcadero Center, especially along Post and Montgomery streets, you will find a world of famous names: Saks Fifth Avenue, Macy's, Wedgwood, Alfred Dunhill, Elizabeth Arden, Polo/Ralph Lauren, Brooks Brothers, Gucci, and locally-born Banana Republic to name a few. But San Francisco has its own home-grown stores from high fashion to funky. (For specifics, see San Francisco Shopping, page 342.)

INSIDERS' TIPS

Sunday may appeal to those who would just as soon miss the mobs of weekday office workers and shoppers. The Hyatt Regency puts on a famous brunch in its soaring atrium (with a 4-story-high aluminum ball sculpture that's worth a peek). Call 788-1234. And summer Sundays offer outdoor concerts at the Plaza Theater. Call 722-0585 for details of Embarcadero Center events. The poinsettia celebrations at Christmastime are another winner.

Embarcadero Center ♛ ♛ is imposing no matter how you look at it. To many San Franciscans this John Portman-designed complex of 4 skyscrapers and a Hyatt Regency Hotel (where Mel Brooks's *High Anxiety* was filmed) represent a resented "Manhattanization" of their city; to others, these are landmarks of "the new San Francisco." You can decide for yourself, but a stroll through this 1970s urban redevelopment project is a must.

Buses, the underground Metro, and the California

Street cable car converge on this bustling business center. If you have not had lunch elsewhere yet, here are two dozen quick-eat food outlets and a dozen leisurely restaurants for lunch or dinner. There are 175 shops that will tucker you out enough to make a sunny seat in the plaza a welcome retreat. Or you could renew your strength in the center's chapel.

The Cannery and Ghirardelli Square

If you missed this colorful corner of the city while at Fisherman's Wharf, it will come as a return to human-scale pleasure after the somewhat intimidating Embarcadero Center. Buses along the Embarcadero will shuttle you to the former Del Monte fruit cannery♕♕ (1894), now a collection of brick arcades, housing 150 shops, galleries, and restaurants. From 10 A.M. to 6 P.M. (from 11 A.M. on Sundays and till 9 P.M. in summer), this complex has musicians, poets, and other performers enlivening its restful plaza, shaded by 100-year-old olive trees and colored with flower carts.

More colorful and upscale than the Cannery is Ghirardelli Square♕♕♕, another shopping-dining complex created from an 1890s factory, this one famed for Ghirardelli chocolate. The light-bulbed Ghirardelli sign has greeted ships entering the harbor since the early 1900s, except during World War II. The cocoa makers moved out in the 1960s, and civic-minded developers saved the complex of crenellated, white-trimmed, brick buildings and clock tower to make this architecturally award-winning playground.

INSIDERS' TIPS

The Ghirardelli Square shops offer unusual and high-quality wares from glass sculpture to Turkish sweets (there is even a Bazaar). A surprise is the most beautiful Chinese restaurant in the city: The Mandarin (673-8812) has graduated many of its chefs to other fine Chinese restaurants, but it remains a preeminent source of superb and original Chinese food. Just as Chinatown abuts Little Italy, Modesto Lanzone's in Ghirardelli is one of the most popular Italian restaurants in town (771-2880).

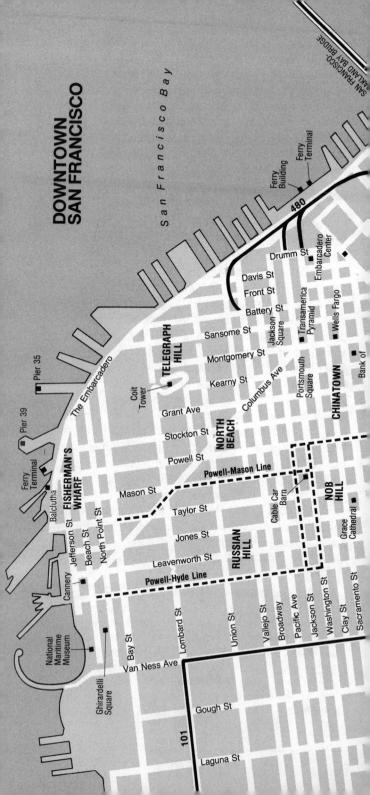

DOWNTOWN SAN FRANCISCO

San Francisco Bay

SAN FRANCISCO-OAKLAND BAY BRIDGE

Ferry Terminal

Ferry Building

480

Drumm St

Davis St

Front St

Battery St

Sansome St

Montgomery St

Kearny St

Grant Ave

Stockton St

Powell St

Mason St

Taylor St

Jones St

Leavenworth St

Embarcadero Center

Wells Fargo

Transamerica Pyramid

Jackson Square

Columbus Ave

Portsmouth Square

Bank of

CHINATOWN

Cable Car Barn

Grace Cathedral

NOB HILL

Powell-Mason Line

Powell-Hyde Line

RUSSIAN HILL

TELEGRAPH HILL

Coit Tower

NORTH BEACH

Pier 35

Pier 39

Ferry Terminal

Balclutha

FISHERMAN'S WHARF

The Embarcadero

Jefferson St

Beach St

North Point St

Bay St

Van Ness Ave

Cannery

National Maritime Museum

Ghirardelli Square

Lombard St

Union St

Vallejo St

Broadway

Pacific Ave

Jackson St

Washington St

Clay St

Sacramento St

Gough St

Laguna St

101

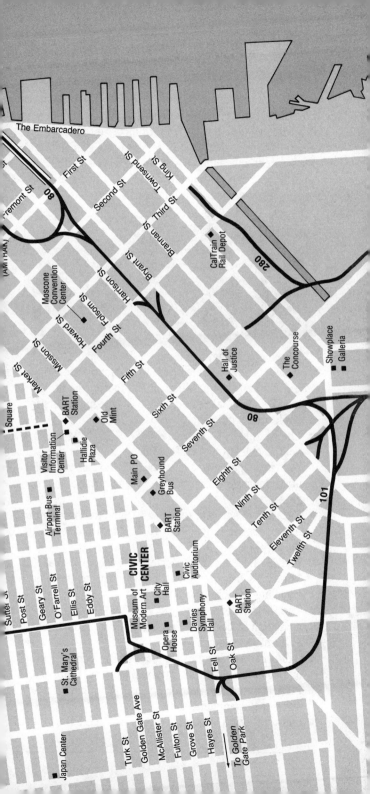

The Embarcadero

First St

Second St

Townsend St

King St

Third St

Fremont St

(AMTRAK)

80

Brannan St

CalTrain
Rail Depot

280

Moscone
Convention
Center

Harrison St

Folsom St

Howard St

Fourth St

Hall of
Justice

The
Concourse

Showplace
Galleria

Mission St

Market St

Fifth St

Sixth St

80

Seventh St

101

BART
Station

Old
Mint

Square

Visitor
Information
Center

Hallidie
Plaza

Main PO

Greyhound
Bus

Eighth St

Ninth St

Tenth St

Eleventh St

Twelfth St

Airport Bus
Terminal

BART
Station

Civic
Auditorium

CIVIC
CENTER

BART
Station

Sutter St

Post St

Geary St

O'Farrell St

Ellis St

Eddy St

Museum of
Modern Art

City
Hall

Davies
Symphony
Hall

Opera
House

Fell St

Oak St

St. Mary's
Cathedral

Japan Center

Turk St

Golden Gate Ave

McAllister St

Fulton St

Grove St

Hayes St

To Golden
Gate Park

Golden Gate Park

All the way across town sprawls one of America's most pleasurable parks. By day's end, its paths will be jumping with joggers, but there is an incorruptible serenity among the massive trees, the Japanese gardens, and the stately museums that make Golden Gate Park ♛ ♛ ♛ ♛ so unique as an urban preserve (what other city park has a buffalo herd?).

PERILS & PITFALLS

Golden Gate Park has precious little sustenance for the energy it requires. The museums have token food services, but saving the Japanese Tea Garden till last may be the best advice. Only tea and cookies are served here, but they make a great pick-me-up—and this is where fortune cookies were invented!

Three miles long, half a mile wide, this park, despite its name, is several miles from the Golden Gate Bridge (the Presidio is the parkland at the foot of the bridge). Among its many lakes and meadows, the highlights for a quick visit would include:

- The Japanese Tea Garden ♛ ♛ ♛ ♛ (1894): A corner of old Kyoto with pagodas, arched bridges, a Zen rock garden, a thatched teahouse, and 350 pink-blooming cherry trees. This is a national treasure.
- The Asian Art Museum ♛ ♛: Olympics impresario Avery Brundage gave his 10,000-item collection to the city.
- The M. H. De Young Memorial Museum ♛ ♛ ♛ ♛: The city's best art museum and home to its major traveling exhibitions.
- The Flower Conservatory ♛ ♛ (1878): Modeled after a pavilion in London's Kew Gardens, it holds seasonal bursts of blooms.
- California Academy of Sciences ♛ ♛: 3 museums in one complex—natural history, astronomy (Morrison Planetarium), and marine science (Steinhart Aquarium—with penguins, too).
- Sporting types will appreciate the park's myriad

activity areas: baseball and soccer fields, tennis courts, lawn bowling, horseback trails, bicycle and roller skate rentals (the main drive is closed Sundays to the delight of skating aficionados).

Japantown

Now you are in just the right mood for Japantown ♛ ♛, this city's second largest Asian community (though the 12,500 Japanese are far outnumbered by the 150,000 Chinese). Japantown is a mostly modern creation focused on Japan Center, a sterile cement slab of shops and restaurants that become fun once you are inside them.

INSIDERS' TIPS

The Westin Miyako Hotel at Japan Center offers a novel experience in Japanese hospitality with its tatami-matted Japanese suites (rice-paper sliding doors, indoor bamboo-and-rock gardens, and futons), ideal for the romantically minded. (Call 922-3200.)

Major spring, summer, and fall folk festivals are staged at Japan Center's open-air plazas and in its teahouses and theaters, the best of them at cherry blossom time in late March or early April. A perfect day's-end treat is the Kabuki Hot Spring ♛ ♛, a Japanese bathhouse with spotless, tiled baths, and relaxing and revitalizing Shiatsu massages. You will feel like a new person.

Japan Center's Ginza-like restaurant corridor features Japanese, Chinese, and Korean foods, including a sushi bar that serves its dishes on tiny boats floating around a channel between you and the knife-wielding sushi chefs. If you see something you like, just take it off its boat and pay according to the number and color of plates you pick. Very reasonable prices throughout.

SAN FRANCISCO WITH PLENTY OF TIME

Few cities have such good "secondary" attractions or such a diversity of special-interest pleasers. The flood of so many ethnic groups and social types to cash in on the riches promised here in the wake of the 1849 gold rush forced San Franciscans to be tolerant of diversity. Thus, each group contributed its culture to the city—its art, customs, costumes, and cuisine.

The raucous Barbary Coast days spawned a tradition of bawdy diversions only a bit less tolerated and more tame today. San Francisco's renown as a city comfortable for gay men and women is only the latest wave of welcome for a subculture ignored, if not resented, in many other cities. The gay community has contributed strongly to San Francisco's creative arts and culture scene, and its voice is politically respected, too.

Two free publications, *Key* and *Where*, both available in most hotels, will detail "This Week in San Francisco" with general overviews of shopping, dining, and sightseeing attractions—with advertisements for nearly every tour service in town. The Visitor Information Center at Hallidie Plaza (900 Market Street near Union Square) is a wealth of information. Round-the-clock recordings of special events and sight-seeing tips can be heard by phoning 391-2001.

The excursion you might not have found time for in a shorter stay—a Bay cruise ♛ ♛ ♛ ♛—can be booked through 2 major operators: Blue and Gold Fleet (Pier 39, tel. 781-7877) and Red and White Fleet (Pier 41 and 43½, tel. 546-2810), each named for the school colors of their competitive owners—blue and gold for the University of California/Berkeley, and red and white for Stanford University, both in the Bay Area.

PERILS & PITFALLS

Call ahead for weather conditions. Where you are could be sunny while the Bay is fog-shrouded. A foggy-day cruise can be novel with the bellowing foghorns and mysterious mist, but if city views and snapshots are your goal, wait for a later hour or day.

The two lines make similar loops under the Golden Gate Bridge, around Alcatraz Island and under the Oakland-Bay Bridge. Each takes an hour and a quarter to make the trip with daily departures every 30 or 45 minutes from 10 A.M. to late afternoon, with sunset cruises in summer. Prices average about $10 for adults, $4 for children, $5 for seniors.

Walking tours are perfectly suited to compact San Francisco. A volunteer organization called City Guides leads tours of the city's most famous sites and scenes. Call 558-3981 for times and details of tours to City Hall, Coit Tower, historic Market Street, the new Moscone Convention Center, North Beach, Nob Hill, and Pacific Heights Victorian homes among others.

Other walking tours at nominal or no cost include:

- Haas-Lilienthal House, 2007 Franklin Street, a Queen Anne-style home that survived the Great Earthquake and Fire. Tel. 441-3004.
- Dashiell Hammett Walks from the main library at 200 Larkin; for details of the *Maltese Falcon* tour, phone 564-7021.
- Golden Gate Park including the Japanese Tea Garden (221-1311).
- Mission District Murals with slide-show preview (285-2287).
- Sutro Heights, spectacular coast scenery (556-8642).

Of numerous splendid churches in San Francisco, the most impressive are probably Grace Cathedral (Episcopal) ♕, a Gothic beauty atop Nob Hill with a renowned men and boys' choir singing each Sunday morning at 11 A.M. and St. Mary's Cathedral (Roman Catholic) ♕♕, a modern landmark atop Cathedral Hill with dramatic stained-glass windows soaring to a 190-foot-high cupola. Guided tours of each are available. (Grace, tel. 776-6611; St. Mary's, tel. 567-2020.)

In addition to the De Young and Asian Art Museums mentioned in our Golden Gate Park excursion (see page 316), each with free docent tours, San Francisco has other lovely museums on a range of themes:

- California Palace of the Legion of Honor ♕♕♕— Our pick for most impressive museum (all French art) if you have extra time; looks like Napoleon's palace of the same name; astounding Rodin sculpture collection and stunning Louis XVI Room.

- Museum of Modern Art, Civic Center♛♛—20th-century masters, but not as compelling as the modern art museums in New York, Chicago, or Los Angeles; occasionally excellent traveling exhibitions come here.
- Palace of Fine Arts♛♛—That was its role at the 1915 Panama-Pacific International Exposition; now it is the Exploratorium—hands-on exhibits and activities for children—but still monumental for adults for a walk-around.

Of the city's smaller special-interest museums, the Cable Car Barn♛♛, power and control center for the cable-car system (1201 Mason Street), is more fascinating than one might expect. Its Cable Car Museum shows the first century of cable-car development, and its giant gears will captivate young and old. Admission is free.

Shoppers not exhausted by the main areas already described will enjoy a more relaxed pace among the shops set in the Victorian homes of Union Street, an area known locally as Cow Hollow♛. This area up above Ghirardelli Square offers a 10-block row of charming shops and quaint bed-and-breakfast inns—great for unusual and original finds in clothing, jewelry, greeting cards, art, and antiques, plus cozy, neighborhood restaurants.

Animal fanciers will find fun at the San Francisco Zoo♛♛, particularly in its Primate Discovery Center, an airy naturalistic atrium for endangered species; Gorilla World, the world's largest and most natural gorilla habitat; and Koala Crossing, one of the country's 3 permanent koala bear exhibitions.

And for a farewell dinner, why not a dinner cruise aboard a historic steamer or a luxury yacht? Hornblower Yachts♛ (tel. 362-1212) has perfected the art of romantic, cruise dining with nightly dinner sailings, weekend brunch cruises, and special event celebrations on the Bay. You'll find their boats at Pier 33.

Students of urban development may like to take a look at downtown San Francisco, to see what stage the gentrification process has reached. Of special note is the Haight-Ashbury district, the flower-people capital of the world in the late '60s and a mecca for the gay population in the '70s. After a period of decline in the early '80s, it has now begun to make a comeback, with many interesting shops and renovated homes attracting a young, almost-yuppie, crowd to the area.

The Upper Haight area, by Golden Gate Park, is famous for its nightclubs, including the Full Moon Saloon (R&B and reggae), and the I-Beam and Nightbreak, both of which are popular with punk rockers. You can meet old hippies at the Chattanooga Cafe, or more modern folk at the Golden Coin or Persian Zum-Zum Room.

The Lower Haight area, around Fillmore Street, is less gentrified, but has very unusual stores, funky galleries, and nice cafés opening up all the time.

Downtown proper, note the many interesting restaurants which have sprung up near the Design Center.

Another city area of recent changes is 16th Street, between Mission and Dolores streets. Here you'll find the revival and foreign cinema, the Roxie, plus foreign-language newsstands, and bars where the local artists and other residents mix with transvestites and ethnic groups. A good café here is the Picaro.

CHILDREN'S SAN FRANCISCO

Keeping children entertained in San Francisco is as easy as hopping a clanging cable car, walking backwards up a steep hill, or eating an outdoor crab cocktail with sourdough bread at Fisherman's Wharf. Jugglers and magicians perform at Ghirardelli Square, the Cannery, and Pier 39. Pier 39 also has Funtasia (981-2638) with electronic and arcade games and rides, and the multimedia San Francisco Experience ♛ ♛ (982-7394). Nearby are the Wax Museum at 145 Jefferson Street ♛ (885-4975), and the National Maritime Museum ♛ ♛ (556-8166) including the historic ships at Pier 43 and Hyde Street Pier.

Golden Gate Park ♛ ♛ ♛ ♛ has endless treats for kids, from the children's playground with its beautifully restored carousel to Stow Lake (boating available), the Japanese Tea Garden, the vibrant floral designs outside the Conservatory of Flowers, Strybing Arboretum with its braille "touch and feel" garden, and countless other floral wonderlands and trails to explore. There are free concerts and 3 museums. Kids will love Morrison Planetarium, Steinhart Aquarium, and the Natural History Museum at the California Academy of Sciences♛♛♛♛ (750-7145 for tape information). Across the Music Concourse is the M. H. de Young Museum (221-4811) and the Asian Art Museum (668-8921).

The San Francisco Zoo♛♛♛, on Sloat Boulevard at the Ocean (661-4844), has a children's zoo, playgrounds, and the Primate Discovery Center. Kids will also love the Exploratorium at the Palace of Fine Arts♛♛♛♛, 3601 Lyon Street at Marina Boulevard (567-6642), where they can tinker with some 600 exhibits. Try also the Cable Car Museum♛ at Washington and Mason streets (474-1887), San Francisco Fire Department Pioneer Memorial Museum♛, 655 Presidio Avenue (861-8000, ext. 365), the Mexican Museum at Fort Mason♛, Building D (441-0404); or Mission Dolores♛, 16th and Dolores streets (621-8203).

It's worth a trip across the bay to Berkeley's beautiful Charles Lee Tilden Regional Park♛♛♛. Over 2,000 acres in the Berkeley hills offer dramatic views of San Francisco and the entire Bay Area, as well as pony rides, a wonderful steam train ride, a Little Farm, Environmental Education Center, Botanic Gardens, another wonderfully restored carousel, and Lake Anza with a sandy beach and swimming May–September (531-9300).

The Oakland Museum♛♛♛, 1000 Oak Street (834-2413), is a delightful place to explore California's history, ecology, and arts, while Children's Fairyland♛, set on the edge of Oakland's Lake Merritt at Grand Avenue and Park View Terrace (832-3609), brings storybook characters to life, along with excellent puppet shows.

Check the Pink Pages of the Sunday *San Francisco Examiner & Chronicle* for special children's theater and events listings. Watch especially for performances of the Pickle Family Circus (826-0747). Also pick up a free copy of *Parents Press* at children's retail stores, public libraries, or Safeway. This has an excellent monthly calendar of events for kids.

At Cliff House, 1090 Point Lobos Avenue, you might enjoy the Musee Mecanique, a collection of old-time penny arcade machines, some of which you may play with. Tel. (415) 386-1170.

EXCURSIONS FROM SAN FRANCISCO

Within an easy drive of the San Francisco Bay Area are the vineyards of the Sonoma and Napa Valley wine country (see page 267), the rugged coast of Big Sur, and wealthy art colony of Carmel. Marin County (see page 265), known for hot-tub hedonism and the good life, is just across the Golden Gate Bridge; a hike in Marin's Muir Woods or a shopping trek to Sausalito are all a ferry ride away from The City, as San Franciscans offhandedly call their corner of the world.

But here we want to point out some perhaps lesser-known but worthwhile directions to explore from The City. Instead of taking the Golden Gate Bridge, head for the silvery San Francisco–Oakland Bay Bridge or hop the ultramodern BART (Bay Area Rapid Transit) underground—and underwater—trains to Oakland.

Oakland

Formerly the western terminus of the Pony Express, Oakland is still a lively transportation and visitor hub. Amtrak stops here and Oakland International Airport is as convenient to San Francisco as San Francisco's own, via AIR/BART bus connections to BART every 7–10 minutes. Lots of deluxe rooms are available here at more affordable rates than in San Francisco, including the only full-fledged resort in the Bay Area, the Claremont Resort Hotel and Tennis Club.

Oakland and its neighbor Berkeley (also reachable by BART) are the points of interest in the East Bay—

Berkeley♛♛ primarily for its famous campus of the University of California (where *The Graduate* was filmed), a real beauty, and its funky shops and eateries hip to the latest in college crazes.

Lake Merritt with its 3-mile shoreline is the centerpiece of Oakland. Sailing, bicycling, and roller-skating are popular here. Among the bordering acres of prize-winning gardens and near the nation's oldest, state-operated Wildlife Refuge (great for birdwatching), is Children's Fairyland♛, a fantasy-styled park of fairy-tale tableaus that supposedly inspired Walt Disney.

Adults may be more interested in Jack London Square♛♛, a 6-block dockfront area named for Oakland's best-known, native author and rich with culinary, historical, and sight-seeing pleasures. Here, too, stand the sod-roofed Yukon cabin where London spent the winter of 1898, and the First and Last Chance Saloon where he wrote some of his novels.

The Oakland Museum♛♛, nicknamed "California's Smithsonian," is a 4-block large, 3-level collection of state history, art, and nature—an excellent place to see the development of this pioneer Golden State. Look carefully for the museum: As large as it is, visitors have been known to miss it, given the lush vegetation enshrouding it.

INSIDERS' TIPS

For information on sports events, call the Oakland-Alameda County Coliseum at 415-639-7700. For tickets to the Oakland A's, call 415-638-0500 and, for the Warriors, 415-638-6000.

Sports are king in Oakland, and there is sure to be some game in progress during your visit. The Oakland A's baseball season runs from April to September; the team has won 3 World Series, which makes for longer seasons; the Golden State Warriors, onetime NBA World Champions, play basketball from October to April.

Silicon Valley

The South Bay, 45 minutes to an hour south of San Francisco, has surged into prominence on the heels of the semiconductors and computer chips pioneered here. Officially it is the Santa Clara Valley, but to everyone these days it is known as Silicon Valley. San Jose, once an agricultural center, has become the fourth largest city in California thanks to the high-tech boom here.

Several unusual sights make this otherwise workaholic area a colorful side trip. The Winchester Mystery House ♛ ♛, built—and built and built—by rifle heiress Sarah Winchester at the turn of the century, is mysterious to this day. Sarah was told by a psychic that she had to pacify the spirits of those killed by Winchester guns by building nonstop on the house. So carpenters worked year-round adding empty rooms (160 total), useless stairs, and dead-end doors 24 hours a day for 38 years. Call 408-247-2101 for information.

In San Jose itself, the Rosicrucian Egyptian Museum ♛ exhibits the largest collection of ancient Egyptian, Babylonian, and Assyrian artifacts in the western U.S. It is the one local museum of widespread interest to visitors. (Call 408-247-2101).

Gardens, parks, and wildlife sanctuaries abound in the area, making it ideal for picnics and leisurely strolls. More than a dozen wineries in San Jose, Santa Clara, and Saratoga offer tours and tastes. Also in Santa Clara is Great America amusement park, tel. 408-988-1800, with 100 acres of action just off Highway 101.

Santa Cruz

Out to the coast from inland San Jose, the land rolls into gentle hills and then redwooded mountains. Located an hour and a quarter from San Francisco, Santa Cruz at the northern tip of Monterey Bay is known as a recreation and relaxation mecca. Another scenic campus of the University of California covers 2,000 acres here, and the city's Boardwalk ♛ ♛ ♛ (1907) is one of the few original, oceanfront amusement parks left in the world (it includes an old-fashioned, wooden roller coaster for thrill lovers).

The wealthy have left Santa Cruz a legacy of beautiful Victorian homes, many viewable on walking tours of 15 to 35 minutes in length led by the Santa Cruz County Convention and Visitors Bureau (tel. 408-423-6927). Begonias, Monarch butterflies, and pristine white-sand beaches explain why the rich lived here.

INSIDERS' TIPS

Redwood-burl tables, clocks, and other gift items are sold at many roadside shops along Highway 9 to Roaring Camp near the mountain town of Felton. At the base of Bear Mountain, take the 6.5-mile steam train ride ♛ ♛ ♛ up to where 19th-century lumberjacks timbered redwood logs for the sawmills down below. This one-hour, narrow-gauge railway trip is breathtaking.

One last curiosity you may find irresistible: The Mystery Spot ♛. No, it's not a dog which disappears, but a place on earth where you can apparently defy gravity. *Ripley's Believe It or Not* has featured this strange phenomenon where visitors lean unexpectedly toward the southwest—more and more as you come closer to the center of the spot. No one, not even a physicist, can explain it. Located at 1953 Branciforte Drive in Santa Cruz. Tel. 408-423-8897.

San Francisco Peninsula

The drive to or from San Francisco can take you past interesting places on the peninsula which the city crowns. Let's imagine you are coming back from a southerly day trip to Santa Clara or Santa Cruz.

Highway 1, the same Pacific Coast Highway that winds south past Big Sur and Hearst Castle to Los Angeles, is lined here with unspoiled beaches and spectacular views of the vast Pacific. Half Moon Bay, a romantic, little town, calls itself the pumpkin capital of California (northern California is full of vegetable and fruit capitals, it seems). Moss Beach and Bean Hollow State Beach are fun for tidepool exploring.

The roads winding inland from San Jose curve

through lovely mountain passes to Palo Alto, home of Stanford University, where campus tours are available. Or, if you are a "Dynasty" fan, drive on to Filoli, the estate for which Blake and Alexis have fought. A 2-hour guided tour of the ground floor and formal gardens is a floral delight. Orchid fanciers may drive farther yet to South San Francisco's Acres of Orchids (415-952-7600) for tours including an orchid laboratory and thousands of blooms. After that, you are back where you left your heart.

INSIDERS' INFORMATION FOR SAN FRANCISCO AND AREA
(area code 415)

WHERE TO STAY

Campton Place ♛♛♛♛♛
340 Stockton St., S.F. 94108; tel. 781-5555, or 800-647-4007 nationwide, 800-235-4300 in California
Single room, double occupancy: $170–$230
Fresh and innovative, this chic hotel sits on San Francisco's busiest corner—but inside, intimacy pervades. The 123 apricot-and-taupe rooms are on the smallish side, but big on warmth. Unpretentious, with Henredon armoires and travertine marble bathrooms. The hotel restaurant (♛♛♛♛♛) is one of the city's best (see Where to Eat, page 333).

Four Seasons Clift Hotel ♛♛♛♛♛
495 Geary St., S.F. 94102; tel. 775-4700 or 800-268-6282
Single room, double occupancy: $135 and up
Book a room here if you want to be pampered. Elegant and understated, the hotel is small enough to feel important in. Redwood Room bar is one of S.F.'s most distinctive.

The Stanford Court Hotel ♛♛♛♛♛
905 California St., S.F. 94108; tel. 989-3500
Single room, double occupancy: $145–$235
This 408-room Nob Hill hotel has a lobby which welcomes you like a private club with wood paneling and a

warm atmosphere. San Francisco designer Andrew Delfino mixed modern design with period pieces for a very residential flavor. Accommodations have canopied beds, marble bedside tables, and Old San Francisco etchings.

The Huntington ♛ ♛ ♛ ♛
1075 California St., S.F. 94108; tel. 474-5400, or 800-227-4683 nationwide, 800-652-1539 in California
Single room, double occupancy: $130–$220
Across from Grace Cathedral on Nob Hill stands this very well established jewel of a small hotel. Nobility, opera stars, and politicians frequent the Huntington for the tasteful rooms and the friendly, familiar service. Ask anything of Cynthia Reid, concierge extraordinaire—she's been known to perform miracles.

The Mandarin Hotel ♛ ♛ ♛ ♛
222 Sansome St., S.F. 94104; tel. 885-0999, or 800-622-0404
Single room, double occupancy: $175–$260
Located on the top 11 floors of the California Center in diagonally shaped twin towers that afford all 160 rooms unobstructed bay and city views. Contemporary style with an Asian flair. Health club, fully equipped business center.

The Portman ♛ ♛ ♛ ♛
500 Post St., S.F. 94102; tel. 771-8600
Single room, double occupancy: $150–$240
A block off Union Square, this sophisticated property is big on informality and Asian-style hospitality. The 348 rooms have marble baths and private dressing areas. No specified checkout time, 3 telephones in each room and call-waiting. Bar, library. Private club with outdoor patio.

The Sherman House ♛ ♛ ♛ ♛
2160 Green St., S.F. 94123; tel. 563-3600
Single room, double occupancy: $170 and up
One of San Francisco's biggest surprises. A 15-room wonderland in Pacific Heights (close to Union Street boutiques) with a 3-story recital hall and luxurious library/lounge. Rooms are magnificent with marbleized wood-burning fireplaces, feather down mattresses, rich

tapestries, and Chinese slate floors. The house car is a 1961 Jaguar Vanden Plas limo.

Fairmont Hotel and Tower ♛ ♛ ♛
950 Mason St., S.F. 94108; tel. 772-5000, or 800-527-4727
Single room, double occupancy: $140–$235
This is the grand dame of hotels; visitors to the city come by to drink in the lobby even if they aren't checking in. You'll recognize this place as the model for the television show "Hotel," and you'll remember it for all of the wonderful facilities like a bang-up nightclub featuring big-name performers and a lively restaurant (♛ ♛), surrounded by a pool of water where a floating barge carries musicians to entertain. Great fun on Nob Hill.

Hotel Diva ♛ ♛ ♛
440 Geary St., S.F. 94102; tel. 885-0200
Single room, double occupancy: $95–$105
For the contemporary traveler, this 105-room, high-tech, Italian hotel has everything: VCRs, a video library, IBM personal computers, and plenty of pizzazz. Italian lighting, Eileen Gray tables. Lobby is nothing special.

Hotel Meridien ♛ ♛ ♛
50 Third St., S.F. 94103; tel. 974-6400
Single room, double occupancy: $170–$225
This elegant member of the French chain prides itself on excellent service for an international clientele. The 36-story hotel towers over the city for great views. Dine in the Pierre Restaurant (♛ ♛ ♛ ♛) for divine French fare. Concierge, guided morning jog. 700 rooms.

The Mark Hopkins ♛ ♛ ♛
999 California St., S.F. 94108; tel. 392-3434
Single room, double occupancy: $145–$235
Great choice for a business traveler, this 402-room hotel is equipped to cater to every need. In one of the oldest buildings on Nob Hill and steeped in tradition. Well-stocked business publication library. Nob Hill Restaurant (♛ ♛ ♛ ♛) gets much kudos for its creative Continental cuisine.

Westin St. Francis ♛ ♛ ♛
335 Powell Street, S.F. 94102; tel. 397-7000, or 800-228-3000
Single room, double occupancy: $120–$235
Queen Elizabeth and Ronald Reagan have stayed here, and you should too if you're looking for a big hotel offering the perfect mix of modern and old world. 5 glass elevators whisk you from the ground to the top of this 32-story hotel for an amazing city view. On Union Square. 1,200 rooms.

The Bedford ♛ ♛
761 Post St., S.F. 94109; tel. 673-6040
Single room, double occupancy: $79
In the heart of the theater district, this cozy, European-style hotel radiates San Francisco charm in all 144 rooms. Free limousine service on weekdays to the financial district. Café Bedford (♛ ♛ ♛) grows its own vegetables.

The Donatello ♛ ♛
501 Post St., S.F. 94102; tel. 441-7100
Single room, double occupancy: $150–$185
An elegant touch of Northern Italy in San Francisco. Extra-length, double and king-sized beds, 2 telephones, and complimentary local calls. 95 rooms, a block from Union Square.

Hyatt on Union Square ♛ ♛
345 Stockton, S.F. 94108; tel. 398-1234
Single room, double occupancy: $159–$214
The 694 rooms in this stately hotel are sunny and spacious, offering sweeping views of the area. Right on Union Square for great shopping temptations at your doorstep.

Petite Auberge ♛ ♛
863 Bush, S.F. 94108; tel. 928-6000
Single room, double occupancy: $95–$185
Warm and cozy French-country-inn atmosphere. Cherry-wood-burning fireplaces and vases of fresh flowers in the 26 rooms. 2 blocks from Nob Hill.

Ramada Renaissance ♔ ♔
55 Cyril Magnin, Market at Fifth St., S.F. 94102; tel. 392-8000
Single room, double occupancy: $115-$130
The perfect convention hotel in a neighborhood that's making strides to clean up its act. Stylish rooms, protected by one of the city's most stringent security and life-safety systems. Heated pool, fitness facilities. 1,015 rooms.

Sheraton Palace ♔ ♔
639 Market at New Montgomery, S.F. 94105; tel. 392-8600
Single room, double occupancy: $125–$165
A few blocks from the Moscone Center, this 500-room hotel has hosted presidents, literary types, and regular folk. Comfortable place to stay. Sunday dinner is accompanied by the San Francisco String Quartet.

Galleria Park ♔
191 Sutter St., S.F. 94101-4595; tel. 781-3060
Single room, double occupancy: $84–$99
Located in the heart of the financial district, this hotel is not overdone—just pleasant. All the charming rooms are soundproofed, nice lobby with skylight. Fitness facilities. 177 rooms.

Hyatt Regency ♔
5 Embarcadero Center, S.F. 94111; tel. 788-1234
Single room, double occupancy: $195–$258
Located near the financial district, this is the city's to–be–expected John Portman–designed atrium–style hotel, with 804 rooms and recorded bird sounds in the lobby. Sometimes in this property the powers that be do achieve the desired effect of making you feel as if you're outdoors when you are, indeed, indoors. The Equinox (♔), a revolving eatery, is adequate as far as hotel restaurants go.

Kensington Park ♔
450 Post St., S.F. 94102; tel. 788-6400
Single room, double occupancy: $85–$115
Steps from Union Square, this 81-room hotel was built in 1924 to house the Elk's Club. Queen Anne and Chippendale furnishings, mahogany furniture, Chinese vases, and frills. Tea and sherry served in the lobby.

Majestic♔
1500 Sutter at Gough, S.F. 94109; tel. 441-1100
Single room, double occupancy: $75–$115
Near the Performing Arts Center and built in 1902, the Majestic is convenient and steeped in tradition. French Empire and English antiques. Limo service and valet parking.

The Mansion♔
2220 Sacramento, S.F. 94115; tel. 929-9444
Single room, double occupancy: $74–$200
An eccentric, turn-of-the-century, Victorian building in Pacific Heights; a B&B with a twist. Visit to learn all the folklore. Music and billiard rooms. 19 rooms.

The Orchard♔
562 Sutter St., S.F. 94102; tel. 433-4434
Single room, double occupancy: $85–$105
A quaint hotel on a posh street with exemplary hospitality and European-style service. No-smoking rooms. 96 rooms.

Vintage Court♔
650 Bush St., S.F. 94108; tel. 392-4666
Single room, double occupancy: $89
Near Union Square, tastefully decorated rooms are a great value for the price. 106 rooms. No room service, but Masa's (♔♔♔♔♔) French restaurant on the premises.

White Swan Inn♔
845 Bush St., S.F. 94108; tel. 775-1755
Single room, double occupancy: $130–$225
Cozy English inn with 27 spacious, Laura Ashley-decorated rooms. Fireplaces and wet bar in all rooms. 2 blocks from Nob Hill.

The York♔
940 Sutter St., S.F. 94109; tel. 885-6800
Single room, double occupancy: $84–$94
You may remember this place; this is the location for the Hitchcock movie *Vertigo* (the hotel was then known as the Empire). Wet bars, walk-in closets, and window seats in the 100 rooms. No-smoking rooms, fitness facilities. Plush Room is a night spot that was once a speakeasy.

WHERE TO EAT

Campton Place ♔ ♔ ♔ ♔ ♔
345 Stockton St., S.F.; tel. 781-5155
Average dinner: $60
The mountain came to Muhammed when midwesterner Bradley Ogden moved to San Francisco to open this highly regarded, American regional-cuisine citadel in the elegant Campton Place Hotel.

Chez Panisse ♔ ♔ ♔ ♔ ♔
1517 Shattuck, Berkeley; tel. 548-5525, café, 548-5049
Average dinner: $45
No California restaurant guide would be complete without listing this pioneer, vanguard restaurant, still serving the same high-quality, innovative, fresher-than-fresh food, by Alice Waters who some credit with creating California cuisine.

INSIDERS' TIPS

Phone ahead for reservations downstairs at Chez Panisse. Upstairs is Siberia.

Square One ♔ ♔ ♔ ♔ ♔
At corner of Pacific and Front sts., S.F.; tel. 788-1110
Average dinner: $40
The Chez Panisse graduate who owns this highly successful restaurant and respected food establishment serves not California cuisine, but New American cuisine, a blend of diverse, ethnic ingredients with the bounty of California produce.

Stars ♔ ♔ ♔ ♔ ♔
150 Redwood Alley, S.F.; tel. 861-7827
Average dinner: $35
Jeremiah Tower, Chez Panisse alumnus and the handsomest chef this side of the Rockies, works wonders day in and day out at his decidedly American brasserie. Superbly executed, highly inventive California cuisine. Excellent California wine list.

China Moon Café ♛ ♛ ♛ ♛
639 Post St., S.F.; tel. 775-4789
Average dinner: $23
A Chinese bistro owned by a first-rate scholar of Chinese culture and food. The restaurant serves splendid, light and zesty Chinese foods, accompanied by Western wines and Western desserts.

Donatello ♛ ♛ ♛ ♛
501 Post (in the Donatello Hotel), S.F.; tel. 441-7182
Average dinner: $40
This pricey northern Italian restaurant, located outside of North Beach, offers a wide variety of esteemed regional fare with attentive service in elegant surroundings. Fortunately, the prix fixe menu changes every few days.

Fleur de Lys ♛ ♛ ♛ ♛
777 Sutter St., S.F.; tel. 673-7779
Five-course dinner: $47, à la carte: $19.50–$22
Not the classic, old-guard restaurant of yore. Chef Hubert Keller tips his toque to American cuisine and offers such unchauvinistic fare as American foie and other French dishes incorporating California's wonderful food bounty.

Amelio's ♛ ♛ ♛
1630 Powell, S.F.; tel. 397-4339
Average dinner: $36
Despite its Italian name and its French-born chef, the food at Amelio's is fanciful American with a sometimes oriental influence. Artful presentations of unusual flavor combinations are beautiful and delicious to eat.

Cadillac Bar and Restaurant ♛ ♛ ♛
1 Holland Court, S.F.; tel. 543-8226
Average dinner: $13
This barnlike, often raucous, Mexican restaurant near Moscone Center offers excellent grilled meats accompanied by spicy salsa, along with the noise!

Ciao ♛ ♛ ♛
230 Jackson St., S.F.; tel. 982-9500
Average dinner: $25
This bright and cheerful, upbeat Italian restaurant near San Francisco's designer district is built on pasta, offering tasty, undreamed-of combinations of in-

gredients to nestle in the perfect strands, as well as a menu which includes other standard Italian fare.

Fog City Diner ♕ ♕ ♕
1300 Battery, S.F.; tel. 982-2000
Average dinner: $25
There is no elbow room in this attractive diner, bar, and grill, and it's a bit too trendy—but worth it to dine on impeccable and imaginative California cuisine.

Greens ♕ ♕ ♕
Building A, Fort Mason Center, S.F.; tel. 771-6222
Average dinner: $25
Vegetarian restaurants belonged in the health-food category until Greens came along. The ultimate in so-phisticated vegetarian dining; elegant, inventive, and impeccably fresh. You'll never miss the meat.

Janot's ♕ ♕ ♕
44 Campton Pl., S.F.; tel. 392-5373
Average dinner: $25
Outstandingly simple, brasserie-style food is served in this long and narrow, brick-walled, fashionable restaurant. The casually dressed will feel quite comfortable here. The interiors are lively, with a definite French ambience and clientele.

Khan Toke Thai House ♕ ♕ ♕
5937 Geary Blvd., S.F.; tel. 668-6654
Average dinner: $15
"The only Thai restaurant in town" is the oft-heard praise for one of the first, and still one of the best Thai restaurants, considered the Chez Panisse of Thai cook-ery. Pleasant ambience.

Oliveto ♕ ♕ ♕
5655 College Ave., Oakland; tel. 547-5356
Average dinner: $20
Food author Maggie Klein opened Oliveto (olives being her pet subject) to approximate the hearty, rustic, and succulent country fare of Italy, Spain, and France. The downstairs restaurant is open all day, serving full meals, plus wonderful pizzas and tapas. Dinner only is served in the formal upstairs restaurant.

Zuni Café ♛ ♛ ♛
1658 Market, S.F.; tel. 552-2522
Average dinner: $30
A solid example of the unique southwestern cuisine is offered at this informal, little restaurant with regional motif, serving the freshest of fish and the requisite mesquite grill, accompanied by an excellent California wine list.

Yank Sing ♛ ♛
427 Battery and 53 Stevenson, S.F.; tel. 362-1640 and 495-4510
Average dinner: $15
Make a fine luncheon of the extraordinary hot or cold Chinese tea pastries served, in a breakaway from the "plain pipe rack" ambience of most dim sum parlors, at 2 well-appointed and attractive restaurants. Also open for dinner.

Ernie's ♛
847 Montgomery St., S.F.; tel. 397-5969
Average dinner: $45
Alfred Hitchcock's old hangout, where Jimmy Stewart met Kim Novak in *Vertigo*. Magnificent ambience, good (but not outstanding) food, warm feeling of money all around you.

Isobune ♛
1737 Post, S.F.; tel. 563-1030
Average dinner: $1–$1.95 per plate (charged by the plate)
Great for the novice sushi diner, all the traditional varieties of sushi are placed on a revolving counter, to be chosen by eye appeal rather than inscrutable Japanese-named dishes.

Mifune ♛
1737 4th St., S.F.; tel. 922-0337
Average dinner: $12
A typical buckwheat-noodle restaurant from the Osaka region of Japan. The noodles are carefully prepared and topped with tasty Japanese ingredients. Choose from the look-alike wax models displayed in the window.

La Palma Mexicatessen♥
2884 24th St., S.F.; tel. 647-1500
Average dinner: $13.50
A microcosm of Mexican tradition in the Mission district. This shop offers take-out fare, including fresh-made tortillas, fresh Mexican panella cheese, nopales (cactus salad), and other excellent Mexican foods to go.

BARS AND CAFÉS

Alta Plaza Bar and Restaurant, 2301 Fillmore St., Fillmore; tel. 921-4646. Gay, yuppie bar.

Balboa Café, 3199 Fillmore St., Fillmore; tel. 921-3944. Popular bar, great restaurant.

Bentley's. Galleria Park Hotel, 191 Sutter, Union Square, S.F.; tel. 989-6895. Bar and restaurant are very in on the weekdays with the downtown working crowd.

Blue Light Café, 1979 Union St., S.F.; tel. 922-5510. Hip, high-tech café owned by Boz Scaggs.

Brasserie, Fairmont Hotel, 950 Mason St., S.F.; tel. 772-5000. Open 24 hours, draws all kinds of socializers.

Buena Vista Café, 2765 Hyde St., Fisherman's Wharf, S.F.; tel. 474-5044. Home of the Irish coffee.

Le Central, 453 Bush St., Union Square, S.F.; tel. 391-2233. San Francisco's movers and shakers congregate at the bar at lunchtime.

The Cliff House, 1090 Point Lobos Ave., Land's End, S.F.; tel. 386-7630. Come for the view of the ocean and Seal Rocks, especially at sunset.

Enrico's Sidewalk Café, 504 Broadway, North Beach, S.F.; tel. 392-6220. A North Beach institution.

L'Etoile, in the Huntington Hotel, Nob Hill, S.F.; tel. 771-1529. Classy and intimate bar with society pianist Peter Mintun providing the music.

Hard Rock Café, 1699 Van Ness Ave. at Sacramento, S.F.; tel. 885-1699. In spot for the young crowd. Great burgers and shakes.

Harrington's, 245 Front St., in the financial district, S.F.; tel. 392-7595. After-work crowd drinks here.

Harry's, 2020 Fillmore St., Fillmore/Pacific Heights,

S.F.; tel. 921-1000. Hangout for yuppies and an older crowd.

Lily's, 4 Embarcadero Center, S.F.; tel. 398-3434. Yuppie heaven, especially Friday from 6 to 10. Live band on the outdoor patio.

London Wine Bar, 415 Sansome St., in the financial district, S.F.; tel. 788-4811. Good wines, jammed after work.

Lord Jim's, 1500 Broadway, Pacific Heights, S.F.; tel. 928-3015. Singles congregate amidst ferns and Tiffany lamps.

Top of the Rock, 817 China Basin, S.F.; tel. 621-5538. Waterfront bar.

Mulhern's, 3653 Buchanan, Marina District, S.F.; tel. 346-5549. Popular spot for professionals.

Perry's, 1944 Union St., S.F.; tel. 922-9022. Very popular yuppie hangout.

Redwood Room, Four Seasons Clift Hotel, 495 Geary St., Union Square, S.F.; tel. 775-4700. Stunning art-deco room. Piano music.

Rosalie's, 1415 Van Ness, S.F.; tel. 928-7188. Classy place with piano entertainment.

Royal Exchange, 301 Sacramento St., S.F.; tel. 956-1710. English pub.

Specs' Twelve Adler Museum Café, 12 Adler St. off Columbus Ave., S.F.; tel. 421-4112. Filled with North Beach characters.

Sutter's Mill, 77 Battery St., S.F.; tel. 788-8377. Gay professionals jam the place Friday afternoons.

Tommy's Joynt, Van Ness and Geary, S.F.; tel. 775-4216. Beer hall featuring buffalo stew and great sandwiches.

Tosca Café, 242 Columbus at Broadway, North Beach; tel. 986-9651. 65-year-old bar is a classic. Opera on the jukebox.

Vesuvio Café, 255 Columbus Ave., North Beach; tel. 362-3370. Classic artist and writer hangout.

Washington Square Bar and Grill, 1707 Powell St. at Union, North Beach; tel. 982-8123. A crowd of journalists, politicians, and the literary set.

Caffe Soma, 1601 Howard at 12th Street, South of Market; tel. 861-5012. A famous hangout, with good espresso, cappuccino. Closes at midnight Fri. and Sat., earlier other days.

Billboard Café, 299 Ninth St. at Folsom, South of Market; tel. 558-9500. Practically an institution.

The Warehouse, 333 11th St., South of Market; tel. 621-5902. Good eats, all-round fun restaurant.

NIGHTLIFE AND ENTERTAINMENT

Nightclubs

Cesar's Latin Palace, 3140 Mission St., Mission, S.F.; tel. 648-6611. Dance to live salsa music in this large ballroom.

Club DV 8, 55 Natoma St., South of Market, S.F.; tel. 957-1730. San Francisco's preeminent club to dress up, spend money, and mix in style—black tie or black leather.

Club Fugazi, 678 Green St., North Beach, S.F.; tel. 421-4222. San Francisco's longest-running musical revue is a fun-filled extravaganza in a cabaret setting. Advance reservations are necessary.

Finocchio's, 506 Broadway, Broadway/North Beach, S.F.; tel. 982-9388. This revue of female impersonators still draws capacity crowds after 50 years.

The Great American Music Hall, 859 O'Farrell St., Downtown, S.F.; tel. 885-0750. Betty Carter and Carmen McRae performed together here. That's indicative of the level of talent drawn to this premier cabaret, restored from a turn-of-the-century building.

Holy City Zoo, 408 Clement St., Richmond district, S.F.; tel. 386-4242. Comedy.

Kimball's, 300 Grove St., Civic Center, S.F.; tel. 861-5585. Fine jazz in a comfortable setting.

Lipp's, 201 9th St., South of Market, S.F.; tel. 552-3466. Comedy.

Milestones, 376 5th St., South of Market, S.F.; tel. 777-9997. A lively spot to catch some fine jazz.

The Plush Room, at the York Hotel, 940 Sutter St., Downtown, S.F.; tel. 885-6800. Intimate cabaret featuring musical revues and solo performers.

Punch Line, 444 Battery St., Financial district, S.F.; tel. 397-7573. Comedy.

Trocadero Transfer, 520 4th St., South of Market, S.F.; tel. 495-0185. Late-night club. Dancing, mixed gay and straight clientele.

Venetian Room, at the Fairmont Hotel, Mason at California, Nob Hill, S.F.; tel. 772-5163. San Francisco's most sophisticated supper club, featuring world-renowned performers.

Wolfgang's, 901 Columbus Ave., North Beach; tel. 441-4333. This Bill Graham-owned club showcases rock, jazz, reggae, country, blues, and comedy. Saturday nights are for dancing with DJ and videos.

Yoshi's, 6030 Claremont Ave., Oakland; tel. 652-9200. Worth the short trip across the bay to hear good jazz in a beautiful club, part of an excellent Japanese restaurant and sushi bar complex. World-class performers are showcased monthly.

Theaters

American Conservatory Theater, 415 Geary St., Union Square, tel. 771-3880. Fine resident theater company presents the classics as well as modern and experimental works in repertory.

Asian American Theater Co., 1881 Bush St., Union Square, tel. 346-8922. Forum for professional plays written, directed, and performed by Asian-American artists.

Berkeley Repertory Theater, 2025 Addison St., Berkeley; tel. 845-4700. More than 2 decades of tradition and national reputation; an eclectic mix of classical revivals and contemporary premieres.

Curran Theater, 445 Geary St., Union Square; tel. 673-4400. Broadway musicals and plays performed by national touring companies.

Eureka Theater Company, 2730 16th St., South of Market, tel. 558-9811. Outstanding company deals with contemporary, political and social issues. Arena for new playwrights as well as those who are established.

Golden Gate Theater, 25 Taylor St., Union Square; tel. 474-3800. Touring musicals with major stars. Lavish, restored, 1920s theater.

Julian Theatre, 953 De Haro St. at 23rd, Potrero Hill; tel. 647-8098. For more than 2 decades the Julian has been committed to producing new plays of social and political importance.

Lorraine Hansberry Theater, 620 Sutter St., at Mason, Union Square, tel. 474-8842. Multicultural theater, devoted primarily to putting on works by black playwrights. Comedies, musicals, dramas, and experimental works.

Magic Theater, Fort Mason, Marina district; tel. 441-8822. Experimental and original works by known and unknown playwrights.

Marine's Memorial Theater, 609 Sutter St., Union Square; tel. 771-6900. Variety of performance modes from one-man shows to the Chinese Magic Circus.

Orpheum Theater, 1192 Market St., downtown; tel. 474-3800. Broadway musicals.

INSIDERS' TIPS

The San Francisco Mime Troupe is the Bay Area's oldest theater company, internationally acclaimed for its political musical comedy. The troupe performs free in Bay Area parks in the summer. When you're in town, call 285-1717 to find out where.

Theater Artaud, 450 Florida at 17th., South of Market; tel. 621-7797. Original and experimental dance, theater, and collaborative works.

Theater on the Square, 450 Post St., 2nd floor, Kensington Park Hotel; tel. 433-9500. Intimate 750-seat setting for musicals and dramas.

Theater Rhinoceros, 2926 16th St., South of Market; tel. 861-5079. While the aim here is to entertain and enlighten the gay and lesbian community, many of the excellent revues appeal equally to a straight audience.

SHOPPING

The Cannery

Bazaar Cada Dia, 2801 Leavenworth. Latin American, African, and Native American folk art, jewelry, and clothing.

The Great American Short Story, 2801 Leavenworth. Fashions and accessories for women 5'3" and under.

Embarcadero

Edwards Luggage and Gifts, 3 Embarcadero Center. Quality luggage.

Ingear, 1 Embarcadero Center. Life-style enhancers from kitchen gadgets to gardening tools.

The Nature Company, 4 Embarcadero Center. Outdoor discovery tools for all ages.

Fillmore

Brian Fedorow, 1900 Fillmore St. Sophisticated women's sportswear by Brian Fedorow. Custom orders.

The Company Store, 1913 Fillmore St. Well-priced, large-size clothing.

C. P. Shades, 2121 Fillmore St. Understated, comfortable clothing.

Fillamento, 2185 Fillmore St. Urban life-style store specializing in uptown furniture, china, crystal, and office supplies—all with flair.

The Producer, 2133 Fillmore St. Classic men's clothing with a touch of modern influence.

Fisherman's Wharf

Cost Plus, 2552 Taylor St., at North Point. Sprawling, warehouse-style complex offering some terrific prices on imports, from housewares to jewelry, temple rubbings to brassware.

Left Hand World, Pier 39. Scissors, watches, and other necessities of life for the left-handed minority.

North Beach Leather, 1365 Columbus. Fine leather in innovative styles.

Galleria at Crocker Center

Trilevel, Milan-style galleria under arched skylight. Elegant shops; classic local eatery, the Old Poodle Dog Restaurant (♛ ♛ ♛) is expensive, but the place to see *tout* San Francisco.

Ghirardelli Square

Folk Art International, 900 North Point. Hand-woven rugs, textiles, and toys mainly from Mexico and Central America, Japan, and Southeast Asia.

Xanadu, 900 North Point. African and tribal art including textiles, sculptures, and jewelry.

Potrero Hill

Esprit Outlet, 499 Illinois. If you're a woman who loves a bargain, but you want to be in fashion, shop here.

Union Square

Banana Republic, 224 Grant Ave. Travel and safari clothing in natural fabrics. Fine travel bookstore downstairs.

Comme des Garcons, 70 Geary St. High-styled, contemporary clothing by Rei Kawakubo.

Emporium Capwell, 835 Market St. Full-line department store.

Findley's Fabulous Fudge, 397 Geary St. 12 varieties of addictive fudge, including Grand Marnier, bittersweet macadamia, and peanut butter.

Gump's, 250 Post St. Museumlike emporium filled with oriental silks, deluxe gifts, and incredible jade.

I. Magnin, Geary and Stockton. Premier, local department store, best known for womenswear, but strong in menswear and fancy foods too.

Jeanne-Marc, 262 Sutter. Unique women's clothing by local design team.

Jessica McClintock, 353 Sutter. Romantic laces and silk numbers by popular San Francisco designer.

M.A.C. and Todd Oldham at M.A.C., 812 & 814 Post St. Smart, simple, very wearable contemporary clothing for men and women.

Macy's, Stockton & O'Farrell Sts. Need we say more?

Neiman-Marcus, 150 Stockton St. A Texas company makes it big in San Francisco. Top-quality department store.

Obiko, 794 Sutter St. One-of-a-kind, handwoven, hand-dyed clothing. Bay Area designers.

Pearl Empire, 127 Geary. Excellent prices for pearls and jade. Around for more than 3 decades.

Saks Fifth Ave., 384 Post St. A touch of New York City chic in the city by the bay.

White Duck, 517 Sutter St. Women's clothing in wonderful fabrics by Bay Area designers.

Wilkes Bashford Ltd., 375 Sutter St. Top-of-the-line and top-priced mens- and womenswear. Trendy and traditional styles with the lower level devoted to local designers.

Williams-Sonoma, 576 Sutter St. The flagship store of this nationwide kitchen-supply chain.

Union Street (Pacific Heights)

Bebe, 1954 Union St., 1977 Union St., 1323 Polk St. Latest European look for men and women.

Carnevale, 2185A Union St. High-fashion, creative clothing and accessories.

Elizabeth's, 2758 Octavia at Union. One-of-a-kind European and American designer dresses.

Enchanted Crystal, 1771 Union St. Fine quartz collection, art glass, crystal stemware.

Mario Fantana, 1796 Union St. at Octavia. High-fashion, Italian clothing for women.

Ricciani, 1799 Union St. Chic designer clothes and shoes for women.

USEFUL TELEPHONE NUMBERS (area code 415)

Emergency Telephone Numbers

911: Emergency dialing to reach police, fire department, or ambulance
Alcoholics Anonymous: 661-1828
Ambulance: 431-2800
California Road Conditions: 557-3755
California State Automobile Association (AAA): 565-2012
Fire: 861-8020
Narcotics Anonymous: 621-8600
S.F. Bar Association Lawyer Referral: 764-1616
S.F. Dental Society (Dentist referral): 421-1435
S.F. Medical Society (Doctor referral): 567-6230
Senior Citizens' Information: 626-1033
Suicide Prevention: 221-1424
Traveler's Aid Society: 781-6738
Western Union: 433-5520

Travel and Business Information

BART information—Bay Area Rapid Transit (underground): 788-BART (788-2278)
BASS Charge by Phone: 762-BASS, 762-2277
Berlitz Language and Translation Services: 986-6474
Deak-Perera Foreign Currency Exchange: 362-3452
Events Hot Line, in English: 391-2001
                         French: 391-2003
                         German: 391-2004
                         Japanese: 391-2101
                         Spanish: 391-2122
Gay Switchboard: 841-6224
Haight Ashbury Switchboard: 621-6211
International Visitors Center: 986-1388
Jazz Line: 769-4818
MUNI information—S.F. Municipal Railway System, buses, streetcars, cable cars: 673-MUNI (673-6864)
S.F. Convention and Visitors Bureau: 974-6900
S.F. Visitor Information Center: 391-2001
Weather: 936-1212

INDEX